from
X mas, 199-

✓ I completed reading this book
on 20-1-94.

Mark of Protest

VICTOR GRIFFIN

GILL & MACMILLAN

Gill & Macmillan Ltd
Goldenbridge
Dublin 8
with associated companies throughout the world
© Victor Griffin 1993
0 7171 1874 6
Index compiled by Helen Litton
Print origination by
Seton Music Graphics Ltd, Bantry, Co. Cork
Printed by ColourBooks Ltd, Dublin

A catalogue record is available for this
book from the British Library.

2   4   5   3   1

Misprint on p. 143 ?

To Daphne

whose courage and cheerfulness in her
wheelchair taught me always to be thankful
for the use of my legs and not to make
mountains out of molehills

Contents

Acknowledgments

Ecclesiastes tells us that 'of making many books there is no end'. However in the making of this book there were many hands. Wendy Fitzgerald prepared an early draft with me. Louis McRedmond gave invaluable editorial advice on structure and historical accuracy. Betty Clarke typed my original script. Marjorie Hampton and my nieces, Sandra Morrow and June Greene, gave generously of their time to research.

The number of books on Northern Ireland grows, quite literally, by the day. Two that I have found to be both valuable and influential are *The Narrow Ground* by A.T.Q. Stewart and *Ulster, Conflict and Consent* by Tom Wilson. They are required reading for anyone seeking to gain an insight into the political and religious complexities of Northern Ireland.

I am grateful to Faber & Faber for permission to quote from Louis MacNeice's *Entirely* and to the *Irish Times* for permission to reproduce photographs.

Finally, it should be remembered that autobiography is a selfish activity. Despite many helping hands, the opinions expressed are entirely my own! Others, on some issues, may have a different perspective. That I recognise and respect. Pure objectivity is an illusion — often a dangerous one. 'No one can jump out of his own skin', as the philosopher, Hegel, so aptly put it.

1

Childhood

THE day I was born, 24 May 1924, my father went out and bought a farm. It was intended as my inheritance, purchased, I suppose, in the hope that I would be a farmer. An entrepreneur who speculated for the sheer love and adventure of it all, he was nevertheless a true countryman with a deep-rooted fondness for the land. The farm was the one enterprise of which my grandfather wholeheartedly approved. The descendant of generations of small farmers and a clerk on Earl Fitzwilliam's Coollattin estate, set among the oak woods of Shillelagh in south Co. Wicklow, my grandfather believed that security lay unshakeably in the land.

Carnew, a small town of about 500 people where I first saw the light of day, is five miles from Shillelagh. To the south, near Ferns, stands Slieve Bhuide (Slieve Wee) with its rounded summit of gorse and heather dominating the skyline. The Wicklow mountains reach out to the north. From the many vantage points on the outskirts of the town, the woods, fields, hills, mountains, rivers stretch away into the distance as far as the eye can see. This immensity of landscape, luscious, fertile, with its scenic contrasts and varieties of shade and colour, a thing of exquisite beauty, has earned for Wicklow the accolade of 'the garden of Ireland'. Incidentally, I would credit Donegal with being the 'rock garden' of Ireland. Both counties are breathtaking in their scenic beauty but in contrasting ways.

I was brought into this world by the redoubtable Miss Sixsmith, an excellent midwife deferred to throughout the community with a respect sometimes bordering on fear. I never heard her called by her Christian name, Maude. Not one to suffer fools gladly, she ran her nursing home in Carnew with Victorian rigour. Babies were regarded as wayward creatures who needed a good dose of corrective discipline. So my life began in an encounter with authority. When I rebelled, screaming at her attempts to force-feed me, she promptly grabbed me by the nose and dug her thumbnail into my nostril. The mark remains to this day — the mark of protest. An omen perhaps? For in retrospect I find a large part of my life has been involved in protest of one sort or another.

Miss Sixsmith was a product of her time. What she would make of society today, if she were to return, I shudder to think. Always most assiduous in her religious duties and a firm believer in original sin, she did not favour sparing the rod even with the very young, for Satan had to be beaten out. To a certain extent my mother, who was to undertake the task of disciplining my younger sister Evelyn and myself, followed Miss Sixsmith's Victorian line though she tempered it with loving care. It was a common punishment then to whip children around the legs with a sally switch when especially naughty, and I can remember frustrating her attempts to switch me by taking refuge in an armchair, sitting huddled up, hugging my knees.

Miss Sixsmith's brother, a self-contained bachelor of impeccable orthodoxy, was a Canon of the Church of Ireland and onetime rector in Kilrea, Co. Derry. Later, when I worked in the North, I heard that he possessed the first 'velocipede' in those parts. Another bachelor brother Erskine, of doubtful orthodoxy, mysteriously appeared out of the blue to take up residence with his sister. I think he was looked upon as the black sheep of the family. The house which was once the nursing home still stands on the road to Ferns, the Carnew end of which was locally known as the Mill Lane.

According to my mother, there was a dispute in the family as to what they would have me called. Although they agreed on Gilbert, after my father, and Benjamin, after my grandfather, the choice of first name was the subject of some debate. For some reason best known to herself, my mother wanted to call me Reginald, but my father remained unconvinced. Uncle Bob

was an ageing relative with a great interest in history who lived
in Victoria Street off Dublin's South Circular Road. My parents,
though residents of Carnew, had been married in St Kevin's,
Dublin, from the uncle's house in Victoria Street. 'Why don't
you call him Victor?' chirped up Uncle Bob. This intervention
produced instant unanimity and promptly settled the question.
Years later I discovered that I had the same birthday, 24 May,
as Queen Victoria!

My paternal grandfather, Benjamin, spent his entire working
life in the service of Earl Fitzwilliam in Coollattin. Most of the
estates fielded cricket teams in those days and Coollattin was no
exception. My grandfather often boasted that he was once a
member of the team which played an eleven numbering some
Australian cricketers whom the Earl brought over from England
at the beginning of their tour. Young Ben apparently took a
memorable catch. I never knew whether to believe my grandfather's story or not. However, when I discovered a village in
Yorkshire with strong cricketing associations called Fitzwilliam
(near Wentworth), an estate which the Earl also owned, I
decided that the tale might well be true.

The Griffins lived in Coolroe village near Tinahely and Jane
Gilbert, Benjamin's bride, in neighbouring Coolafancy. The
couple took up residence in one of the Coollattin houses on the
main street in Carnew, for the Earl owned not only the village
of Shillelagh but also property in Carnew, including the castle.
My father, named Gilbert after his mother's family, brought *his*
bride in turn to live there with his parents. It was an ample
mid-Victorian house with five bedrooms and a shop beneath,
situated not far from the castle. Beside our family house stood
an identical one linked by an archway and above that archway
was a room which I often used.

My father eventually acquired both houses, having opened a
grocery store on our side. His brother Joseph and his family
came to live in the other house whose shop my uncle used for
his drapery business. The garden was opposite, on the other
side of the street. When the houses were built there was very
little traffic, but the street became in time much busier and

noisier. My grandfather's garden was his pride and joy. On one occasion, fooling around with some school pals, we trampled on his flower beds. I remember how he stormed and stamped and shouted at us for this wanton destruction of his carefully planned horticultural symmetry.

After he died part of the garden was sold as a site for a cinema. Vigorous opposition from the parish priest, Canon Prandy, marked the construction and opening of this invention of the devil. He objected on the grounds that allowing young people of both sexes to sit in close proximity in the dark would lead to immorality, roundly denouncing from the altar those responsible for bringing the cinema to Carnew and advising his flock to have nothing to do with it. The first film due to be screened was, ironically enough, *The Keys of the Kingdom*, based on the A.J. Cronin novel about a missionary priest in China. We were wondering how many of our Roman Catholic friends would run the gauntlet of the Canon's disapproval. A few brave souls who resolved to move with the times did so, but the cinema led to a split in the parish. As long as Canon Prandy remained, some steadfastly refused to go to the pictures. The affair was by no means unique. In Clones, Co. Monaghan, about that time, a priest decreed that boys should sit on one side of the cinema and girls on the other.

In those early days the houses would resound with the laughter of children. We had five cousins: Stanley, Cyril, who was my age and therefore especially close to me, Edna, Meta and Gilbert. On Sunday evenings there was family hymn singing around the piano or to Auntie Maude's harmonium accompaniment next door.

From a child I felt I was destined to be ordained. I never really had anything else in mind. If anyone asked me at seven or eight what I was going to be, I invariably answered 'a clergyman'. On Sunday evenings I would play 'church', dressing up perhaps somewhat self-importantly in an old sheet for a surplice and conducting the service, saying the prayers, reading the lesson and preaching the sermon, encouraged by my grandmother who told me she would like to see me ordained. Indeed, she had an indirect influence on my decision by bringing me into contact with the devotional life. I can visualise the plump, matronly figure seated in her armchair beside her work-basket, hands busy crocheting, while avidly reading the *Irish Times*.

In the mornings, after breakfast in bed, she would set about her devotions, and anyone around would be invited to share them. I remember, as a very small child, snuggling into bed beside her and hearing her read from *Daily Light* the bible passage and thought for the day, after which she would say the morning prayers. She read another portion of Scripture every evening, often joined by my father and mother.

It was a tribute to her practical Christianity that I never sensed any tension between herself and her daughter-in-law. She left the running of the house entirely to my mother.

My grandfather was a man who knew his own mind. Once determined he became inflexible. He was a typical Victorian patriarchal figure, a cautious man who was suspicious of some of my father's novel ideas.

His behaviour on the night of the guns raid entered family folklore. During the Civil War some Republicans or Free Staters came to our house looking for guns. My father was at pains to assure the men that there were no guns in the house. At this point my grandfather, who possessed a shotgun which he had prized from his youth, emerged in his night-shirt and, to the consternation of my father, leaned over the banisters shouting, 'Bert, for goodness sake don't give them my good shotgun'. My father recovered himself in time to save the situation.

'Don't mind *him*,' he urged the men, 'he's imagining things.'

My mother, Martha Violet Crowe, came from Newbliss, Co. Monaghan. Her people were small farmers, like so many Protestants there. We made train journeys in unheated carriages to visit them, the porters bringing my mother footwarmers freshly filled with hot water at stations along the route: Shillelagh station via Woodenbridge to Harcourt Street, then over to Amiens Street and the GNR to Monaghan via Dundalk. She received an excellent primary education, being taught not only the three Rs but also a fair amount of Latin and French.

Her sister Emma went on to become a teacher, and she herself could have continued her education but she chose to exploit her flair for fashion, for hats in particular, and so was apprenticed in Clones to learn the millinery business. She moved south to Carnew to become millinery buyer in Correll's department store and there she met my father who was a grocer by profession, but also a man of many parts, one of nature's successful speculators. He was the first man in Carnew to buy a motor car and, seeing potential in the growing motor business, built a garage there in 1920. Having no knowledge of motor engineering he employed a mechanic and electrician named Wells. He picked Wells' brains and soon became an expert himself. The garage not only sold petrol and undertook repairs but also hired out cars, mostly 'Model T' Fords. There were also at one time a Vulcan, an Armstrong-Siddeley and a charabanc seating up to seven for seaside trips. During the Civil War both Republicans and Free Staters would arrive at all hours looking for cars.

My father survived by never taking sides; he had a strict policy of first come, first served. Not surprisingly, the cars would often come back the worse for wear. He even lost some. I think it was doubtful whether he was always paid for the hire or the repairs. I have a sheaf of unpaid bills in my mother's neat handwriting — it was she who kept the accounts — held together by a large, long-since-rusted safety pin, itemising the Carnew IRA account for October 1922.

He was known throughout the locality for his generosity and courage which at times came very close to recklessness. Furthermore, all religious denominations were secondary, of little concern, and he would say, 'There is one God over us all. We are all travelling the same way. So why should we worry about what church we attend?'. He told me of a memorable trip to Galway and back during the Black and Tan period. The relative of a Carnew Roman Catholic family had died in Galway and no one was prepared to bring the coffin home to Carnew for burial. In desperation the family approached my father. A journey across a country in insurrection was fraught with danger and my grandfather advised against it, as did my mother. But my father, never one to resist a challenge, set off with his driver, William Birch, to make a two-day journey to Galway. Finding overnight accommodation was far from easy, for people were naturally suspicious of travellers. In one place they were given little more than a floor to lie on. There were roadblocks all the way, but the return journey took longer because the coffin was frequently opened and searched for arms. When the funeral finally took place the parish priest made a moving reference to the kindness and courage of Mr Bert Griffin, and members of the deceased's family came up to my father to shake him by the hand, tears of gratitude in their eyes.

Funeral undertaking was for him a logical extension of his car-hire service, and before long he had his own joiner, Bill Hope, making coffins for him and the other undertakers in the locality. Bill used to work in a loft down on our farm on the Ferns road and we would often go there and lie in the coffins. Rest in Hope, we would say. Death and coffins and funerals held no fears for us. Nothing macabre — all entirely natural. And if my father's coffins were in great demand, the brass plaques or breastplates which he engraved to affix to the coffins were even more widely sought after, there being no one else within miles offering this service. Undertakers would come from far and near, even from Bunclody (then Newtownbarry), Arklow and Gorey, with breastplates and inscriptions. Entirely self-taught, he had an inborn sense of design, fashioning the breastplates in different shapes, for each had to recognise the individuality of the deceased, and engraving in ornate lettering RIP, name and details. Sometimes he would stay up half the night to finish two or three orders in time for the burials. I can still see him, bespectacled and crouched over the kitchen table first tracing and spacing out the letters and then engraving them and blowing away the scrapings as he went along.

He brought the first wireless set to Carnew. I remember the excitement the first time he put the earphones on me and I watched him twiddle the knobs on top of the little brown box until through the crackling and atmospherics I was at last able to detect a human voice. The locals were invited in to sample the novelty. Some were so suspicious they wouldn't even listen. One or two were scared out of their wits. My earliest memory is of electric rather than lamp light in our house because my father had a generator installed in his garage across the street, and Wells the mechanic fixed up a connection from it. We became the first family in Carnew to enjoy electric light.

My father was never interested in making money. He never speculated in order to make himself rich. Indeed, if he'd any money on him and saw a beggar, particularly a destitute mother with a child in her arms, he just couldn't pass by on the other side. It was a miracle that he survived financially. In the Thirties and Forties, there was a great deal of poverty and people often came into his grocery shop for provisions with no means of paying. He always served them without a second thought. My mother was generous too, but more prudent. 'What are you doing to your family?' she would ask him. 'If this goes on *we'll* be on the street.' It was similar with his other business enterprises. When he did work for which he wasn't paid he never had the heart to take debtors to law to recover what he was owed. I don't suppose he ever asked a solicitor to write a letter to anyone.

Sometimes, when family finances were pretty desperate, as in the Economic War, my mother would lie anxiously awake at night while my father slept the sleep of the just. She used to say to me, 'If that man was to be executed in the morning he'd have a good night's rest in the condemned cell.' I inherited that same ability: I may have problems during the day but I never carry them to bed. It's a great blessing, for health is damaged, not by worrying during the day, but at night. I think I may have inherited some of my father's soft heart, too. I find it hard to turn away anyone who comes looking for help and it is almost invariably money, not spiritual consolation, which is sought. Sometimes while seeing through the fiction one has to admire the ingenuity which supplies an air of credibility to what is obviously, and from past experience, a 'tall' story. Once in St Patrick's Deanery I was so thrilled when one 'customer' said,

'Dean, I'm not going to tell you a lie. I want the price of a pint' that I rewarded him there and then for his honesty. This was exceptional. The usual line was a near relative dead or dying in Belfast, Cork or Liverpool. Would I please help with travelling expenses to enable attendance at the funeral? 'I'm not asking you for money, only to lend me £20 or so until I get my allowance next week!'

I remember coming home for Christmas after my first term at Trinity College, Dublin. The weather was bitterly cold and on the edge of the town was a line of small cottages called Coollattin Row. One of them was occupied by a widow. 'That poor woman hasn't even a fire,' said my father. He brought me with him into the yard and we began splitting logs together. I had then to shoulder a sackful all the way to her cottage.

'My father sent these over to you.'

'Ah,' she replied, 'your father's a good Christian man.'

Looking after people in need was something I was also expected to do.

2

Farm

I REGRET never having served in a country parish during my ministry, but when I was in Derry I used to enjoy making pastoral visits to a number of farmers on Sheriff's Mountain which stood on the outskirts of the parish. Walking round their farms as we talked of country concerns, I was grateful for the renewed contact with surroundings familiar since my earliest years. Such roots go very deep. I relished the exhilarating sense of freedom and space in open fields. This was especially true of school holidays once I started at Kilkenny College which was, like most boarding schools of the time, a virtual prison. Life became once again uncomplicated on my return home for holidays. I was as free as air.

Even the task I found irksome, thinning turnips, was a welcome relief. Wearing sacks tied on with binder twine to protect my knees, the sun beating down on my back, the seemingly endless drill of tiny plants stretching ahead of me, I experienced the loneliness of the long-distance turnip thinner. Reaching at last the end of one drill, I had to turn and begin the next.

But if the farm workers, Lar Rossiter or Jim Doran and occasionally Maurice Molloy from a neighbouring farm, were with me the drudgery disappeared as we talked to each other across the drills. Lar was lean and sinewy with a weather-beaten face and work-hardened hands, a man of few words. He impressed by his total lack of fear of rats. When we were threshing and the rats that had been living and feeding in the ricks of corn in the haggard finally had to make a dash from their refuge, Lar had no binder twine round his trouser bottoms to stop them running up his legs as the other men had. If any rat had the audacity to run up one of his trouser legs he promptly caught it and squeezed the life out of it. Then, quite unruffled and to our amazement, he would shake out the corpse.

Jim, on the other hand, was a shy, callow youth, the willing helper, almost the overgrown schoolboy, who lived with his mother in a cottage outside Carnew. Jim had a knack with rabbits. He knew exactly when and where they would leap. When the rabbits in a hay or cornfield were being slowly deprived of their home as the mower or binder was drawn in ever-decreasing circles around them, Jim would anticipate their bolts for freedom and pounce on them, catching the frightened creatures in his hands.

Maurice was tall and slim with a quiet and relaxed manner for whom nothing was too much trouble.

Rabbits were a great source of food. We often snared them. I remember Jim showing me where and how to set a snare in a rabbit's run. A rabbit in mid leap would catch his head in the looped snare wire attached to a slender wooden stake in the ground. Like all country children, I accepted snaring, hunting and shooting as part and parcel of country life. The fox, hunted in open country with a chance of escaping but sometimes torn apart by hounds, is himself a ruthless hunter and killer in the chicken run. But I could never tolerate the contrived cruelty of letting out a hare in an enclosed space to be savaged by grey-hounds, nor could I bear to see a horse being beaten or a cat or dog ill-treated.

I sometimes helped Jim and Lar to make a scarecrow. We nailed two pieces of wood together in the shape of a cross and made the head from a white cloth flour bag stuffed with straw, marking out the features with a finger dipped in black shoe polish. (At Hallowe'en we made disguises for ourselves in the same way from flour bags with holes cut out to see through.) An old jacket and pair of trousers were stuffed with straw and tied on the frame, like the head, with binder twine. A battered hat completed the outfit. It is possible that for the first twenty-four hours a scarecrow might have had some salutary effect, but no longer. I have seen birds perching on scarecrows, the final indignity.

In winter we would talk of the hunt: where the fox had gone; how many foxes had been killed. My Uncle George hunted with the Coollattin Hounds, kept originally by Earl Fitzwilliam, who died in a plane crash and had no male heir. When the Earl's widow died, the estate was sold and the hounds taken over by a local group. There were also the Island Hounds which hunted in North Co. Wexford. Both packs had a great following around Carnew. Whatever about hare coursing, the farmer or countryman will never be convinced that fox hunting is wrong and should be declared illegal. Hunting, shooting and fishing are second nature to him, an accepted and normal part of country life.

On fair days the main street of Carnew was full of cattle, pigs and sheep with farmers haggling over prices. A third party would sometimes step in and negotiate a deal which was clinched by a ceremonial spitting on and slapping of hands. The farmer who had been paid usually said to the third party, 'Come on, I'll stand you a drink.' And they would adjourn to the nearest pub. On occasions one of the more affluent members of the farming fraternity might be described as a 'snug man', the 'snug' being a cubicle in a pub providing privacy, often used for negotiating business deals or for matchmaking. The 'snug man' was comfortably off and no 'dozer' when it came to business deals.

On the farm we used the Wicklow-Wexford farming terms like 'sprong', meaning four-pronged fork. The 'fork' was a pitchfork which had two prongs. A briar was called by its Irish name, a *sceach* or *sgeach*.

All the local farmhands, or farm labourers as they were called, were Roman Catholics. I never remember religion being discussed except perhaps what the priest had said about some misdemeanour (or serious parochial financial problem) the previous Sunday. Neither was there any sense of social or class distinction between us as we worked in the fields together.

Haymaking took place in June. When I was at national school I could look forward to this but later, as a boarder at Kilkenny, I would miss bringing in the hay. Hay bogies were becoming popular, having the novelty of winching the haycock up the tilted surface until with a thud the horizontal was reached. Rides on the backs of bogies were always fraught with danger, for the additional weight might cause the bogey to up-end and deposit its load on the free riders.

I was always at home for the harvest, the busiest and, for a child, the most exciting time of the farming year. Extra labour was called in and, as was the custom, neighbouring farmers came to lend a hand. I can still see myself sitting high up on the piled sheaves in the cart as the horse pulled it towards the haggard, and then pitching the sheaves up to the rick which gradually grew higher and higher, hard work for the first ten minutes until a rhythm of forking and pitching was established.

Throughout the harvest my mother was busy in our kitchen with Brigid and Theresa, who helped in the house, preparing meals for the men. Whole hams were bought and boiled in big pots on the large kitchen range which was black-leaded every week until it shone. I can still smell the mouth-watering aroma of bacon-flavoured steam. The hams were sliced to fill great sandwiches spread with my mother's own butter. Sandwiches, mugs and cups were put into large sally baskets, to send down to the haggard along with lidded cans and buckets of strong tea.

Although my mother trained as a milliner, she was a farmer's daughter and fulfilled her duties as farmer's wife with quiet, controlled efficiency. I remember one year the threshing went on for nearly a week because a damaged piston in the threshing engine took two days to replace and then the rain set in. The men, of course, turned up every day expecting work and had to be fed.

As a child I awaited the arrival of the threshing engine, mill and straw pitcher with mounting impatience. Steam traction engines were sometimes used for deliveries of bulky products. Davis's of Enniscorthy had one which puffed up the street quite fast, like a little railway engine, pulling a truck of bags of flour. But the steam engine which slowly pulled the threshing mill and pitcher was special because its arrival heralded the transformation of the normally tranquil haggard into a noisy, bustling hive of industry, a delight just to watch from a distance until I was old enough to join in.

Into the haggard went this whole threshing apparatus with much shunting and shouting and swearing to get the correct position between the ricks. All in order, the driver and fireman, my boyhood heroes, would then snatch a few hours sleep in a shed before getting up at the crack of dawn to light the fire and get steam up. A whistle from the engine signalled that threshing was about to begin.

Sacks were hooked below on the mill to collect the grain. Straw vomited from the large gaping mill mouth was caught on the pitcher, a spiked conveyer belt sending it to the men building the rick. The whole scene was a rhythm of intense activity. My earliest contribution to this activity was to watch the filling of the sacks and tell the man beside me when one was almost full. Later I would have unhooked the full sack myself and hooked on a new one. Dogs were invariably present, barking and chasing any rat which emerged from the corn rick, its squeaks of alarm drowned by the noise of the engine. I can remember having to take parts of machinery damaged during the harvest for repair at the forge and also frequently bringing a horse to be shod.

Ned Lyons had, like all blacksmiths, great sinewy arms. There was not an ounce of surplus fat on his body. Indeed, it is impossible to imagine a blacksmith ever being rotund. Entering the forge, leading the horse, I encountered sparks flying in all directions and was rather hesitant to proceed further, fearing that one of them might get into my eye. There was Ned at the anvil, hammering away at a glowing red horseshoe which he plunged into water with a sudden hissing of steam. Then, starting high up, he ran his hand little by little down the horse's leg, finally lifting it gently. At this point the horse would become uneasy and it was my job to reassure him, patting him on the neck and saying, 'Yo, yo. Quiet now. Come on, now.' Ned pared the hoof with a curved knife to suit the new shoe, then tried the shoe against the hoof and if alterations were needed it was fired and hammered again. The process of fitting, heating, hammering, cooling, fitting again continued until he got it right. At last he nailed the shoe on and the horse was released to admire it.

I looked forward to going to the forge because a few locals could always be found there telling yarns. It was a popular meeting place for those for whom work was not particularly attractive or who were genuinely unemployed. They read the *Independent* or *Irish Press*, particularly the racing pages, and, having chosen likely winners, they sent their sixpenny bets up to the bookmaker in Carnew. Often in the evening I sat listening to the BBC six o'clock news on the radio to get the racing results for the lads outside, marking numbers 1, 2, 3 in each race in the racing section of the newspaper. I would then emerge waving it like someone with the election results. Shouts of joy if they'd won. Groans of disappointment if they'd lost again.

My father used to bet twice a year, on the Derby and the Grand National, compulsory rituals as far as he was concerned, and at point-to-point races. Mild flutters always. A shilling or maybe half-a-crown but no more. My grand-uncle Joseph Gilbert, my grandmother's brother, would bet more often. He had been a land steward and had an eye for the horses, and when he retired he came to live near us in Carnew. He bought the *Irish Independent* and, having studied the form, would place a small bet or two. Following the horses or studying form, as it was commonly termed, was a favourite leisure time activity of the retired in the country. We read the *Irish Times* — Irish Protestants were the original 'Smyllie's people', Irish through and through although never anti-British — but perhaps the racing coverage was better in the *Independent*!

Sometimes Uncle Joe went to stay with a farmer friend in Kilcavan in the Wicklow hills, about five miles from town. He had an arrangement with the driver of the van which transported Protestant school children living in remote areas to deliver his bets to the bookmaker in Carnew. One morning the driver was sick and the rector, Mr Forrest, took his place at the wheel. Joe Gilbert had everything prepared as usual. Then to his horror he noticed the rector was driving. 'Hello, Mr Gilbert. Can I do anything for you?' Uncle Joe hesitated, then handed over his envelope, the contents of which he described as a 'message' for immediate delivery to the accustomed driver whom the rector told him would soon be on duty as usual. Next day Uncle Joe discovered that one of his horses had come in at 20–1. He'd won a not inconsiderable sum for those days. A day later the driver returned.

'I backed the right one,' said Uncle Joe.

'What are you talking about?'

'Didn't you get my message?'

'I got no message,' said the driver. 'Who did you send it down with?'

Meanwhile, Mr Forrest, going through his pockets, found the envelope and delivered it. When he apologised for his forgetfulness, Joe Gilbert couldn't say a word.

Over the years we had a number of horses on the farm. Horses, unlike dogs, had no names; they were referred to as 'the chestnut' or 'the grey' or 'the frisky one' or 'the mare'. Like all farming children, I begged to be put on one of the horses at an early age. I would ride the animal bareback, clutching its mane. A carthorse's back stands very high off the ground but while my father or one of the men was leading the horse I was unafraid, even when it began to trot. That was the sum total of my riding experience because there was no opportunity of riding at boarding school. Times had changed since Jonathan Swift's schooldays in Kilkenny College when he bought a nag at a local fair which dropped dead under him not long after.

Country children soon learn the facts of life and I was no exception. Bringing the cow to the bull at the right time and seeing the bull mount her afforded practical instruction of the most natural, healthy kind. And I vividly remember waiting in the cow house with Jim and my father through the small hours with a cow that was ready to calve, all three of us wrapped up against the cold, the wind howling outside and me holding the storm lantern. Eventually the two front legs and head would appear, the signal to tie the rope round the legs and start to pull for all we were worth to assist the birth. Once the membrane was broken and my father had taken deep breaths and blown air into the newborn's mouth, we rubbed the calf with bran and salt to encourage the mother to lick it. Then she would suckle the calf and whatever was left of the thick, creamy first milk, known as the 'beastings', was used to make pancakes.

I occasionally tried my hand at milking. While the men were emptying milk out of a pail into a creamery can, I might sit down and manipulate a cow's teats, but I don't suppose I ever milked one completely. I remember the swishing sound as the thin stream of milk hit the side of the bucket held between my knees. If the cow kicked that bucket over, my services were promptly dispensed with.

My mother was an expert butter-maker. Our house in the town had a large, cool, stone-flagged dairy at the back. The milk was brought there and poured into big earthenware vats, kept on wooden benches round the walls. Some was set aside for the kitchen, three or four gallons laid by for butter. I used to turn the end-over-end churn for my mother. Churning would take about an hour. When the butter began to form in blobs on the top of the milk, the churn had to be shaken to make them congeal. Then my mother skimmed off the butter, and placing it on a butter board she slapped it with two wooden platters to remove the buttermilk. The skill lay in squeezing out all the moisture and in knowing how much salt to add. She would often decorate the finished product by impressing a design from a wooden block. A rose, I think, was her favourite.

Buttermilk was a heavenly drink, especially on a hot summer day, and was also used in making bread. Eating home-baked bread from our own flour spread with home-churned butter and home-made blackberry jam or crab apple jelly was, for a child, the nearest thing to paradise.

Food continued plentiful on farms during the Economic War, waged between Ireland and Britain for over six years during the Thirties as a consequence of the de Valera government's decision to withhold the land annuities payable twice yearly by Irish farmers to the British government. In retaliation, Britain taxed imports of Irish cattle, thereby depriving Irish farmers of their principal market. There was a glut of cattle in Ireland and stock prices plummeted. New-born calves were left to die in ditches, milk was poured away and cows slaughtered. Growing grain crops became uneconomic. A barrel of oats sold for two shillings instead of fifteen. There was food to eat — potatoes, vegetables and meat in plenty — but no hard cash. Bill Harte, the local postman who also acted as butcher, visited us more frequently than usual in order to despatch an animal in one of the outhouses. These executions were a sight I never witnessed, nor had I any desire to do so.

There is a story told about a farmer in Enniscorthy which illustrates graphically the effect of the Economic War. He was told by his wife to take a calf to the fair and get what he could for it. 'Get rid of it,' she instructed him, 'even if you only get a shilling for it.' Having a soft heart, presumably she did not wish to leave it to die. So he brought it to the fair in his cart with the creels round it. No one would so much as look at it. On the way home he stopped at a pub and leaving the calf in the cart went inside. 'Would anybody like to buy a calf for sixpence?' Still no takers. After talking to the boys for a while and drinking a proffered pint, he went out and found two calves in the cart instead of one!

I remember how scarce money was then. My father struggled to survive, but his generous treatment of needy customers in his grocer's shop (he had already handed over the garage to his brother-in-law) did not help matters. The week before Christmas at the height of the Economic War my mother remarked to my father that she had only a ten shilling note left in her purse. Ten shillings was a considerable amount for some people then, but it was unusual for her to have so little. 'Look what we've come to,' she said. 'Times are hard when I've only got ten shillings at Christmas.' And they continued hard until de Valera settled the annuity dispute by paying Britain a capital sum of ten million pounds in 1938.

Today's farmers have a long folk memory going back to the time of the Economic War when they were its chief victims, treated as second-class citizens. In the Thirties the farmer had a low standing, far beneath that of the merchant or the member of a profession. He was the 'hewer of wood and the drawer of water', the 'mullocker', up to his knees in mire or 'clabber', making the best he could of the few resources he had. Small wonder then, that with such a history of gloomy insecurity, his modern descendant regards the European Community's Common Agricultural Policy, with its stable markets and guaranteed prices, as a sacred cow.

While segregation was the rule in schools and churches, it never obtained in the local farming and business community. Protestants and Roman Catholics mingled together, would drop into each other's homes for an evening fireside chat, when the talk usually centred on the price of bullocks, the state of the crops, what so and so got for letting his land, recent marriages and deaths. The only hint of embarrassment came when there was a mixed marriage. Both sides remained silent. I suppose by a sort of tacit mutual agreement mention of such matters was ruled out. Strange to think that the Christian religion, which should have been a unifying force, was the only issue which divided Protestant from Roman Catholic, Christian from Christian. How untrue to the teaching of its founder. I used to wonder, what has gone wrong? How can this be in so-called Christian Ireland, the island of saints and scholars? And if talk turned to politics it was strictly limited to their internal dimension, never extending to questions which might involve Protestantism and its identification in the public mind with the British connection.

I remember the Kinsellas and the Brownes with whom we were on particularly friendly terms. And there was Dick Doyle who had some land down in Beechmount adjoining my father's fields. My father would sit for hours in Dick's house yarning away the time. Dick was the tallest man in Carnew at six feet seven. He was a gigantic man, large of frame as well as tall of stature and with a deep powerful voice — a veritable Goliath — and he had to drive with his seat pushed back to the furthest possible extremity in his car in order to accommodate his extraordinary length of leg. Dick was a big man in every sense, large hearted and generous, one of nature's gentlemen.

Our immediate neighbours in Carnew were of our own religious persuasion. When I was a boy all the houses on the square belonged to Protestants. My uncle, aunt and cousins lived on one side and my grand-aunt Susie and her brother, the betting man Joseph Gilbert, resided further up the street. Aunt Susie was a spinster who lived alone before Uncle Joe retired. Her house stood beside the castle. The Roman Catholic schoolhouse was about 100 yards down the road. During the Civil War when the bullets began to fly between the Free Staters entrenched in one building and the Republicans in the other, she found herself in the crossfire. But she refused to leave home, retreating to her big oak wardrobe, even sleeping in it at night, to the whine of bullets bouncing off the walls outside.

Opposite us lived another spinster, Miss Stone, a strict Protestant who would have felt uncomfortable in this ecumenical age. She took in lady teachers as lodgers, one at a time, all of them Roman Catholics. But, avoiding theology and sharing the kitchen, while enjoying their separate sitting rooms, Miss Stone and her lodgers lived amicably together. She was an elderly countrywoman who complained often of the arthritis which caused her to limp. Her grey hair was pulled back severely in a bun, and like all women of her generation she wore long skirts. As was the custom then she always wore a cross-over pinafore while at home. When visitors arrived she whipped it off. The moment they left, on it went again. I remember my mother doing the same.

There were many in those days who barely managed to eke out a living. Labourers were housed in rough stone whitewashed thatched cottages with half-doors. Large families were raised in three rooms, a central kitchen which also served as a living room with a bedroom on either side. Next to the hearth stood the fanners, a metal contraption with a fan inside belted onto a wheel which was turned by hand to encourage the logs and turf to burn.

There was an old country saying, which we firmly believed as children, that the surest way to persuade a bird to talk was to split its tongue with a sixpence. Mrs Quigley's talking jackdaw, which, it was said, she kept in a cage in her cottage in Coollattin Row on the edge of town, was reputed to be proof positive of the efficacy of this method.

Mrs Quigley's husband worked for a gentleman farmer called Hammond, supervising his stables. One of Hammond's horses, a powerfully built black gelding named after Mr Quigley, was particularly successful in winning prizes at point-to-point races and was therefore much fancied. Quigley was always entered in the last event of the Coollattin Hunt Point-to-Point Races held in Shillelagh, a race which we children endeavoured never to miss. He was ridden by an amateur jockey, a man from Carlow called Burgess, a farmer, I think, who rode with the hunt.

The school management naturally saw no reason to suspend classes on race days, but if we really hurried we could make it down to Shillelagh to witness Quigley's anticipated triumph. My father and friends would have driven down earlier, so we had to thumb a lift from a passing motorist. If we were lucky, we would sometime pile into the post van with Matt Kennedy who had collected the four o'clock post in Carnew to bring it to Shillelagh in time to catch the train for Dublin.

Many labourers' children went barefoot all the year round and wore cast-off clothing from older children or items purchased for a few pence at jumble sales. Some lived in tied cottages, their father working for the farmer who paid a wage of about ten shillings a week and supplied the family with some potatoes and vegetables and perhaps a bit of meat and a chicken or two.

The lot of casual labourers was even harder. They found occasional work with the County Council repairing the roads or shovelling the weeds and mud from drainage channels or trimming the hedges with shears or a billhook. Sometimes they had to break stones sitting on a sack on top of a huge pile, hammering away at stone after stone. Before tarmacadam, stones were used to make a foundation. Clay was scattered on top, sprayed with water and the job completed by levelling out by a steam roller.

Then there was always the emigration. They headed in droves for England, sending home what they could spare of their earnings to support their impoverished parents and younger brothers and sisters.

I remember very few country Protestant general practitioners, since most Protestant doctors tended to practise in the cities and larger hospitals. Dr King was one of the few. He resided in the doctor's house in Shillelagh but he sometimes had patients who lived in Carnew. He was a staid, gaunt, elderly gentleman, a real Victorian, complete with waistcoat, watch and gold chain and white wing collar, a kindly family doctor whom I will always associate with the character Dr Cameron in A.J. Cronin's, *Dr Finlay's Casebook.*

He was called in when I broke my leg at four years of age. The accident happened while one of the men was crossing the yard carrying an iron gate on his back to secure the pigsty. I foolishly climbed up on it. Feeling himself pulled backwards by the additional weight he let go and the gate landed on my leg. Dr King decided to treat the fracture himself. He applied plaster of paris there and then in our house, but after six weeks the leg was more crooked then ever and I had to be sent to the Adelaide Hospital in Dublin to have the bone broken and reset.

An eminent surgeon called Ball performed the operation. I remember vividly white figures encircling me, holding me down as I kicked and screamed on the operating table. 'Now be a good boy and blow into this big bag,' they coaxed as they forced it down over my face. Then suddenly appearing out of nowhere were balloons in all the colours of the rainbow floating around in the terrible darkness as I struggled against the ether and then lost consciousness. But Mr Ball did an excellent job on my leg and the injury did not stop me from playing rugby later when I had entered the formidable portals of Kilkenny College.

I remember on winter mornings, after porridge and fried bread, my mother with her tablespoon ladling into me a clammy treaclelike concoction from a brown jar, called Virol, said to be the complete answer to all the rigours of winter. And there was castor oil, the infallible cure for tummy upsets, and cascara or syrup of figs, the sure answer to constipation. Children today are spared such medicinal tortures. Dinner was always at midday. Lunch consisted of the sandwiches and bottle of milk brought to school if distance ruled out getting home for the midday break. In our case this wasn't necessary as the school was literally on the corner about fifty yards away. Two courses were on offer for dinner, potatoes, meat and vegetables followed invariably by a milk pudding, sago, rice or tapioca. Soup, either mutton or chicken broth, was generally reserved for elevenses on cold mornings or afternoons and was served in mugs. Tea was the evening meal with bread, butter and jam, perhaps also scones or ginger cake supplemented sometimes by a boiled egg, especially a duck egg if available, a salad in summer and in cold weather an ample fry of eggs, sausages and rashers. Supper at bedtime meant tea or cocoa and cheese or occasionally spring onion sandwiches. Only the shining ones up in the castle, Captain Woodhouse and his wife Beatrice, had dinner at 7.00 p.m., announced every evening to the Carnew townsfolk by the ritualistic ringing of the castle bell. Lords of the Manor or the Ascendancy, with the exception of the Woodhouses, always referred to the locals by their surnames, Griffin or Molloy, not even prefixed by 'Mr'. His female partner was simply called his wife, never 'Mrs'. Class distinction was rigidly observed. Protestant and Roman Catholic were looked on or looked down on with equal dispassion. No special degree of intimacy was extended to Protestants. Whatever crisis of identity the Ascendancy may have had, the ordinary Irish Protestant, farmer or businessman, had no doubts that he was thoroughly Irish, though he may secretly have regretted the ending of the British connection and his political separation from the English, the Welsh and the Scots who made up the United Kingdom under the Crown.

'We are going to Courtown Harbour.' Nothing in our young minds could compare with the thrill and excitement of such an announcement. In cars, with our sandwiches, cups and kettles and later on bicycles, we made our way through Gorey to our seaside mecca, Courtown, whose maritime delights seemed like a magnet irresistibly attracting what appeared to be the entire population of Carlow, South Wicklow and North Wexford every

Sunday and church holiday during the summer months. Swimmers and splashers, farmers and their families made this pilgrimage, many on the off-chance of meeting some friends, distant cousins or old acquaintances. Weather-beaten sons of the soil, dressed in Sunday best, would sit together on the wall gazing out to sea, discussing the price of land or bullocks or the state of the crops before adjourning to a crowded pub to down a pint or two. Then at the approach of darkness all were homeward bound, except the cinema goers or dance-hallers. But for Protestants, no cinema or dance-hall. Such breaking of the Sabbath was frowned on in Protestant circles, and any infringement was seen as a lukewarm attitude to the faith and the first step on the road to a mixed marriage with the inevitable and dreaded consequence of capitulation to Rome. Apart from seaside outings, those who were fortunate enough to have a week or fortnight's holiday spent it at home, with perhaps, for some, a few days with relatives elsewhere in Ireland.

Protestant thoughts were occasionally turned from the domestic religious scene when a returned missionary would arrive complete with magic lantern and bulky slides of foreign parts. Huddled together in a darkened classroom with the hissing and pungent smell of carbide as the lantern was activated, we gazed in awe and admiration on one who had actually been to Africa or Asia and escaped the cannibals' cauldron. The last slide was always the words of a missionary hymn. As the piano thumped out the tune we all joined in. Our pennies and sixpences clinked on the collecting plate and the strains of *From Greenland's Icy Mountains* reverberated over the silent street outside. We were left in no doubt that the poor, blind, 'benighted heathen, bowing down to wood and stone' needed us to lighten their darkness. We must be prepared to bear the 'white man's burden' and from our lofty spiritual pinnacle look down and be ready to introduce the 'lesser breeds' to the benefits of Western Christian civilisation. Thankfully things have now changed with the realisation that we all have something to learn from as well as to teach each other.

3

Living in a Minority Community

AFTER Independence Protestants in the South, or in the Irish Free State as it was then called, were a beleaguered minority. The vast majority of them were of the Unionist tradition and had a soft spot in their hearts for the monarchy. They felt that leaving the United Kingdom was a mistake, that Ireland's future, from a political and economic point of view, would have been better served as part of the United Kingdom. There was an exodus on the part of those who could not bring themselves to accept the new order, while those who remained resigned themselves to the inevitable. Protestants felt vulnerable and kept a low profile. This was understandable, since Protestantism was associated in the minds of the majority community with the British Ascendancy. Keep your head down, look after your family and business, avoid religion and politics in conversation with your Roman Catholic neighbours — this was the Protestant manifesto.

The Protestant minority depended very largely on the good-will and support of their Roman Catholic neighbours, especially if they were in business in small towns. In Fethard-on-Sea, as late as 1957, a boycott was imposed by Roman Catholics on the Protestant community because of the break-up of a mixed marriage when the Protestant wife made off with her children to Belfast, and the local Protestants were accused by a zealous priest and others of collusion in the affair, an accusation which they utterly rejected. The pressures on mixed marriages imposed by Roman Catholic teaching (the *Ne Temere* decree), resulted in a further diminution of the Protestant community. 'He (or she) has turned' meant a conversion to Roman Catholicism, usually by marriage. This was spoken of by Protestants in whispers, with a certain sense of embarrassment, a feeling of being let down, of one of our own going over to the enemy. Even our baptism was not recognised. Having to be baptised conditionally a second time in a Roman Catholic church before being married was a great indignity for a Protestant to bear. And in politics too we were seen as outsiders, not truly Irish, in the nation but not of it. To be Irish meant being Roman Catholic, Nationalist, Gaelic and anti-British. As a result, the Protestant community as a whole opted out of the political scene, thankful for any crumbs thrown it in the form of educational funding, grateful for toleration which it regarded not as a right but as a favour bestowed by a government which could withhold it if it chose to do so. This passive, almost subservient attitude had an unfortunate effect on the Roman Catholic community and on the Northern Protestants. It sent the wrong signal, the effects of which are still with us.

Roman Catholics in the South saw the Protestants apparently happy with the status quo, accepting without demur the dominant influence of the Roman Catholic Church. True, from time to time, some lone Protestant voices, such as W.B. Yeats in the Senate, could be heard protesting at the confessional nature of the State and the denial of democratic rights to the minority. Alas, such courageous souls were not supported by the Protestant community at large and were therefore regarded by Roman Catholics as eccentrics and unrepresentative of Protestant opinion.

Roman Catholics deduced from what they saw around them that it was not Protestantism which prevented the reunification of Ireland, since Protestants could apparently live happily under a government imbued with the Roman Catholic ethos. Therefore, they concluded, there must be some other factor responsible for keeping Ireland divided. No prizes for guessing the identity of that *bête noire*: the British, of course, the source of all our ills. So the argument went, if the Brits were sent packing, the Protestants of the North would come in. Britain was using the

Northern Protestants for her imperialistic and colonial objectives. Brits out. Unity in. This simplistic and totally invalid conclusion was nevertheless understandable. For their part, the Northern Protestants saw no hope for the survival of Protestantism in the South, and this view seemed to be borne out by the continuing decline in the Protestant population and the total acceptance by the Southern Protestants of the Catholic ethos of the State. This hardened the resolve of the Northern Protestants never to become part of a united Ireland.

I remember so well my mother constantly warning me: 'Victor, steer clear of religion and politics.' She would write to me at Trinity when she read or heard of some controversial chord which I had struck in student debates and she would add, 'You'll get us all burnt out if you go on saying things like that.' I continued to ignore such admonitions. Years later she mellowed, and when many Roman Catholics mentioned to her, with approval, my outspoken pleas for a pluralist society I think she felt rather proud. But in those days she was frankly scared of me.

I had taken up a protesting stance at a very tender age, having been taught not to think of St Patrick as being the exclusive property of the Roman Catholic Church. Miss Moody, our teacher at Carnew Church of Ireland National School told us that St Patrick believed what we believed and that the Pope in the time of St Patrick did not make claims to universal jurisdiction or infallibility. These only came much later. We in the Church of Ireland were taught to be true to St Patrick's teaching founded on Holy Scripture. What divided us from the Church of Rome were doctrines which had been added to the old faith, such as papal infallibility, the Immaculate Conception and the Assumption of the Blessed Virgin Mary. We were warned always to speak of *Roman* Catholics, never just Catholics, and to resist any attempt to call us non-Catholics. We belonged to the one Holy Catholic and Apostolic Church and affirmed this in the Creed which was said during every act of public worship. The Church of Ireland, it was emphasised, did not begin at the Reformation. The Reformation was a protest against additions to the old Catholic faith which was the faith held always, everywhere and by all. Protestants were protesting Catholics or reformed Catholics, certainly not non-Catholics, an insulting title equivalent to non-Christian. Non-Roman Catholic certainly yes. Non-Catholic certainly no. We had the Catholic Scriptures, the Catholic Creeds, the Catholic Sacraments, the Catholic ministry and we looked back to St Patrick and the Celtic Church for our origins with a due respect for the See of Rome as the primatial See of the West but with a firm rejection of later Roman claims and innovations.

This was all in our Church teaching, so necessary to preserve our sense of identity. It was always positive, and never do I remember any words of bitterness directed against Roman Catholics. On the contrary, it was emphasised that we are all God's children and, while not agreeing about everything, we must always, as Christians, love and respect one another. We were not non-Catholics, but protesting, Protestant Catholics. No contradiction was involved in being a Protestant *and* a Catholic.

I brought all this home from school and told it to Brigid, a local young Roman Catholic girl who lived with us and helped my mother. 'Brigid, do you know St Patrick was just as much a Protestant as he was a Catholic'! Much later, after I was ordained, I would often meet her on visits home. 'Remember the debates we used to have about St Patrick?' she would ask me. 'Do you still think he was a Protestant?' And we would laugh.

When I was a baby Brigid wheeled me out in my pram and later took me on my first walks when we often passed her church in Tomacork, a couple of miles from Carnew. She brought me into the church while she said a prayer in front of a statue of the Virgin Mary. Brigid later told me that I invariably knelt down beside her and said the Lord's Prayer so audibly that I almost shouted out the petitions, much to the amusement or annoyance of those who were silently practising their devotions.

Some Protestants in those days would have objected to their child being brought into a Roman Catholic church. My parents never did. Social and business relationships between the communities were by and large very cordial but when it came to the practice of religion there was complete segregation.

Although the best of friends in life — visiting one another's houses, dealing together at fairs and markets, helping each other in haymaking and harvests — in death there was the great divide. It was the custom to stay outside the church while a funeral mass or service was being conducted and to stand some distance from the graveside in order not to hear the words of the priest or clergyman.

Much comment has been made about the funeral in St Patrick's Cathedral of President Douglas Hyde when the members of the Cabinet sat in their cars in St Patrick's Close while the service was taking place, only joining the procession as it left the Cathedral. A similar situation obtained with weddings. People would wait outside the church and join the other guests at the reception. While the Roman Catholic faithful were forbidden by Church law to be present at worship in a Protestant church, Protestants were not bound canonically in the same way. My father was one of the few who did not hesitate to attend weddings and funerals in Roman Catholic churches.

We had to learn large portions of the Authorised or King James Version of the Bible by heart, and although a certain amount of drudgery was involved, retaining these passages for life has been to me a pearl of countless price. The poetry, the rhythm, the cadences, the sense of mystery or 'numinous' embodied in the language, have always gripped me. Indeed, I believe that the sublime language of both the Authorised Version and the Book of Common Prayer had a marked influence on writers such as Yeats, Synge and O'Casey. One can almost hear the poetry and lilt of the Authorised Version in their works.

Textbooks used in national schools were written from the Roman Catholic, Gaelic, Nationalist point of view. Such a version of Irish history made us, to say the least, feel uneasy, especially when we read of the oppression under the Penal Laws. But, as Percy French said, there are two sides to everything in Ireland 'except Harcourt Street Station'. Thankfully today Irish history is rightly seen in its European context. The argument from persecution is not the exclusive preserve of any one denomination. The persecuted in turn became persecutors and vice versa. Protestants persecuted Roman Catholics and Roman Catholics also persecuted Protestants, especially the Huguenots. So every denomination has its martyrs. Religious persecution is a stain on the history of Christianity, an evil out of which no denomination should seek to make capital, but for which all should be penitent before God and ask forgiveness one of another.

There were two primary schools in Carnew: Roman Catholic and Protestant. We had the same playground, a field near the castle, but we occupied it at different times. We led segregated lives, neither playing together nor learning together. Any friendships we made with Roman Catholics were outside the context of the school. Later a vocational school was built in Carnew, and those who attended it, including my sister Evelyn, as far as I know found nothing strange or unusual in sharing the same school with Roman Catholics.

I am convinced that to remove prejudice and misunderstanding children of all denominations from the earliest age should be educated together. By segregation we plant in their young minds the seeds of suspicion: 'There must be something wrong with them since they go to a different school.'

'You Protestants don't believe in the Virgin Mary.' How often have I heard this. Of course it is utterly false. As members of the Church of Ireland we hold the blessed Virgin Mary in high honour as the one chosen by God to be the mother of our Lord and as a wonderful example to us of humility and obedience to the will of God. Her hymn of praise, Magnificat, is appointed for use daily in Evening Prayer. We observe in our Church calendar two special days in connection with the Virgin Mary, 2 February, the Feast of the Purification or Presentation of Christ in the temple, and 25 March, the Feast of the Annunciation, or the announcement by the angel to Mary that she had been chosen by God to be the Mother of Jesus. But the Immaculate Conception, decreed by Pope Pius IX in 1854, that Mary was preserved from original sin, and the Assumption, proclaimed by Pope Pius XII in 1950, that Mary was assumed or taken up into heaven, are not part of the teaching of the Church of Ireland, for those doctrines have no scriptural or historical support. Anglicans and members of the Church of Ireland make a clear distinction between what we see as the essential doctrines of the Catholic faith contained in the creeds, witnessed to in Holy Scripture, held always, everywhere and by all, and later additions such as the doctrines of the Immaculate Conception and Assumption. We regard these later additions as optional extras or pious opinions which may or may not be believed but which are in no way essential to the Christian and full Catholic faith.

It has been said to me, 'You Protestants don't believe in the Body and Blood.' The reference here is to Transubstantiation, which is a philosophical way of defining the presence of Christ in the Eucharist or Mass. Certainly we don't believe in Transubstantiation but we do believe that Christ is really present in the Eucharist 'in a heavenly and spiritual manner' and that the Body and Blood of Christ are 'verily and indeed taken and received by the faithful in the Lord's supper'. We believe that Christ is truly present but we do not resort to any philosophical formula to explain *how* He is present.

'The Queen is the head of your Church.' Another fallacy. The Queen is prayed for in Northern Ireland as the Head of State, as is the President in the Republic of Ireland. The Church of Ireland is autonomous, governed by the General Synod consisting of the Bishops, elected clergy and laity. The Church of Ireland is a member of the Anglican Communion which is a family or fellowship of equal, autonomous or self-governing Churches in many lands whose aim is to uphold and propagate the ancient Catholic, apostolic faith and order without any additions or subtractions. These Churches are in full communion with one another and with the See of Canterbury. They look to the Archbishop of Canterbury, not as Pope or supreme ruler, but as one among equals who nevertheless occupies a position of considerable esteem and honour. Neither the Archbishop of Canterbury nor the Queen has any authority over the Church of Ireland.

'Your Church was founded by Henry VIII.' Wrong again. Henry VIII was never a reformer. Indeed, he wrote a book against Martin Luther for which the Pope gave him the title 'Defender of the Faith'. He lived and died a strong supporter of mediaeval papal theology, however much he may have quarrelled with the Pope over the annulment of his marriage. There would have been a reformation had Henry never lived, for reformation was in the air. Henry supplied the spark which kindled the fire of the Reformation in England but, had he not done so, others certainly would have, for reformation was inevitable.

And it is not all on one side. Protestants are also guilty of misunderstanding and malice evident from such remarks as, 'Roman Catholics worship idols and images', or 'Roman Catholics worship the Virgin Mary and make her greater than God for they call her the "Mother of God" . . . Roman Catholics can sin as much as they wish provided they confess to the priest who forgives them and leaves them free to sin over and over again with a clear conscience. . . . If the Pope is infallible and so powerful, why doesn't he stop war and violence? . . . The Church of Rome is the great whore of Babylon, drunk with the blood of the saints. . . . Monasteries and convents are unnatural and should not be allowed. We'd like to know what goes on in secret behind those walls.'

These old canards, both of the Roman Catholic and Protestant variety, so prevalent in my schooldays, can still be heard from time to time, in spite of the ecumenical movement and its laudable attempts to remove misunderstanding and to create an atmosphere of mutual respect which can only come by the removal of ignorance and the knowledge of what each really believes and why.

4

Kilkenny

A T OUR national school in Carnew the instrument of punishment was the pointer, a wooden stick about eighteen inches long which tapered to a point and was used in geography lessons to point out places on the map. A slap of this on the hand could sometimes cause bruising. If we complained to our parents about the severity of the blow the invariable retort was, 'You got what you deserved.' On one occasion I remember kicking Miss Moody's shins when she endeavoured to remove me from sitting beside a girl with whom, even at the tender age of four or five, I had fallen deeply in love. I kicked and punched and screamed in protest. All to no avail. The pointer was promptly produced to ensure obedience to lawful authority. Miss Moody also tried to teach me the piano. I am blessed — or cursed — with having the ability to play by ear. Learning to play by sight was sheer drudgery. Once I had heard the melody I could play it. I just wouldn't settle down to the monotony of having to concentrate on practising scales and chords and playing exactly the notes on the music sheet. I was scolded and there was the occasional slap on the hands for not practising but I think Miss Moody knew all along that she was fighting a losing battle. However, as compensation I enjoyed the English, history and geography lessons and had also a liking for Irish. Arithmetic did not interest me. Every day from 12 noon until our break at 12.30 we had religious instruction given by the rector, Mr Forbes, who used to walk the 400 yards up from the rectory, puffing his pipe, a practice which was frowned on by some of the more puritanical members of the Protestant community. Mr Forbes left to become Dean of Ferns and was succeeded by Mr Forrest, young, forward-looking, energetic.

Miss Moody and Mr Forrest apparently saw a measure of academic promise in me and encouraged my parents to allow me to sit for a scholarship awarded by the Protestant Incorporated Society which ran several boarding schools, including Kilkenny College. Kilkenny was the nearest Protestant secondary school to Carnew. Roman Catholic children in Carnew were more fortunate in that they had secondary schools located much nearer — in Bunclody, for instance — which allowed them to continue their education without having to leave home. But Protestants had to go to a boarding school which meant more expense on the family.

Sitting the scholarship examination was a rare event as far as Carnew national school was concerned, although a few years previously a Carnew boy called Tom Hannon had won a scholarship to Kilkenny. On a sunny May morning in 1936 my mother sent me off to Enniscorthy by garage car driven by Willie Birch to sit the exam, putting into my pocket a little toy black cat, as a lucky charm. I had to wait for a month or so to hear the result and when Mr Forrest announced to the school the news of my success a great cheer went up. The following Sunday at church he emphasised to the assembled congregation the importance of this achievement in bringing honour to Carnew parish.

My mother, while delighted at my success, had strong reservations about losing me to Kilkenny and indeed about boarding schools in general. She believed that children should remain as long as possible in the warmth of the family circle. My father, on the other hand, saw no disadvantages whatever. He had no hesitation in encouraging me to grasp this opportunity with both hands. 'It's a great new adventure, Victor,' he enthused. 'It'll do you the world of good.'

For myself, I had mixed feelings about leaving home. I knew nothing about boarding schools. Had I known then what lay in store for me I would have departed from home with far greater foreboding. Tom Hannon, who had by this time left Kilkenny, was working in Davis's flour firm in Enniscorthy did not, mercifully, give me any inkling of what to expect. He simply said, 'I hope you enjoy Kilkenny,' and presented me with his hockey stick. Little did I know that my backside would be frequently beaten by hockey sticks, the favourite punishment inflicted by seniors on unfortunate juniors. Boarding schools have since changed for the better, but in those days such brutality was accepted by boys and parents as a normal part of school life. Parents never protested. Indeed, I sometimes think that if a boy had gone home at the end of term with stumps instead of hands his parents would merely have remarked, 'You probably deserved it.'

After the announcement of my scholarship there followed some weeks of preparation for my first term, such as the purchasing of a school uniform and the stocking of a tuck box. Kilkenny, founded by Piers, Earl of Ormonde, in 1536, imitated the English public school and was once proudly known as the Eton of Ireland.

It is the second oldest school in the country (the oldest being St Patrick's Choir and Grammar School, attached to St Patrick's Cathedral in Dublin). Its Sunday uniform was identical to Eton's traditional schoolboy garb: short black jacket, black trousers with a grey stripe, white shirt with Eton collar, black tie and mortar board. On other days, when we were spared the mortar board and Eton outfit, we had to wear the school cap, black with red KCK letters over the peak.

The contents of the tuck box constituted not special treats, but an essential addition to our spartan school diet. Pots of home-made jam, home-made butter, brown sugar (to spread on bread) and eggs wrapped singly in pieces of newspaper and placed in a separate cardboard box. A home-baked cake or two, ginger or fruit cake or jam sandwich.

Stanley, my older cousin, who lived in the adjoining house to ours, started Kilkenny at the same time as myself, in 1936. It was good to have each other for companionship and at times for mutual commiseration. Cyril, my cousin of the same age, did not go to secondary school. He stayed at home, went to vocational school, took up motor engineering (and golf!), and inherited Uncle George's garage. We would often tease him that in financial terms he was the most successful of us all. Alas he is no longer with us. After three years retirement, enjoying his golf and his garden, he was struck down by a rapid throat cancer which carried him off within six months.

We always drove to Kilkenny in one of the garage cars. Uncle George insisted on collecting us at the end of term but would never leave us there. He did not like 'goodbyes'. About four miles before we reached Kilkenny we passed a roadside pub called the 'Fox and Goose'. It had a signboard depicting a haughty-looking fox with the neck of a goose in its jaws and the goose's body flung across its shoulders. When Stanley and I saw this sign our hearts would sink, for we knew that there was now no turning back — the end was nigh! Like the goose, we were in the jaws of the school with no hope of escape and would not see a single relative for a whole term. At home we had been treated as individuals who mattered, called by our Christian names, had experienced the loving care of our families. Now we faced the harshness of a system designed to 'toughen us up'. Conversely, our spirits soared when we passed the 'Fox and Goose' on our way home at the end of term.

The journey to school for the second term was by far the most dismal. The Christmas festivities had kept at bay the dread of going back, but as soon as these were over old fears returned with a vengeance. The initial drive to Kilkenny had been undertaken in a spirit of blissful ignorance; now I knew all the pitfalls. It was like returning to prison after being out on parole. How I envied my sister Evie, safely at home, still attending the national school. Later on after vocational school training she became a book-keeper with responsibility for the garage accounts.

Kilkenny College, then typical of schools of its day, has now changed out of all recognition. It stands on a different site, is co-educational and much more enlightened in its treatment of pupils. During my time it was housed in a fine Georgian building which still stands on the banks of the river Nore, directly opposite Kilkenny Castle. At that time it catered for about seventy boarders up to Intermediate Certificate. I cannot honestly say that the happiest days of my life were spent in Kilkenny College but it wasn't all misery either. It had its moments of fun and light-hearted relief.

A rigid hierarchy was in place, a pyramid of which the first years, or 'grabbers', as we were called, formed the base. Above these juniors came, in ascending order, what was called the 'second set'; then third year seniors and fourth year prefects. After that came the teaching staff and at the very apex stood the headmaster, a man who enjoyed absolute power in his domain. There were all kinds of petty traditional pupil-imposed sanctions and privileges. For instance, a grabber was not allowed to pass beyond the huge iron stove in the centre of the long classroom cum assembly hall, where we relaxed, read or fooled about, especially during wet weather. He had to ask permission from a second year boy. A grabber also had to seek out a third former to get permission before entering an adjoining smaller room. As grabbers we had to fag for the prefects, one fag to one prefect to act as his personal slave. Our duties were principally to clean his rugby and hockey boots, to wash his togs after a game and to run messages which consisted mainly of fetching items from the tuck-shop. My prefect was a decent fellow. When he needed anything he would shout, 'Fag. Fag. Griffin.' He would occasionally give me chocolates. But there were, also, some ferocious prefects and other seniors who took a sadistic delight in using the hockey stick. I was one of the more fortunate fags.

Soon after arrival grabbers were subjected to a cruel initiation ceremony known as the 'christening' or 'dipping', its sole purpose being to scare the wits out of us. We, the victims, were caught by seniors one Sunday morning and brought one by one on all fours into the washroom, past basin after basin after basin, up to a huge tub at the end which had been filled with cold water and suds. We were then hoisted on high by able-bodied seniors and our heads ducked twice in the tub and held under the water for a terrifyingly long period. When we were finally let go we were forced to walk between twin lines of mocking seniors who, revelling in our plight, slapped us with wet towels as we struggled to make our way along the wooden slatted floor. This was already well lubricated with soap which made our progress to the door and merciful release more difficult.

The ceremony was eventually stopped. During my time the staff knew what was going on but turned a blind eye. But some parent may have objected to the headmaster. I took part in the ceremony as a senior, although by that time the worst excesses were disappearing. But I remember thinking how stupid and infantile the whole ritual was, 'full of sound and fury signifying nothing'.

During the 'dipping' all grabbers were given a nickname. I was christened 'Cong' for some reason which escaped me, but it didn't stick. I was always known as Griffo. Stanley was named Danno after a celebrated Irish wrestler of the day, Dan O'Mahoney, probably because Stanley's physique in the eyes of some resembled that of a wrestler.

School food was basic. The main meal, dinner, was served in the middle of the day. It consisted of three courses, varied greatly in quality and was sometimes very good. For breakfast and evening meal we received plain fare: under- or overcooked porridge in the morning followed by bread with butter scrapings and weak, milky tea; bread and scrape and tea again in the evening, hence the necessity of a tuckbox to supply the deficiencies. Eels which we caught in the Nore were a welcome supplement.

At night we would sometimes set lines baited with worms and attached to overhanging branches. Returning in the morning we might be lucky enough to find a couple of eels caught on our hooks, still alive and wriggling. It's hard to kill an eel. School lore convinced us that it could be stunned by hitting it on the tail with a stone. Then its head was cut off. I became expert at skinning an eel before taking it to the kitchen to be fried. The cook would fry but would not skin.

The cook also boiled the eggs from home. We presented them with our names pencilled on the shell. Griffin 1 (Stanley) and Griffin 2 (myself). Such dietary supplements helped to keep us fit, and when ailments such as sore throats or chilblains afflicted us we had a most understanding nurse to turn to and from her we received not only medical treatment but sympathy — without the tea.

One of the saddest things about school in those days, looking back, was not knowing anyone's Christian name. It was considered perhaps a sign of unmanliness to call one another by our first names, and the masters would never demean themselves by addressing us in this intimate way. There was a great gulf between staff and pupils. Nobody got too close to anyone else. Any boy who became a favourite of the staff was called a 'soak', a term of disapproval. Years later, when asked 'Did you know John or Leonard so-and-so at Kilkenny?' I have been unable to identify the boy because I only knew his surname.

The Nore not only supplied eels but had a wide, tree-lined path in the school grounds sweeping down to it known as Swift's Walk. Kilkenny legend had it that Jonathan Swift planted the trees while a College pupil, but there is no historical evidence for this. It is, however, true that Swift took a great interest in the environment, improving the rectory grounds in Laracor, Co. Meath, and later St Patrick's Deanery and churchyard grounds by planting trees.

For many decades it had been the custom for every Kilkenny schoolboy to carve his name somewhere in the college. Skirting boards and lockers were festooned with names and initials. Not long after I arrived word went round that Swift's name had been found inscribed on top of one of the lockers. The boy who apparently made this momentous discovery called a group of us together to view it. There it was. D. Swift, beneath a patina of dust and grime which gave it a mildly antique appearance. It occurred to one of our number that Swift's name was Jonathan.

'That wasn't his name,' he protested.

'Of course it was. He was Dean Swift,' replied the exposed hoaxer as, humiliated, he withdrew from the scene to a chorus of much taunting and jeering.

Swift and other celebrated alumni such as Congreve and Berkeley, the eighteenth-century Irish philosopher, and Admiral Beatty, member of a prominent Wexford family and hero of the First World War naval battle of Jutland, were no more than names to me at the time. Later, as a student at Trinity College, I became aware of their notable achievements in literature, philosophy and naval prowess and the unique contribution made by Kilkenny College to Irish education.

There is a plaque in St Canice's Cathedral in Kilkenny on which are recorded the names of distinguished past pupils. The only unsupervised freedom I experienced during my time at the College was as a chorister in St Canice's when we were allowed to walk to the Cathedral and return on our own. On all other occasions it was the custom for us to be marched two by two in a crocodile under the watchful eye of masters. Church-going was compulsory twice on Sundays and non-choristers processed to nearby St John's Church. Arrayed on Sundays in Eton suits and mortar boards, Kilkenny boys were figures of fun or, at the very least, objects of curiosity to the local populace. 'Proddy Woddy cups and saucers,' jeered some in reference to our religion and our mortar boards. This unusual garb served to increase our sense of alienation. Not only did we attend a Protestant school but we were compelled to wear the badge of our peculiar separateness.

In the local theatre Anew MacMaster, with his touring company, occasionally provided us with a feast of Shakespeare. At a performance of *Hamlet* I was haunted by some music I heard coming over the loudspeakers prior to the performance. What is it? Who composed it? I wondered. Months later I found out. It was the ballet music from Gounod's *Faust*. I saved up and bought the record, my first classical purchase, an old 78. That whetted my taste for ballet and opera. I soon became hooked on Wagner, Puccini and Verdi and when in Trinity used to queue for the gods in the Gaiety: hard wooden benches, towering steeply and dizzily high above the auditorium, admission one shilling. Music was in the family. Mother and Father, especially Father, loved to sing — hymns, ballads, folk songs, Percy French. My sister Evie was a competent pianist, played the organ in church and was an active member of the Carnew Musical Society.

In Kilkenny we had a flourishing debating society which met on Saturday evenings in the autumn and spring terms. This was to be my first experience of controversy as we tried to produce convincing arguments either for or against such matters as co-education and compulsory games. I loved the debating society and felt very much at home in the chamber, enjoying every moment of the cut and thrust of debate.

It was decided during my time at Kilkenny to install contraptions erroneously known as fire escapes in every upstairs dormitory. These consisted of a pulley and a coiled asbestos-covered steel cable housed in a drum which was affixed to one side of the window inside the room. At one end of the cable was a harness with straps for the shoulders and a belt to be worn under the armpits. After the installation we were summoned to the window and the method of use was explained to us. The first boy would buckle on the harness which, attached to the cable, would allow him to be lowered slowly to the ground. He would then relinquish the harness which was drawn up to the window for the next boy to use. We were lined up for a rehearsal during the course of which we were each pushed out bodily in turn.

We could not help wondering what would happen if flames were emerging from the windows on the lower floor as we descended inch by inch. They would not consume the asbestos-covered cable, but God help the unfortunate individual strapped to it. The main intention of the manufacturers of this peculiar contraption was, it seemed, to preserve at all costs the cable rather than human life. We were obviously expendable; the cable was not.

This dubious method of escape was fortunately never put to the test, at least not during my time. There was, however, another more immediate danger of which everyone in those days was blissfully unaware. Boys being boys, we used to fool around with the cable in the dormitory and pieces of the covering would come off in our hands, releasing potentially lethal asbestos particles into the air we breathed.

The teaching of English, French and history at Kilkenny was excellent. The first two were taught by a shy, retiring master who nevertheless had the ability to communicate his immense enthusiasm for his subject, especially Shakespeare. He made us feel on stage as we read *Julius Caesar*, *Hamlet* and *Macbeth*, *The Merchant of Venice* and *As You Like It*. I was always interested in dramatics and have retained to this day large portions of Shakespeare learned by heart under his tutelage. Though he must only have been in his thirties, he seemed to us somewhat advanced in years. The baldness from which he suffered compounded this impression. He had a very round head and a rotund frame and he walked with a stoop or, perhaps more exactly, an inclination to the right. In his younger days he had taught in Athlone where he played rugby for a team called the Shannon Buccaneers, which has long since ceased to be. He was a good conversationalist but was happiest, I think, alone with his books.

We were subjected to a particularly rigorous regime on the games field. Whatever the weather, we had to go out and play, unless there was a hard frost and frozen ground, in which case we were required to walk in a crocodile for miles around Kilkenny, a master at the head and another at the tail. Although by no means outstanding in the field, I enjoyed the games. I never resented their compulsory nature and was not unduly worried by harsh conditions. I remember, though, playing rugby one day in a thunderstorm with the rain lashing us. Even with heads down in the scrum we could see the lightning flashing through the tunnel. Eventually, and very reluctantly, the master called off the game.

Science held nothing but terror for us all. It was taught by the headmaster, a man who could be very charming in relaxed company but who ruled his school with a rod of iron, always austere and unsmiling. A tensed figure with glaring, penetrating eyes, he appeared to us always ready to pounce at the least provocation.

One lesson I shall never forget concerned an experiment requiring the use of a conical flask which had to be dipped into boiling water. We were working in pairs and my companion rather carelessly plunged the flask with such force into the water that he fractured the bottom. The headmaster approached.

'What's wrong with that flask? Take it up.'

'It won't float, sir.' The headmaster seized it by the stem.

'Of course it won't float,' he thundered. 'You've broken the bottom out of it, you blithering idiot.'

Then we were subjected, trembling, to a long, humiliating tirade as he walked round and round, bellowing and scaring the wits out of us.

He had no reservations about wielding the cane, no 'soft' notions about the physical or psychological damage its free use might occasion. It was still very much taken for granted that sparing the rod meant spoiling the child. The cane put a youth on the right track and kept him there. Wickedness must be beaten out of the sinner. When summoned to his study we knew the experience would be, to say the least, a painful one. Some of us tried stuffing a towel down the seat of our trousers to soften the blows, but he soon became wise to this and if a towel was detected the caning was doubly severe.

Boys who had perpetrated some singularly reprehensible act were subjected to a public flogging, as it was called, an event which transformed the drab monotony of school life. Some of our number, like spectators at Nero's circus, eagerly awaited the blood-letting, others experienced varying degrees of sympathy for the victim, all wondered exactly how he would stand up to the ordeal. At evening prayers the headmaster would solemnly appear with his cane, place it reverently with priest-like precision on the desk as on an altar, after which the offender, as the sacrificial lamb, was summoned forth, put on display and arraigned in front of the assembled company. This miserable wretch had departed from the path of righteousness, declared the headmaster, had turned aside into the path of iniquity and was now to be severely punished in public as a warning to us all of the consequences of evil doing. When at last the homily ended the culprit had to bend over and submit to swishing and slashing while we counted the strokes of the cane, one, two, three . . . until the requisite atonement price was paid and the ordeal ceased.

One heinous crime which met with this chastisement was the raiding in the dead of night of examination papers from the masters' common room. But the flogging might have the opposite effect from that intended, for those who had undergone such public humiliation were regarded as popular heroes marked out as having achieved an extraordinary distinction. It was counted

to them more for righteousness than for wickedness, to parody
St Paul.

Time changes all. Years later I met my old headmaster in
the front square of Trinity. No longer the awesome forbidding
figure of my schooldays but now mellowed with age and keenly
interested in my academic progress, he took me for coffee in
Bewley's and we chatted about old times in Kilkenny. I think
he was proud of the fact that I, an old Kilkenny boy, had been
elected a Scholar of Trinity.

I had no great ability in art but I entered for it in the
Intermediate Certificate knowing that I had sufficient subjects
without having to worry about a pass. We were required to do
a still life drawing and to paint an imaginary scene. The others
who were good at art were all earnestly doing the necessary
measuring and getting their perspectives right. I was not. I
enjoyed myself scribbling lines out of perspective and splashing
paint around. When the results came out I was well to the fore
of the class. Everyone thought there had been some mistake.
The examiner may well have imagined he had found a pupil
with avant-garde propensities, perhaps even a budding Picasso.
My offering would certainly have been very noticeable amongst
those which were meticulously executed according to the then
recognised canons of school artwork. The experience taught me
not to take way-out modern art too seriously.

In Kilkenny we were an enclosed celibate order. The only
contact we had with the opposite sex was a furtive wink at
some desirable young thing in church or on summer evenings
whistling or throwing kisses across the Nore at those who, like
Rhine maidens, paraded on the opposite bank.

Sports day at the end of term in June was the great event of
our school year. Parents and friends gathered to cheer, to
congratulate or to commiserate. Flags and bunting lent a festive
air with sandwiches and other goodies in plenty for all. For
weeks we had trained every evening on the track beside the
Nore. I concentrated on the mile as I was a 'stayer' rather than
a sprinter. In my last year I came second.

On our last Sunday in Kilkenny College after evening church we hurled our mortar boards into the air with a great triumphant shout. We then proceeded to the Nore where we set them on fire and watched as, consumed by flames, they floated down the river like stricken battleships. This was indeed *Götterdammerung*, the final act.

So, having served my time at Kilkenny I transferred in 1940 to Mountjoy School in Dublin, where I was to spend two years preparing for matriculation to Trinity College.

5
Mountjoy

THE atmosphere in Mountjoy School was far less repressive than that which I had known in Kilkenny. We were that much older and were given more freedom and responsibility. I cannot recall any form of corporal punishment in Mountjoy. On Sunday afternoons we were allowed to visit relatives in Dublin provided we supplied a name and address. I must confess that we sometimes used such information as a cover for going to the pictures, in those days an unheard-of activity for Protestants on a Sunday.

One such clandestine visit proved particularly memorable. Three or four of us were in the old Regal Rooms cinema in Hawkins Street, next to that impressive building, the Theatre Royal, now, alas, no more. When the lights came on at the interval we saw, to our horror, sitting at the end of our row one of the senior masters from Mountjoy. We turned our heads instantly and never discovered whether he had spotted us or not. But there were no repercussions since he also stood condemned.

The school was situated in Mountjoy Square and the games fields were out in Clontarf. We thought nothing of the trek to Strandville Avenue to play rugby in winter and cricket in summer. And there was the long walk back to school after a hard game, an arrangement which would hardly be tolerated by transport-conscious pupils or parents of today. For us the streets of Dublin were a source of constant interest, and, being allowed to walk unsupervised with our friends in groups of twos and threes like ordinary human beings, we revelled in a freedom unthinkable at Kilkenny. Mountjoy's headmaster placed a great deal of trust in us which was very rarely abused.

Our route took us first down to the North Circular Road past a chip shop with its warm, enticing aroma, especially on a winter day, then along Jones's Road where I surveyed the forbidden portals of Croke Park. Little did I know that years later I would probably be the first Protestant clergyman, certainly the first Dean of St Patrick's, to make my way to a GAA final there, and on a Sunday too.

Playing or watching games of any sort on Sundays was then out of the question, a flagrant breach of the Sabbath. Rugby, which many Protestants played, was of course a Saturday sport. It never occurred to Protestants that the biblical Sabbath fell on Saturday and to be true to the literal interpretation of the commandment Saturday sport should have been ruled out. No biblical restriction could be applied to Sunday sport.

At Kilkenny the uncharacteristically liberal decision to allow boys to play tennis on Sunday afternoons had caused uproar among some parents who protested, in vain, that their sons were being encouraged to break the Sabbath. In addition to playing their games on Sundays, the Nationalist ethos of the GAA did not appeal to Protestants, who associated the organisation with the Roman Catholic Church and a very extreme form of anti-British Republicanism. The GAA ban preventing its members playing, or even attending, non-Gaelic games also meant that the few Protestants who might have ignored their community's disapproval of 'Sabbath' sport and taken up hurling or football were unwilling to forego their rugby, hockey, soccer or cricket to comply with GAA regulations. Passing this bastion of the GAA I was bewildered by an attitude which decreed that to be truly Irish one had to renounce all interest in 'foreign' games.

Even in those days there were some Roman Catholic teachers in Protestant schools and they were totally accepted. Religious affiliation made no difference. Our Irish master was one. He was not only a great devotee of Gaelic football and a member of the GAA but also an avid follower of rugby. As a member of the teaching staff no doubt he felt bound to support our school matches as a spectator. There was a rumour that he occasionally made his way to Lansdowne Road in a clandestine manner, furtively looking out for GAA spies, for fear of summary excommunication from the *sanctum sanctorum*. Happily such dissimulation is no longer necessary as the GAA lifted its ban on 'foreign' games in 1971.

Turning from Jones's Road into Clonliffe Road, with its neat houses, we passed the residence of the Roman Catholic Archbishop of Dublin and the adjoining theological college. Sometimes we would catch sight of clerical students and priests in cassocks. Before the birth of the ecumenical movement, most Protestants subscribed to the view that Roman Catholics, if not exactly working in opposition to us, were certainly running on separate rails. There was spiritual apartheid, and never the twain did meet except on the rugby field. As schoolboys we used to gaze into those grounds and wonder, in a superior and self-righteous manner, how people of intelligence could accept such dogmas as the infallibility of the Pope. Every denomination then claimed to be the one true Church, having the truth, the whole truth and nothing but the truth.

This condescending attitude in all Churches towards other denominations is exemplified in a apocryphal story of a discussion between representatives of the different Churches as to which tradition Christ would be most at home in were He to return to earth. The Methodist, the Presbyterian and the Roman Catholic all put forward convincing arguments concerning their own religious emphasis, each claiming the approval of Christ. The Church of Ireland representative remained silent. When pressed to give his opinion he remarked smugly, 'I don't think He'd wish to change.'

Each denomination believed they had an exclusive right to God, that God was in their pocket and other poor unfortunates who were not of their theological outlook were to be pitied. They were, at best, second-class Christians, not having the full truth of the Gospel. To be grudgingly tolerated, no more.

Crossing the Tolka on our way to the playing fields we reached the row of shops in Fairview. A fish and chip shop which stood nearby had the same powerful effect on us as the one we had passed near the North Circular Road.

We peered into other windows at a mouth-watering display, even in those early war years, of fruit cakes, apple tarts, scones and sticky buns. The loaves were brown, for the government had outlawed the practice of removing the husks from flour in an effort to ensure that our limited stocks of imported wheat were utilised to the full. Housewives would often sieve the brown floor through a silk stocking, and if anyone visited the North their first act was to look for white bread to bring home. Southern Ireland was dependent on imports to a large extent and, despite its neutral status, suffered the indignity and deprivation of having several of its merchant ships sunk by belligerent action, mainly German.

The fruit in the Fairview shop windows was rather basic, depending on what was home grown: apples, mostly, sometimes pears and crab-apples and plums in season. Passing Fairview cinema we scanned the posters to see what pictures were being shown. Ginger Rogers and Fred Astaire drew in the crowds; Wallace Beery, hero of many Westerns, and Carmen Miranda, the Latin-American star, were household names, beside Errol Flynn, Greta Garbo, James Mason and Laurel and Hardy.

We walked along Clontarf Road, under the railway bridge and then turned left into Strandville Avenue and the playing fields, where we togged out in the pavilion. After the game cold showers and the long trek back awaited us. If playing away on Saturday in, say, Terenure or Castleknock, we were allowed to use bicycles. One one occasion cycling back from Terenure my bike skidded on the tramlines alongside the railings of Harold's Cross park. My head struck the railings, and with blood spouting in all directions I quickly remounted and made off helter skelter for the Meath Hospital where stitches were promptly inserted. I still bear on my head the mark of this unfortunate encounter with the railings of Harold's Cross.

The roads were less busy than before the war because of petrol rationing, although some cars had been converted to run on gas, a somewhat risky option. The gas was contained in a huge white canvas bag which billowed forth from the car roof. There were buses, and trams emitting an incessant ping-pinging sound to warn pedestrians and the many cyclists of their imminent approach. The trams which plied the route to Howth Head and back, the last to be removed from service after the war, went burring past us in Fairview. Alas, there are no more trams in Dublin. With their departure the city lost some of the 'dear old Dublin' atmosphere.

There were the laundry and bread vans, milk floats and brewers' drays, pulled by Clydesdales, delivering kegs of beer and porter. Occasionally we would see a hearse, the driver in his black coat and crepe-trimmed top hat sitting high up in great decorum wearing a suitably funereal expression, reins in hands, as he set a steady, solemn pace for the two black horses. They, with their black covers on backs and white plumes on heads and shining harness, reverently bore the coffin to the cemetery. It was the custom then for everyone to wear headgear, hats or caps, and we wore the obligatory school cap on all outside occasions which, along with other bystanders, we would solemnly take off as the hearse passed by. But for Protestants no sign of the cross, only the removal of headgear.

Coal as well as petrol was scarce, and the trains had to supplement their ration with wooden logs. Farmers complained that crops were being set alight by flying sparks. It was difficult to maintain steam pressure, and one evening returning to school we were stranded at Woodenbridge Station and had to wait nearly three hours for a relief engine from Dublin to rescue us. We arrived at Westland Row around 11 p.m. I trudged through the darkened Dublin streets with my two suitcases, across the Liffey at Tara Street and up Gardiner Street to deserted Mountjoy Square where I stood on the school doorstep repeatedly ringing the bell. No one came, and I was on the point of turning away to spend the night on a bench in the square — for it was a fine warm September evening — when the door was suddenly opened and a wrathful master dressing-gowned and slippered, barked at me, 'What the blazes do you think you are doing?' I offered an explanation and he vanished upstairs, muttering something about a tall story and threatening to ring the railway. But he did let me in and the next day in class never even mentioned the incident. I'm sure he thought he had dreamt the whole thing.

At night German bombers would follow the east coast from Wexford to Dublin, taking advantage of the lights below for there was no black-out, and then head across the sea to bomb Liverpool and other cities. In the playground at the back of the school building, one morning just before nine o'clock, we heard the sound of an aeroplane in apparent difficulty, croaking and spluttering. A huge bomber clearly marked with a swastika, presumably a lone straggler from a night raid on Britain, came limping over the rooftops emitting large quantities of black smoke and so low that we could clearly see the crew in the cockpit. Suddenly we caught sight of an RAF fighter shadowing it. Nothing was reported in the press about the bomber, but rumour had it that it was later shot down off Dun Laoghaire. Whatever ambivalent attitudes may have prevailed elsewhere, there was no doubt that Protestants fervently favoured the British, who were seen as defenders of freedom in the face of the most evil tyranny ever perpetrated on mankind.

Searchlights and anti-aircraft guns were often in operation around Dublin after dark. One night the lights and guns were more active than usual and, more curious than alarmed, we crowded the windows of our dormitory overlooking Mountjoy Square to view the scene. The long, lean fingers of searchlights were sweeping the blackness of the sky and from a distance came the heavy thud of the guns. Suddenly we heard an unforgettable high-pitched whine followed by a tremendous explosion, and a few minutes later one of the house-masters entered the dormitory and shepherded us down to the basement which had been strengthened to act as a shelter against such an eventuality. There we had to remain until the raid was over. Next day we heard of the bombs that had killed a number of people in the North Strand area, only a mile away.

On several succeeding nights we returned to the basement as soon as the searchlights and guns went into action, but when no more bombs fell we were allowed to spend the nights in our dormitory.

Fragments of the bombs dropped were examined and conclusive proof found of their German origin. Official protests were made to the German Government about this infringement of Irish neutrality, but some IRA sympathisers in Dublin pubs put it around that, while the bombs were German made, a British plane had dropped them as a propaganda exercise.

They regarded Britain's enemy as Ireland's friend and Hitler was seen as teaching the arrogant English a lesson they sorely deserved. A similar view was expressed when war had ended and cinema newsreels showed footage of concentration camp victims. This was simply 'Allied propaganda'. No such camps existed. We were being duped by Britain. And the same blinkered attitude bedevils Ireland still, a refusal to face facts which do not conform to our inherited and so often prejudiced attitudes, be they Nationalist or Unionist. We interpret present facts in the light of past prejudices and allow past conflicts to blind our eyes to present realities. For the diehard Nationalist or Unionist the past as he sees it, often with squinted vision, must dominate the present and fashion the future. This is the road to nowhere, except to bigotry and intolerance.

In Mountjoy we were well grounded in mathematics and science. The school concentrated on these subjects. Languages, apart from Irish, came a poor second, especially Latin and Greek. I left with only a smattering of Greek but I was well versed in mechanics or applied maths and how to make sulphuric or nitric acid.

There were the usual schoolboy pranks and misdemeanours. A puff or two on a shared Woodbine behind the toilet block in the school yard, when the ascending smoke caught the eye of a watchful master peering through the commonroom window, brought swift retribution in the cancelling of afternoon leave for three consecutive Sundays and a warning of the risk of expulsion should it happen again. But revenge was sweet when some days later a comb was set alight and the vigilant master, again on the alert for nicotine miscreants and observing not only puffs but a veritable smoke cloud arising from the same venue, betook himself with all speed to apprehend the culprits, only to find the remains of an incinerated comb. In Kilkenny punishment was inflicted by the cane or, for lesser offences, by having to write perhaps a hundred lines ('I must behave myself in school', etc.) or copy out large portions of Shakespeare. Sunday leave was the weapon in Mountjoy. The only times we were marched in crocodile was to St George's Church, Sunday by Sunday. In this fine elegant building, one of the architectural gems of Georgian Dublin, we occupied side pews and by winks and smiles often tried to attract the attention of young ladies from Bertrand and Rutland School who sat centre stage, right in the middle of the nave. 'Daddy' Harrison played the organ. After the services he would let fly, releasing full throttle on Chopin's Military Polonaise or Verdi's Grand March from Aïda. This tiny man, high up on the organ stool in the west gallery, held us enthralled as great rising crescendos and fortissimos of melodic sound flooded the building. We loved it.

My memory of Mountjoy is that of a friendly relaxed school. Boys called each other by their Christian names and we were all, teachers and pupils, one happy family. Who could ask for more?

6

Trinity

AFTER two years in Mountjoy I entered Trinity in October 1942. I very soon discovered that being a former pupil of Mountjoy brought a singular additional advantage on entering Trinity in that Francis La Touche Godfrey, philosopher and classicist and, by reputation, the best tutor in the College, always took boys from Mountjoy under his wing. Mr Godfrey spared no effort to fight his students' cause. He had a nose for uncovering various funds available to help the more necessitous in making ends meet and, if a student had been given a borderline mark in an examination and sought Godfrey's aid, he had a good chance of being pushed over the dividing line into the ranks of the successful.

He was a short man of stout build, unfailingly kind and tolerant, dressed soberly in a dark blue suit over which, in winter, he wore a light raincoat. He cycled unhurriedly to Trinity from his Ballsbridge home. Permanent chaos reigned in his college rooms, books, letters and papers were piled higgledy-piggledy on his roll-top desk, yet he would put his hand immediately on anything required.

He smoked his pipe continuously and was scarcely visible through clouds of blue smoke which filled his study. Any student who entered was greeted with an amiable grunt. 'What can I do for you?' he invariably enquired. And when he had listened to the tale of woe, advised consolingly, 'Oh, I wouldn't let that worry me if I were you.' My first problem was finding digs in Dublin. Godfrey had heard that the Harding Boys' Home, a hostel in Lord Edward Street, originally opened to afford Protestant apprentices and working boys from the country modest accommodation within their means, was now also taking students. He suggested I try for a place there.

The Harding Boys' Home, under the competent but unobtrusive supervision of a a retired army officer, Captain Clarke, was an excellent mix of backgrounds and occupations. There were apprentices to trades, clerks in insurance companies and the railways, shop assistants in Protestant establishments such as Dockrells, Brown Thomas and Switzers, joined recently by veterinary, medical and divinity students. Board and lodging were austere and cost us ten shillings a week. We slept five or ten to a dormitory and supplemented our meals with food parcels from home delivered by friends or relatives visiting the capital. We played badminton and billiards and put on concerts in the assembly hall. I joined the Harding Boys' Rugby Club. Students, apprentices and clerks got on well and no one cared two hoots whether you were a student or a railway porter. We were all pals together, totally and happily unaware of any class or academic distinction. I have never been able to label people into classes or groups. God sees only individuals, persons of value in his sight to be loved and cared for. He sees no label and neither should we. Wars are fought between labels. Individuals do not fight wars. For war, individuals have first to be depersonalised and conditioned to see an opponent, not as a human being with joys and sorrows, hopes and fears, but simply as a labelled object.

So with Godfrey's help I secured cheap accommodation and whatever financial assistance he could dig up towards paying my fees. There was also the possibility of winning by examination various prizes worth from five to twenty-five pounds to supplement a student's slender means. These examinations came up at regular intervals throughout my five-year course and I managed to acquire a number of prizes in the philosophy of Locke and Berkeley, Kant and Hegel. Philosophy in Trinity was termed Mental and Moral Science. While I much preferred philosophy to theology, there were divinity prizes on offer too, and I secured two in sermon composition, which entailed writing a sermon and then delivering it.

Prize money helped to finance modest outings, visits to Bewley's or the Adelphi or some other cinema restaurant for coffee and biscuits, or to an ice cream parlour in Grafton Street for a peach melba or knickerbocker glory. Theatre-going meant invariably the gods! Never had I the wherewithal to furnish myself with a comfortable seat in the stalls or the balcony. But there was more fun in the gods, the 'crack' was always good with comments on play or players, whether in praise or blame, loudly proclaimed for all to hear.

My financial position was further eased after three years when I had the good fortune to be elected a Foundation Scholar of Trinity. Election was achieved by competitive examination and entitled a student to free rooms in College and free commons, or dinner, in the dining hall every evening. A scholar was also exempt from paying fees. The names of the new scholars were read out every year on Trinity Monday from the steps of the Examination Hall by the Provost, flanked by the Fellows. I celebrated my election as a Scholar in Philosophy with some friends in Davy Byrne's in nearby Duke Street. In those days visiting pubs was reserved for special celebrations, when we could afford it, and had not become the regular student habit it appears to be today.

It was the duty of Scholars to take turns by rota in saying two long Latin graces at commons, one before and one after the meal. We received ten pounds a year for our pains. I spent hours walking up and down College Park trying to memorise the graces. When my turn came I stood, with some trepidation, in front of such classical experts as Professor Stanford, seated at the high table. I survived my first night nerves but thereafter was occasionally stopped on my way out and admonished for my incorrect pronunciation of particular words. For example, King Charles is mentioned in the second grace, *Carolo conservatore*. We non-classicists used the pronunciation Car-rolo, whereas I was informed by the experts that it should Carol-o. Sometimes students timed us to find the fastest delivery. Speed of delivery was a great advantage, for it covered a multitude of linguistic sins!

The wearing of gowns to lectures was compulsory, and on becoming a Scholar one was entitled to wear a graduate gown. This differed from its undergraduate counterpart in that it had sleeves. Immediately a Scholar was elected he had to purchase or hire a graduate gown from the Porter, Jimmy Few, who sat in his little office beside the examination hall and continually chewed tobacco obtained, so it was said, from sailors. It came in long tubes looking for all the world like dark brown spaghetti. Presumably it was this habit which gave him his very hoarse voice. He sounded as if he suffered from permanent laryngitis. Jimmy usually kept a stock of graduate gowns in a locker. I went to him the day after the announcement of the new Scholars, and unfortunately he had none left but promised one the following day.

I proceeded to lectures in my old gown. 'Griffin,' remarked the Rev. Dr Luce, Professor of Philosophy, 'you are academically nude. Why are you wearing your undergraduate gown?' I explained the reason. 'That's not good enough. Get yourself a graduate gown and be properly clad before you appear at my lecture again.'

The regulations governing the wearing of gowns to lectures were stringently observed. No student dared appear without a gown. Since attendance at a stipulated number of lectures was compulsory, absence over this limit would mean losing credit for the term's lectures, a serious matter. One student, a devil-may-care character whom I knew quite well, had an undergraduate gown, a gown only in name. It was in ribbons, hanging down like the robe of Charon, the Styx boatman in Virgil's Aeneid, 'in a knot from his shoulders'. One day when so clad he came into lectures the lecturer took one hard, disapproving look at him and promptly ordered him to leave the room for being improperly attired. The student went out bemoaning his fate and sat dejectedly on the chapel steps, lighting a cigarette to relieve the gloom. No sooner had he done this than another lecturer approached and fined him five shillings for smoking while in academic dress, which was strictly forbidden. Bewildered and aggrieved, he complained to his tutor that being found guilty on both counts was inconsistent and unjust. The fine was eventually waived.

Trinity was then very much a Protestant Trinity, more particularly a Church of Ireland enclave, in which college chapel and the School of Divinity played a prominent part. Roman Catholics were forbidden by their archbishop to attend Trinity although some did in spite of the ban. The story is told of a Roman Catholic who defied the episcopal ban and entered Trinity where he graduated, only to be killed in a road accident a few days later. At the celestial portals St Peter was hesitant to admit him because of his insubordination to ecclesiastical authority, but Our Lord, hearing the protests of the graduate, and being informed of the situation, turned and said to Peter, 'Let him in. Don't you know I'm a Trinity man myself!'

There was a residential hostel for ordinands situated in Mountjoy Square — not far from my old school — where I was prepared for ordination. The warden was a tidy, exact and orderly man whose theology was of the Anglo-Catholic or High Church variety. He appeared very aloof at first but on further acquaintance mellowed and delighted in telling sophisticated jokes which often eluded us, or in recounting Trinity tales of long ago. The area round the hostel was a fitting environment for the training of ordinands. The morning walk down to lectures and meetings in Trinity and back again at night through the slums of Gardiner Street and Grenville Street showed us a world far removed from our own. Along these streets we were confronted with life in the raw.

The destitution and degrading conditions of decaying tenements in which human beings were forced to live were appalling. Window panes were missing, front doors in many cases were non-existent, and the passer-by could look right down the hallway of what was once a dignified Georgian dwelling and see a rickety staircase often without banisters. These, like the doors, had long since been chopped for firewood. A few tattered items of what passed for clothing were strung across the doorway to dry. Inside, whole families lived in one room, sharing a tap on the landing and a single toilet. Neglected-looking children roamed barefooted and unwashed. Men wearing cloth caps and ragged trousers sometimes appeared the worse for drink, and from upstairs windows would often come the screeching and screaming and sobbing sounds of a domestic quarrel.

Of course, there were those who said that the tenement dwellers were too lazy to better themselves, that it was all their own fault. But I thought they deserved better and that society had a responsibility towards those thrown on the scrapheap of life. I felt we had failed to show a Christian sense of responsibility and justice to such unfortunates, and I developed a cynicism about politicians who were on the make and feathering their own nests while at the same time professing concern for the poor. Words and promises in plenty, particularly at election times, but no subsequent action.

When I was a student election rallies were held on the streets, the two main venues for such activity in Dublin being College Green and outside the GPO, where all manner of utopian promises were made. One politician who did impress me was Jim Larkin. I can still see him towering over us all from the platform like a mighty colossus in the gathering dusk, arms out-stretched, words thundering forth with fearless and passionate concern and full-blooded commitment to the cause of freedom and justice.

Described by some as the very incarnation of the blood and tears, toil and sweat of the down-trodden working classes, his ideals were sadly and ironically rejected in the ballot box by the masses. The Roman Catholic Church's condemnation of social-ism, allied to the fear that Jim Larkin and his like might under-mine the dominant influence of the Church in Irish society and upset the status quo, ensured that the Dublin poor, although loudly applauding, did not deliver the votes.

Larkin exposed in all its hideousness the Fascism of Franco's Spain and Nazi Germany and instilled in me a lasting abhor-rence of intolerance in any form. Those who, like the Fascists, profess to have the truth, the whole truth and nothing but the truth, whether in the political or religious sphere, are dangerous. Until we all recognise that we know only in part, as St Paul says, that we have only our particular point of view and that others may have an equally valid perspective — only when this is universally recognised can we have tolerance and reconciliation. If we are to behave like civilised human beings we must be prepared to listen, to understand and never to be so cocksure of ourselves that we foolishly believe we have nothing to learn from others.

Perhaps my socialist leanings may be attributed to my admiration for a man of like name, the Rev. E.M. Griffin, with whom I was told as a schoolboy by my Dublin relatives that there was a family connection. Not being strong on genealogy, especially in boyhood years, I am afraid I never pursued this. He was one-time rector of St Barnabas', Dublin, a socialist and champion of the poor whom Seán O'Casey held in high regard and used as a model for the rector in *Red Roses for Me*, written in 1942. Among the workers in the Great Northern Railway were some Orangemen from Belfast who were employed in Amiens Street station and had settled with their families in St Barnabas' parish in the vicinity of the station. They disapproved of Griffin's High Church practices, and O'Casey took up the cudgels on his behalf. O'Casey also dedicated the second volume of his autobiography, *Pictures in the Hallway*, to Griffin, describing him as 'a man of many-branched kindness, whose sensitive hand was the first to give the clasp of friendship to the author'. Years later, when I began to read O'Casey, I remembered being told of the family connection with E.M. Griffin.

Our Church of Ireland Theological College is now situated in Rathgar among green fields and pleasant surburban housing. I regret the loss to divinity students today of what we experienced in Trinity by living on or near the university campus. I am convinced that isolating divinity students in a college far removed from the university campus is a retrograde step. We are in danger of encouraging theological hothouse plants, the greenhouse effect, which shows itself in tense, introverted types who often take themselves far too seriously and tend to be intolerant of those who differ theologically from them. Theological differences or emphases such as between 'High' and 'Low' Church are better contained within the confines of a university than a theological college.

During my time in Trinity ordinands shared the same campus, attended lectures often in adjoining rooms, participated in debates and sports and had commons with those from the medical, engineering, commerce and economics schools, meeting a wide range of students from various faculties. With theological training now largely removed from the context of university life, it is possible for a student to come to ordination without having had any contact whatsoever with those from other disciplines, which is to their mutual impoverishment.

As an aside, let me say here that I believe we would be justified in refusing ordination to the priesthood to women only if Jesus had explicitly forbidden it. Since saintly and scholarly men and women are to be found on both sides of the argument and there is disagreement on what the will of Christ is for the Church, we can only find the answer by experiment. If ordination of women is of God, then this will, in time, become clear to all and in years to come Christians will wonder what all the fuss was about. If it is not of God, then it will soon fade away. There is, therefore, no cause for panic or schism since God will still be there, women priests or no women priests! I often think that those who oppose the ordination of women take themselves and their theology more seriously than God takes them. I cannot see the deity being particularly worried!

When I began my ministry in Derry I joined my fellow curates in playing rugby and hockey for the local clubs. It was generally assumed that curates would be members of some local sports clubs, and play rugby, hockey, cricket or soccer. Golf was usually out of our financial range, but we generally played rugby or hockey and socialised with our team mates and supporters, teachers, bank officials, doctors, engineers, insurance men and so on. Alas, very few curates now appear to be involved in sport, which I believe is to the detriment of the Church's outreach to the many young people who are taking sport more seriously than ever before. Perhaps one of the main reasons for this is the fact that we now have many married curates with families. A married curate in the nineteen forties and fifties was a rarity.

Bishop Boyd, our bishop in Derry, insisted that we should remain unmarried until at least thirty years old. I married at thirty-four and am very glad that I had eleven years free of family responsibility and domestic cares which enabled me to participate fully in community life. Married and unmarried clergy have each a distinctive contribution to make to the life of the Church. All I can say, speaking personally, is that my pastoral ministry would have been the poorer had I not had those early years free from matrimonial responsibilities and subsequently a ministry also enriched by a happy marriage.

Mr Godfrey, who lectured on Kant and Hegel, was an optimist in true Hegelian fashion, believing that justice and freedom were at the very heart of reality and would ultimately prevail: things inevitably and ultimately moved in the right direction in spite of all appearances to the contrary. Absolute spirit worked its purpose out. His style of lecturing reflected his delightfully laid-back nature, lounging in his armchair, leaning forward occasionally to consult the notes which he had been using for years and really knew by heart. His lectures started ten minutes late and ended ten minutes early. I was rather fond of mimicry and one day, while we were waiting as usual for him to arrive, I settled into his armchair and began imitating him, expounding Hegel's philosophy of the triadic movement of thought — thesis, antithesis and synthesis — in his nonchalant, almost grunting manner. Suddenly I became aware of a great silence having descended, and I looked up and saw Godfrey calmly sitting and chuckling in the back row. 'Oh, Griffin, just carry on,' he instructed. 'There's really no need for me to be here at all.'

He had a fine brain, was a classicist as well as a philosopher and a Senior Fellow of Trinity. He could have been a doctor ten times over had he so desired but doctorates held no attraction for him. He was perfectly contented with himself, his students, his fellow academics, his MA and Senior Fellowship of TCD. I knew an academic at Trinity who spent his time adding one qualification after another to his name, much to the amusement of lecturers like Godfrey who saw no point in such academic self-aggrandisement. Collecting degrees can for some become a hobby like collecting postage stamps.

Godfrey retained a remarkable memory for his students. Years later, on a visit to Trinity from Derry, I met him pushing his bicycle across the front square. He recognised me immediately out of the hundreds of students who had passed through his hands. He knew exactly when I was in college, where I had gone as a curate and the name of the parish of which I was then rector.

He had a sister who was for many years Lady Registrar, having charge of the female students, including my future wife, Daphne, who began her studies in Trinity three years after I left. Girls did not have rooms in college or attend commons. Some lived out in Dartry in Trinity Hall. The segregation of the sexes was very vigorously enforced and by and large accepted. Female social life was centred on the college choral society, the ladies' sports clubs and the preparing and serving of refreshments at college rugby and cricket matches. Daphne captained the ladies cricket team and years later when, in all innocence, I asked her if they bowled underarm, I thought our marriage would end in divorce!

Discrimination against women was not a phrase one heard in those days. Indeed, to judge by information received from Daphne and others, it is doubtful whether female students themselves were conscious of unfair treatment. We took the status quo for granted. Lady students were not elected foundation scholars, having only the possibility of winning what might now be termed second-class scholarships funded by lesser bequests. They were barred from college activities such as membership of the Philosophical, Historical and Theological Societies which met in the Graduates Memorial Building, then a male preserve.

I concentrated on the Theological Society or 'Theo' and the Metaphysical. The 'Theo' was flourishing because of the large number of ordinands who constituted its membership. Since at

X They were also involved in the Drama S (D.U.D.S.) & the Elizabethan S. (the latter was for women only, I think.)

that time the very idea of a female ordinand was unheard of, the Society, like the Hist and Phil, was exclusively male. The Metaphysical Society which concerned itself with wide ranging philosophical subjects from art to ethics was more progressive and welcomed all, regardless of sex.

The Dixon Hall in College Park on Saturday nights was a favourite venue for 'hops', the then equivalent of the modern disco, but without kaleidoscopic embellishments. There we danced and flirted to soft lights and sweet music on the strict understanding that our girl friends would not afterwards be admitted to college rooms, but depart immediately from the campus with virginity intact when the dancing was over, usually at 11.30 p.m. We also had the Molesworth Hall attached to St Ann's parish for frequent dances, or socials as they were officially called in the parochial context to avoid taxation. So like most students I danced and I dated. I cuddled in the pictures and drank coffee afterwards in the Adelphi restaurant. But nothing serious. No falling in love.

Since returning to Dublin as Dean of St Patrick's, I have been invited to speak at meetings in the Philosophical, Historical and Theological Societies, and to take part in debates. Standing in the Graduates Memorial Building always brings back old memories and I still feel I can be outspoken, even recklessly so, in Trinity. I was always a bit of a maverick. The character of Trinity has changed to a certain extent in that it has now become more of a Dublin university whereas formerly it was cosmopolitan, with students from England, Northern Ireland and those whose fathers, in many cases Trinity graduates, were in the British Colonial Service. Nevertheless it still retains that liberal, tolerant and controversial atmosphere 'with no holds barred' which I remember so well.

Presbyterian divinity students from Magee College in Derry came to Trinity to complete their degree course. The experience was mutually beneficial, but now that link has been broken and both Trinity and the Presbyterian Church are, I believe, the poorer. There have been other changes too. I remember a student who for many years enjoyed the leisurely atmosphere of college life, having been left money by a doting relative to put him through Trinity. The terms of the Will entitled him to draw a stipulated amount annually while at Trinity. Provided the fees were paid, the college authorities in those days had no objection to such prolongation.

The Theological Society was a vibrant organisation and I can recall lively debates held under its aegis, during which some views I expressed were considered very radical. I was critical of the dominant role of the Roman Catholic Church in Ireland (hence my mother's fears that I would cause Protestants to be burned out of their homes), arguing that all Churches should make their way and commend themselves by their own integrity without having to rely on the State to enforce their moral disciplines. I remember saying that members of the Church of Ireland were altogether too subservient, too timid to stand up for their faith, especially in the case of mixed marriages; we should know what we believed and why we believed it. I also disliked the practice of referring to Bishops as 'My Lord' and to Archbishops as 'Your Grace'.

In the intervening years my views have changed very little. I am still repelled by titles such as 'The Lord Bishop' or 'His Grace the Archbishop' which to me have nothing to do with the Christianity one finds in the New Testament. The only justification for their use is that the recipients of such deference are entitled to membership of the House of Lords! I can honestly say that I never had any ambition to become a bishop but if I had reached that exalted state my first directive to my diocesan clergy and laity would have been: 'Never address me as "My Lord", plain "Bishop" is quite sufficient.'

If my mother worried about the repercussions my debating might have on the Protestant population of Ireland, she was also concerned about my taking the occasional drink with friends. One Whit Monday we had to vacate the Harding Boys' Home for the day to give the staff a holiday. Three of us purchased half a dozen bottles of stout and set off on our bikes for the Wicklow mountains. I carried the stout in my rucksack. As ill luck would have it two of the bottles collided and smashed as my bike went over a bump in the road, and Guinness stout streamed down the back of my shirt. We had to dismount, discard the broken bottles and make do with what was left intact. Not long afterwards I brought home my laundry, including the shirt, which I had thoughtlessly bundled up with the other items, to be washed by my mother. Strictly teetotal herself and being met by a strong aroma of stout when she opened the bundle, she feared I had gone completely to the bad. 'That shirt was smelling terribly of drink,' she scolded, 'Don't tell me you're hitting the bottle at Trinity?' My father took the occasional drink and smoked ten a day until he turned sixty when suddenly he gave up both, not, as he explained, for any health reasons but because he discovered they were a waste of time and money and added nothing to the enjoyment of life. My mother only once agreed to break her lifelong teetotal commitment when, weakened after a serious operation, she was advised to take a bottle of stout mixed with a pint of milk every day for a fortnight. This she did with great reluctance. It had the desired effect for her strength quickly returned. However, her daily libations did not result in her acquiring a taste for Guinness, although I am sure they sharpened her nose to detect its smell.

Trinity Rag Week was a welcome relief from the drab conformity of the war years, and as such seemed much appreciated by the citizenry of Dublin who responded to our high-spirited student pranks with tolerant good humour and generous contributions to our charity collections. The occasional tram would be commandeered with the connivance of the driver, its overhead cable adjusted and set in reverse, so that the unfortunate passengers on a tram bound for Dun Laoghaire and hi-jacked at the end of Dawson Street would suddenly find themselves heading back towards Nelson's Pillar. I do not recall any resistance or ill-feeling. Drivers and passengers invariably entered into the spirit of the occasion.

Dr Jourdan, or Jourdy as we called him, was Professor of Ecclesiastical History. He always lectured to a background of continuous uproar. Paper darts were thrown in great waves to descend on Jourdy, who remained quite oblivious to all and promptly brushed aside any dart which landed on his script. The louder the din the more persistent he became. Once, everyone agreed to stop the noise during a lecture and note the effect. When silence descended poor Jourdy sensed a change in the atmosphere. He looked up from his notes. 'Are you all right?' he asked. He was a good historian and those who listened to him gained much in return. Unfortunately he had no idea of how to keep order.

He fell easy prey to the student clowns among us who asked him outrageous test questions such as, 'Was St Patrick a Roman Catholic, sir?' Jourdy stared at the questioner over his glasses.

'I'll answer that by asking you a question. Did St Patrick ride a motor bicycle?'

'Of course not,' replied the student. 'There were no motor bicycles in St Patrick's day. But I don't see what that has to do with my question.'

And so we managed to spin out the debate on St Patrick and motor bikes, feigning ignorance of Jourdy's analogy which was based on innovations and additions to the Catholic faith since the time of Patrick.

Jourdy was a vigorous protagonist of the independence of the Celtic Church and there was a story, no doubt apocryphal, that he took on two priests of the Roman persuasion in heated debate in a railway carriage. The argument eventually came to fisticuffs. Jourdy was, in fact, a Zacchaeus in stature, a little terrier of a man. The guard, it was said, attracted by the commotion had to intervene and separate the contestants, threatening to stop the train and put the three of them off, if they didn't stop fighting about the Pope.

Once an alarm clock was placed under the lecture platform set to go off halfway through the lecture. Suddenly an almighty jangle began to reverberate around the lecture theatre.

'Stop that, stop that,' shrieked Jourdy.

'We can't, sir. That's the fire alarm.'

The lecture ended in shambles with everyone, Jourdy included, evacuating the building.

Latin and mathematics were compulsory subjects in the first major Trinity examination known as Littlego. All students had to prove by passing it that they had achieved a general standard of education before being allowed to specialise in the subject of their choice. Many would fall by the wayside in Littlego. Part of the preparation consisted of frantically swotting up and committing to memory translations for a Latin oral, especially sections favoured by examiners known as 'snips'. Many non-classicists would learn great passages from the 'key' by heart before appearing for examination, carrying their Virgil or Horace. Sir Robert Tate was Professor of Latin, and the terror of timid females. It sometimes happened that students who thought they recognised a prescribed piece in the oral would mistakenly begin to recite a translation which did not corre-spond to the text before them. This would send Sir Robert into paroxysms of rage. He seemed to rant especially at the girls and they would emerge from the examination in tears. As public orator he held forth at Commencements (degree-conferring ceremonies) with Latin perorations which were punctuated by aggressive shouts of 'translate' from some of the more unruly students in imitation of Sir Robert in Littlego.

Arthur Aston Luce, Professor of Philosophy, left his mark on many a student, including myself. He couched his lectures in such picturesque language that they became works of poetic description. I can see him now, with perhaps twenty of us at nine o'clock on a bleak winter morning, sitting huddled over a turf fire reading out his lecture. He was erect, well-built and completely bald. His wife, Lilian, after whom a memorial philosophy prize had been named, and his daughter had both drowned in a tragic fishing accident. Besides lecturing at Trinity he was Precentor of St Patrick's, a position next in order of precedence to the Dean. He claimed to be tone deaf, but this in no way lessened the impact of his preaching or reading, which was always highly articulate, with ringing tones gripping and holding the attention of the congregation. He loved the King James version of the Bible and the Book of Common Prayer and dismissed out of hand contemporary revisions as banal and devoid of any linguistic or theological merit. I later had the embarrassing experience of being his superior, although he would constantly say when perhaps I was feeling a little diffident: 'Remember you are the Dean and Ordinary, you and you only have the right to give the orders here in St Patrick's.' Tradition and protocol had always to be meticulously observed, for Luce, also a fine classicist, had a sense of history and the right ordering of things. All things, following St Paul, must be done 'decently and in order'.

He was master of an acerbic wit. On one occasion having preached in the college chapel, a fellow professor, likewise in holy orders, reminded him to sign the preachers' book in order to be paid his five pounds preaching fee. As he was signing it the professor informed him:

'You know, Dr Luce, when I preached in America I was paid the equivalent of fifty pounds for one sermon.' Luce, who did not see eye to eye theologically with the professor, looked at him.

'Your own?' he enquired.

On another occasion, when he was somewhat hard of hearing, a visiting preacher in St Patrick's anxious to make an impression ranted on for half an hour. Afterwards Luce, in the hearing of the unfortunate preacher, remarked in an aside: 'I heard every word of that sermon and I wish I hadn't.'

A.A. Luce wrote many of the standard works on George Berkeley, his hero, believing that Berkeley had given in his clear, concise, well-reasoned and stylish writings the most convincing answers to important philosophical questions. He was also a very dedicated angler. Fishing and thinking were his twin occupations; he even wrote a book about them. One of his colleagues in the philosophy department, not a Berkeleian, when asked his opinion of the book retorted somewhat unkindly, 'Better on the fishing.'

There was Professor R.R. Hartford, nasal in voice, friendly in manner, practical in theology. In sermon preaching class the unfortunate student who dared announce 'My text is taken from . . . ' was promptly put down with 'It's not *your* text and you have no right to take it. Put it back, and don't say Harvest

Festival. It's not one of the five Church Festivals. Say Harvest Thanksgiving.' How often have I felt like standing up in church and doing a Hartford correction on sermon and church announcements.

And the Provost, 'Tubby' Alton, whose rotundity naturally gave rise to the nickname and who, when presiding at a meeting, always gave the impression that he was trying to read the agenda upside down.

And Max Henry, a mathematician attractively heretical in religion, which he tried in an uncomfortably unorthodox book to reconcile with science: a sort of Uri Geller who, it was said, attempted single-handed in his rooms by a supreme act of concentration to stop the Dublin traffic and so prove the supremacy of mind over matter.

And I remember dear George Simms, later Archbishop of Armagh, and at that time college chaplain or Dean of Residence. Always exceptionally kind and considerate, even-tempered and gentle, he never forgot a name. An authority on the Book of Kells, a man of immense learning, he was without doubt the most humble and holy man I have ever met. Words of Isaak Walton are a fitting epitaph:

Of this blest man
Let this just praise be given,
Heaven was in him, before he was in heaven.

Many years later when he as Archbishop of Dublin welcomed me to St Patrick's he said: 'Victor, when I am in St Patrick's you must tell me what you wish me to do, for you are the Ordinary.' Once when he was Archbishop of Armagh I forgot to ask him to give the blessing at a General Synod service and he remained in his Primatial stall until I sent my verger over to request him to do so. With a discreet nod and smile, he complied.

The war impinged considerably on Trinity life. The college was very pro-British, and victory over Hitler and the Nazis and Fascists was earnestly desired and prayed for. A large number of students enlisted in 1939, the majority of them joining the British Forces. Due to their absence the proportion of male to female students appeared more balanced until 1946, when many former undergraduates returned to Trinity and women once again became a small minority in the student community.

I well remember the ugly riot in College Green on V.E. Day in May 1945. Pro-British and Allied supporters displayed their colours. A number of Trinity students (mainly from Northern Ireland) wearing red white and blue rosettes celebrated the victory triumphantly, shouting and dancing and singing 'Rule Britannia' on the streets. Some Northern Irish students climbed on the roof at the front gate of Trinity and hoisted the Union Jack. Republicans in College Green, mostly students from University College in Earlsfort Terrace, were furious and in retaliation produced and set fire to a Union Jack. Then the fat was really in the fire, for the students on the roof, incensed at this insult to their flag, set fire to an Irish tricolour and hurled it down in flames into College Green. Running scuffles and much shouting and jeering ensued. I and some Trinity students in College Green made ourselves scarce, having no desire to be confronted by a hostile mob and so, preserving our anonymity, we all walked up Grafton Street.

Meanwhile the Garda Síochána were occupied trying to keep the rival mobs apart. Anyone who looked like a student was suspect and fair game for a garda baton. I was set upon by a guard in Grafton Street but somehow escaped his truncheon. However, my friend was not so fortunate. He was clouted on the head. The riot did not, however, even remotely approach the level of violence sometimes unleashed on the streets of the world's cities today. No tear gas or water cannon were needed to disperse the angry crowds. There was no attack on the gardaí, only on each other, no looting and little destruction of property. I cannot recall seeing any shop windows broken. One or two may have been smashed accidentally, certainly not deliberately. Those were the days before protective steel shutters. Now, alas, they are a common sight in Dublin and a poor reflection on our society.

Examinations were held at the beginning of term, which gave an opportunity to study and prepare during the preceding vacation. We had time for participation in college activities without the prospect of an exam looming ahead at the end of term. In the war years travelling abroad was out of the question and so I had little else to do during the vacation except study, lend a hand on the farm or visit our popular seaside resorts, usually Courtown Harbour. In the evening I often cycled the seven or eight miles to the Togher, near Tinahely, where our friends, the Willoughbys, lived. There, well into the night, we played cards, rural Irish games called 25 and 45 and I would arrive home in the small hours to be warned by my mother, still awake, that 'you and those Willoughby boys will come to no good'. I think her puritanical conscience was disturbed by the idea of a card-playing son, particularly one preparing for ordination although I hasten to add, we never played for money. So far, thankfully, her prophecy has remained unfulfilled. Of the three Willoughby card players, Noel became a bishop, Charles an archdeacon and James a highly successful secondary school teacher. I finished up as Dean of St Patrick's. All of which would seem to say something about cards and the Almighty, but what the message is, I'm not so sure!

In 1947 the number of ordinands was inflated by the return of students from the Forces and the Church of Ireland had no difficulty in filling vacant curacies. Forty-two of us were ordained that year. I had previously been accepted for a curacy in a parish near Belfast in the United Diocese of Down and Dromore, but a month or so before my ordination I was left high and dry because the curate who was serving there, and had intended to leave for elsewhere, changed his mind at the last moment. What was I to do?

Out of the blue came news of a vacancy in St Augustine's, Derry. My professor summoned me to his rooms and asked if I would like to go to Derry. Professor Oulton (Gerry as we all called him) was Regius Professor of Divinity, a consummate and careful scholar whose favourite concluding phrase after setting out both sides of a theological argument was invariably: 'It is therefore not unreasonable to suppose . . . '. In my desperate situation I was in no mood to weigh up the pros and cons of a curacy in Derry or anywhere else and so acting on the maxim, 'any port in a storm', I immediately agreed to go, although I had never visited the Maiden City and knew nothing whatever about it, except for its famous siege. Whether the eleventh-hour appointment was coincidental or providential I do not know, but I have never regretted it. I grew to love Derry, or London-derry, to give it its official title. With Kilkenny and Dublin it remains one of my top three Irish cities.

So I left Trinity, dear leisurely, tolerant, friendly Trinity, sad at leaving and full of memories but also proud of having a world-renowned academic foundation as my Alma Mater. As a Trinity man, for all time, I could hold my head high.

7

Derry

M Y FIRST glimpse of the historic city, Derry, the oak grove of St Columba, was when a month before my ordination I made my way to be interviewed by the bishop, Robert McNeil Boyd, and satisfy episcopal requirements for admittance to his diocese as curate of St Augustine's on Derry's walls. Though officially named Londonderry when Derry became the property of the City of London at the Plantation of Ulster, the British connection indicated by the prefix 'London' is frowned on by Nationalists who always speak simply of 'Derry'. Unionists when emphasising their Britishness use the official title 'Londonderry' in correspondence and sometimes in conversation, although paradoxically the Orange Order and the Apprentice Boys are known as the 'City of *Derry* Loyal Orange Lodge' and the 'Apprentice Boys of *Derry*', and Orangemen hail the Williamite victories of *Derry*, Aughrim, Enniskillen and the Boyne! The Church of Ireland bishop is the episcopal ruler of the Diocese of *Derry* with his 'cathedra' or episcopal chair in *Derry* Cathedral. In matters ecclesiastical 'Derry', following its Columban origin, is the official title both in the Church of Ireland and the Roman Catholic communions. Presbyterians also have 'First *Derry* Presbyterian Church' and the Rugby Club, predominantly Protestant in membership since Roman Catholic schools in Northern Ireland do not play rugby, is the City of *Derry* Rugby Club.

I travelled by train from Belfast, approaching the city along the shores of Lough Foyle, on that day glistening in the sunlight. When the train rounded Culmore Point I saw the spires of Derry's two cathedrals, St Eugene's and St Columb's in the distance and, as we drew nearer the city, the stately Guildhall on the other side of the river. The view was impressive, the city rising from the Foyle, set on a hill and surrounded by hills, a perfect location. Arriving at the old Waterside Station I took a bus to Rosemount on the other side of the Foyle where I was to stay. We crossed Craigavon Bridge, and up Carlisle Road. Steep streets appeared everywhere and endless as we climbed to the Diamond and then hurtled down Shipquay Street at breakneck speed — or so it seemed — through a gateway in the City wall which looked at first too narrow to accommodate the bus and entered Guildhall Square before climbing again to Rosemount.

Those hills seem to reflect Derry's turbulent undulating history, but the walls, so well preserved and surmounted with their cannon from the old siege, symbolise the tenacity and resilience in adversity of the citizens. Despite the vicissitudes, the violence and the bombings, one returns to Derry only to see business as usual, its inhabitants still as solid and steadfast as the ancient walls encircling their city.

In July 1947 I returned to Derry and was ordained in the Cathedral Church of St Columb, to serve for a year as deacon after which, if all went well, I could look forward to my ordination as a priest. 'When you are ordained deacon you have arrived,' writes Archbishop Michael Ramsey, 'but being a priest meant far more to me than being a bishop. Becoming a bishop is an incident in the life of a priest. I sometimes forget the day of the year when I was made a bishop. I never fail to remember the day of the year when I was made a priest.' Salutary words, especially in this mass media age with its frequent demands for instant episcopal comments and statements. Between bishops and priests there is a great media gulf fixed. Bishops are seen as the very embodiment of the Church. Priests are regarded as having an inferior status, 'episcopal messenger boys', as someone has put it. This is a far cry from Ramsey's wise and incisive words: 'Becoming a bishop is an incident in the life of a priest.' The priesthood is the central order.

St Augustine's still stands on the walls overlooking the Bogside, despite having suffered considerable damage many times by bomb blasts. It is near the site of the old Walker Pillar, since demolished by the IRA. The Pillar served as a scaffold every 18 December on which the Apprentice Boys burnt an effigy of the city governor, Lundy, who, against the wishes of the citizens, ordered the surrender of the city to King James's armies. This annual ritual, marking the shutting of the gates with its 'no surrender' motif, was intended as an object-lesson to all would-be traitors. Its significance was certainly not lost on the Nationalist Bogside community below the walls. The term 'Lundy' in Protestant jargon was synonymous with 'traitor', with betraying the cause by compromising with the enemy.

The situation in Derry was very different from the one I was accustomed to in the South. There were two separate communities, never meeting except perhaps for some professional and business people who found themselves fellow golf club or Rotary members. I joined the City of Derry Rugby Club but Northern Roman Catholics did not play rugby. The Protestants for their part knew nothing about Gaelic games or the Irish language. The segregated schools went their separate ways with no contact whatever, even on the sports field. There was a Feis Ceol for each community. A few Roman Catholics would occasionally compete in the Londonderry Feis but I never heard of Protestants participating in the Derry Feis. The platform of the Londonderry Feis was festooned with a large Union Jack and the programme each evening concluded with the singing of the National Anthem accompanied on the piano by one of the adjudicators. The audience was left in no doubt as to which Feis it was attending. Although Protestants were suspicious about Irish and had no idea of the origin of place names which they used every day, Belfast, Coleraine, Ballymena etc., they apparently had no problem with Feis Ceol!

As a Southerner I was immediately struck by the number of Protestants who were bus drivers, postmen, labourers drilling the roads or emptying the bins, engaged in all sorts of occupations never associated with Protestants in the Republic. I was suddenly aware of the Protestant working-class population which for me had not existed before.

In those days it was customary for a curate to live in a boarding house until appointed to a parish. He then moved out and his successor as curate would usually take his place. A curate found himself sharing digs with bachelors in secular occupations and possibly also with fellow curates. He never entertained the idea of getting married, a holy estate to be entered upon only after becoming a rector. Besides turning out for Derry City Rugby Football Club I played hockey for Derry Cathedral and joined in the multifarious activities of the younger parishioners with whom tennis and rambling were especially popular.

Canon McKegney, rector of St Augustine's, arranged digs for me in Harding Street, a little row of terraced houses, with two kindly spinsters who were also fervent Presbyterians. A fellow lodger there was a curate in the Cathedral, one of my card-playing friends from Co. Wicklow, Charles Willoughby, and we often engaged in light-hearted doctrinal discussions with the sisters, who generally laughed off our tongue-in-cheek attempts to convince them of the superiority of Anglicanism over Presbyterianism.

Electricity was not permitted in the house, being regarded with suspicion as to its safety, reliability and cost, so we had gas lamps in our rooms. But even gas was not to be entirely trusted and had to be turned off at the main to ensure that the house did not perish in nocturnal flames, a task scrupulously performed by our landladies each night on retiring to bed. We had torches at the ready for this sudden blackout. Downstairs, there was a coal fire but our rooms, like those of any digs then, were unheated. Many a frosty night I wrote sermons sitting up in bed dressed in nightgown and scarf, my breath emerging in steamy clouds, often having to finish my labours by torchlight.

I remember vividly my first Christmas away from home. I spent it alone. Canon McKegney left for Sligo for a brief holiday break with his wife's relations after the Christmas services, naturally taking it as read that I had been invited to spend the rest of the day with one of the parishioners. Unfortunately, no such arrangement had been made. Arriving back in Harding Street after the morning services I found the two

sisters (who had not themselves been to church since Presbyterians did not believe in keeping any church holy day but
the Sabbath, though celebrating Christmas Day when it fell on
a Sunday was in order), both ready to go out for Christmas
dinner.

'Are you not going anywhere for your dinner?' they enquired.

'No. Nobody asked me.'

So I sat alone in the front parlour dining on chicken soup and
some boiled chicken with white bread and tea hastily prepared
for me. No Christmas pudding or cake. I thought wistfully of
the festivities taking place at home. It was my own fault. I could
have gone to many houses and would have been more than
welcome. When later it got round that I had spent Christmas
Day alone, the apologies were profuse. Next Christmas I feasted
unceasingly for a month.

Canon Herbert McKegney came from Belfast with a well-
founded reputation for being 'a great man for the youth'. A
leading scout in Northern Ireland, he was not slow in appointing me cubmaster on my arrival. Having had some experience
of scouting but not the cub movement, I was forced to purchase
a manual and swot up on Akela and Baloo and dib-dibbing and
dob-dobbing. I thoroughly enjoyed being a cubmaster, especially
trekking and camping with my charges. St Augustine's was a
vibrant parish, full of young people, and I felt very much at
home in my ministry there.

During those early months as a raw curate I met with almost
unanimous understanding and encouragement from loyal
parishioners who instantly opened their doors and their hearts
to me without a hint of the northern coldness or aloofness I had
been led to expect.

Northerners are not cold or aloof. They are warm-hearted,
cheerful, kind, generous and considerate. They will do their
utmost to help at all times and I count myself fortunate in
having had the opportunity to work with them and to have
enjoyed their friendship and hospitality for over twenty years.
'Come in, your reverence', they would urge me, 'you're
starving.' Did I really look so thin and emaciated I wondered,

until I discovered that 'starving' meant 'shivering with the cold'. I heard children referred to as 'wains' and choice phrases such as 'he took a skunner at him' meaning 'took a dislike to him' and 'I joined him' in the sense of 'criticised him'. And there was the 'brock man' who collected the 'leftovers' after meals to feed his pigs. 'Thon man's wired to the moon' (he's crazy) or 'he's an auld gulpin' (he's stupid).

Tracing my sense of vocation to the ministry back to my boyhood in Carnew, I am conscious that our local rector, Edward Forrest, influenced me more than anyone. I wanted to be a good listener, communicator and a man of action — someone who, like Mr Forrest, viewed every problem as a challenge to be tackled head on. I came to detest the attitude of 'putting things on the long finger'. I have always been impatient with inactivity and complacency. If anything, I am inclined to be too impetuous, to act on instinct and intuition to get things done, come what may. At Kilkenny College, a very macho establishment, I kept any idea of ordination to myself, fearing that if it became known I would be regarded as too holy by half! A number of boys at Kilkenny during my time were later ordained, but we all kept such thoughts of ordination, if we had them, strictly private and confidential. In the more mature atmosphere of Mountjoy School, the subject was openly discussed and we knew who intended going 'into the Church', as ordination was commonly styled.

While at Trinity I had periods of doubt, especially when confronted in my studies with philosophical arguments about the existence of God, and the problem of how to reconcile the terrible suffering of so many innocents with the existence of a good and omnipotent God. These doubts, though formidable, were not enduring.

I became an agnostic at Trinity from time to time, but never an atheist. We are all agnostics to a degree, having to admit that we do not know all the answers. This is a reasonable position but I find it hard to understand the atheist who asserts with absolute conviction that there is no God. Perhaps reason cannot prove the existence of God. But neither can reason prove that those who believe in God are irrational. As the psalmist says, 'The fool hath said in his heart, there is no God.' The man who says 'I don't know' deserves to be treated with greater respect than the atheist. Since existence is usually related to what we experience by our senses (I see it, therefore it exists), I prefer to speak of 'the being of God' rather than 'the existence of God'.

Preaching in St Augustine's I discovered in the congregation a characteristic common to most Northern Protestants: they commented on sermons, ready to utter a word of appreciation if they found them helpful but, equally, not hesitant in criticising and disagreeing. Feedback of this kind is very useful to a preacher. At times I was taken to task by members of the congregation for what I had said, but at least I knew they were listening and taking my sermons seriously. In the South I find there is not the same tendency to comment. The preacher is left wondering whether the congregation has been listening at all. As our Derry churches had no amplifying system — 'the preacher's ruin', now seemingly a 'must' even in small churches — the preacher had to speak distinctly, articulating every word clearly and projecting his voice to be audible to those in the back pews. No mumbling into mikes in those days.

I believe that preaching must always be relevant and concrete, not confined to generalities. In Derry I began the attempt to relate the Gospel to the situation I saw around me, to come to grips with what was taking place and apply the teaching of the Gospel. It is easy to preach about love and justice in the abstract, but applying these Christian virtues to particular situations and pointing out that this or that state of affairs does not embody Christian love or justice and needs to be remedied, this approach touches a sensitive nerve. 'Why are you criticising the Corporation or Stormont?' I was asked indignantly.

One of my duties, particularly at Christmas and Easter, was taking Communion to the elderly and housebound in their homes. Celebrating Communion on the kitchen table, I had sometimes reached the most solemn part of the service when the front door-bell would ring and the dear lady would interject

My father and mother and *(below)* the scene about 1920 outside my father's garage in Carnew. He is on the extreme right.

The Darlington Band, Carnew, about 1915. My father is on the cello, with Mr Darlington the local merchant on fiddle.

Harvesting on the family farm in the 1930s. My father is pouring tea and my grandfather is partially hidden behind him.

The 1945 scholars with the Provost on Trinity Monday. I am in the middle row on the extreme left.

Many years later, with Noël Browne, supporting David Norris as a Trinity candidate for the Senate. *(Irish Times)*

Pat Fanning, President of the GAA and Seán O Siocháin, Director-General of the GAA, presenting a cheque for £1,000 to St Patrick's Cathedral in January 1973. *(Irish Times)*

Mícheál Mac Liammóir and President Childers receive special editions of sterling plate at Marsh's Library in May 1973. *(Irish Times)*

without a moment's hesitation, 'Hold on, your reverence. That's the bread man.' And out she would go and talk to him quite unconcerned while I sat awaiting her return. This mixing of sacred and secular I'm sure did not worry our Lord. I can imagine him smiling benignly on the scene.

A visit to give Communion to a confused woman of over ninety made a lasting impression on me. She had lost all contact with reality, and her daughter commented 'I don't think she'll understand.' 'We'll try, anyway,' I suggested. Opening the Book of Common Prayer I began the Communion Service and to our astonishment the old woman moved her lips and recited every prayer with me. The time-worn phrases of the Prayer Book had so entered her soul that they alone remained when all else had gone. I can still see the tears of joy of her daughter as the service came to an end.

In those days of greater trust and respect for the property of others, a length of string was often left attached to the front door latch enabling visitors to put their hand through the letter box, pull the string to open the door and let themselves in. I used to announce myself as I pulled the string in order not to surprise parishioners at some activity which they might not wish their clergy to discover. In the evenings I sometimes heard the clink of tumblers and bottles being removed and later, perhaps, caught sight of a hastily secreted tumbler behind an armchair. Puritanical Northerners felt a little guilty in those days about such indulgences.

In the late forties the scourge of TB was still wreaking havoc in Derry, and all too often I sat late into the night to comfort a family where a father, wife or brother was lying emaciated by the killer disease. St Columb's TB Hospital had just opened but waiting lists were long and many died before they could be admitted. It was a sombre spectacle and heart-rending experience to bury these people, many cut down in the prime of life.

Though I soon began to put down roots in Derry I did not lose sight of Southern affairs. Having expressed my belief during Trinity debates that it was a denial of freedom of conscience and democracy for the Roman Catholic Church, or any Church, to dominate the political and moral scene, I was incensed when John Costello on becoming Taoiseach in 1948 sent a message of allegiance to the Pope on behalf of the Irish government (as Eamon de Valera had done on taking office in 1932). I was prompted to write a letter to the *Irish Times* protesting that the Government of a State which professed to be democratic and Republican at that, should not, on election to office, set about publicising their subservience to a foreign pontiff or to any religious leader. Of course they had a right privately to their religious views but had no democratic right to pledge the allegiance of the Irish people as a whole to the See of Rome. I sometimes think it strange that any hint of political allegiance to a foreign monarch is met with accusations of being anti-Irish, a traitor to the national cause, whereas religious allegiance to a foreign bishop resulting in a greater surrender of democratic freedom is unreservedly accepted by so many, indeed exulted in, as being truly Irish.

On a salary of two hundred and twenty pounds a year a curate had no pretensions to owning a motor car. All he could rise to was a push bike for making his pastoral visits. Nevertheless as a result of a remarkable coincidence I, in time, acquired the wherewithal to purchase a motor bike, an infinitely superior means of transport. I am not a betting man, but on the eve of the Grand National one year I dreamed I was riding a horse through a huge mound of coins. I happened to mention this to a rather well-heeled friend who discovered among the runners an outsider called Nickel Coin. Taking my dream as an omen he placed two bets of five pounds — one for me and one for himself — on Nickel Coin. Sure enough, Nickel Coin won at very good odds. With the proceeds I paid back the five pounds and bought a motor bike which I christened Nickel Coin. The news quickly got round, especially in the sporting fraternity where I was regarded as a latter-day Biblical Joseph, also a dreamer who never failed in his prognostications.

There was a once-only repeat performance of sorts when I dreamed the following year that I was playing rugby, kicking frees all over the place, landing the ball straight between the posts. I described the dream to my friend, we looked at the list of runners and there, true to form, was a fancied horse called Freebooter. Bets were duly placed, and Freebooter finished first. The news reached me at half time during a rugby match. Immediately a great cheer went up from my team mates who were also in on the act and had backed the winner. Unfortunately, I was expected thereafter always to dream the winner of the Grand National and for a number of years I was inundated with phone calls on the day of the race. Needless to say it took a long time to live down my reputation as the punter's friend.

My rector at St Augustine's, Canon McKegney, was a no-nonsense man, forthright, meticulous in his attention to detail, one who never suffered fools gladly. Slim and wiry of build, he was blessed with boundless energy and a happy disposition; his walk was jaunty and he whistled a lot. He enjoyed life, but he worked hard and he expected the same of others, giving them due recognition for their efforts. I had to report at the weekly staff meeting on the house visits I had made, a required minimum of forty each week, not to mention hospital visitation and morning teaching sessions in local schools. All visits were recorded in a book. Canon McKegney also taught me one of the most valuable lessons of my life, namely to acknowledge letters as soon as they arrive. 'Clear your desk every day,' he admonished; apposite advice for procrastinating Southerners. I discovered that government departments in the North operated in the same way. Whatever the defects of the Stormont Government, the Civil Service was remarkably efficient at answering letters promptly.

Herbert McKegney's wife, Mabel, was a Sligo girl and a talented cook, who made the rectory a second home, an ever-open door for me. I had a standing invitation to a lavish spread every Sunday after Evening Service. Their first son, John, was born while I was the curate and in St Augustine's rectory I had my first lessons in nursing and baby care! John is now a rector in Armagh with children of his own.

In 1951 the senior curacy at Christ Church, the largest parish in the United Diocese of Derry and Raphoe, fell vacant and

I was appointed to work there under the Rev. Edwin Parke. In appearance and temperament he was the opposite to Canon McKegney. A powerfully built man, he was a former rugby player who over the years had become more corpulent, and whereas my first rector had been outgoing and practical, Edwin Parke was quiet, contemplative and priestly, a firm supporter of the 'Catholic' side of Anglicanism. In short, Herbert McKegney was Low Church and Edwin Parke was High Church. I was privileged to have served my ecclesiastical apprenticeship with two such able men. Indeed, my ministry would have been much the poorer but for the influence of both.

I well remember my first pastoral visit in Christ Church parish.

'I'm the new curate, Mrs Irwin,' I announced to the lady who answered the door-bell.

'Ah,' she said, 'come on in.'

'Mrs Irwin, you don't come from the North with an accent like that.'

'No. I come from a little place down in County Wicklow you've probably never heard of.'

'Where is it?' I asked. 'I come from Wicklow myself.'

'A place called Carnew,' replied Mrs Irwin.

It transpired that her father had been an RIC sergeant in Carnew but had joined the RUC and moved north when the RIC was disbanded. Thus I gained a friend for life. If ever I felt peckish I went to see Mrs Irwin, who always produced the goods.

Charles and I had to leave our digs in Harding Street when the doctor advised our kind landladies to take life a little easier by getting rid of the lodgers. Our next landlady, to put it mildly, was rather eccentric. We had electricity in abundance and a gas hot water geyser, which for the sake of economy she had the habit of turning off at the main while we were running a bath, with the result that the water from the hot tap suddenly turned cold. Amid loud protests from upstairs she would reluctantly be prevailed on to restore the supply.

Another lodger, Michael Franklin, the Cathedral organist, shared the same roof with us. As Christmas drew near cards from parishioners began to arrive for the three of us. To our landlady, however, the very thought of receiving fewer cards than her lodgers was humiliating. Each morning she would announce her count.

'I got twenty cards today,' she would inform us.

'We got twenty-five between us.' Close to Christmas Eve the rivalry became more intense.

'Another fifty arrived for us today,' we would exclaim. Whereupon she would check that our professed totals were correct, carefully counting the cards displayed in our dining room. She was not to be beaten. Always resourceful she suddenly confronted us with a hundred cards — a miracle we thought, until it dawned on us that the stocks of former years had been brought into play to secure the winning count. We surrendered gracefully and she rested victorious until the following Christmas.

Michael Franklin, a lovable eccentric, was a confirmed bachelor in his mid-fifties and splendid company with a dry sense of humour. He came from a musical Sligo family who had been friends of Percy French. Menus forty years ago not being as varied as they are today, the constant fare was becoming monotonous.

'Do you ever cook black puddings?' suggested Michael one day, having seen some tempting examples of the delicacy in Doherty's butcher's window down the Strand. Since puddings black and white were considered in the more genteel Northern circles to be dishes for the poor, our landlady was somewhat taken aback by this unprecedented request, but no doubt thinking they would be cheap and easy to prepare, she overcame her scruples and promised to give us all the black puddings we wanted.

Next evening, however, our anticipation turned to bewilderment and then to horror when she appeared with three plates, each bearing one partially fried, inedible, complete horseshoe of a black pudding. When she had departed Charlie and I rounded on Michael, who saved the day by secreting the three puddings in a paper bag in the pocket of his shower-proof coat hanging on the hall stand; then, as soon as we could reasonably leave the house, we all went down to Yannarelli's fish and chipper.

Approaching the festive board in trepidation the following evening we found our worst fears realised. Our landlady, concluding from the empty plates that she was on to a winner, served up three more horseshoes which joined the others in Michael's pocket. On the third evening when the same fare appeared we tactfully persuaded her to give us some respite from black puddings. Michael was too embarrassed to dispose of the nine puddings in a public litter bin — when he tried to do so everyone seemed to be staring at him — and so he carried them round for days, by which time they were beginning to smell. We caught the landlady sniffing in the hall.

'If she goes to the pocket we've had it, Michael,' we told him. 'We'll be thrown out.'

He promised to rid himself of his obsessive black pudding burden next day during his weekly train journey to Ballymoney to teach music. Selecting an empty compartment he waited until the train reached Culmore Point and heaved the black puddings out through the carriage window and on to the shingle beside the Foyle. As the bag ruptured a flock of screeching seagulls descended on the contents. That was in truth the end of the story, but Michael could not resist adding his own punchline:

'You know, as I was coming back I looked out at Culmore Point and six seagulls were lying dead.'

Church of Ireland bishops then carried with them an aura of great dignity and authority. When Bishop Boyd entered the vestry frock-coated and gaitered, we were immediately aware of an episcopal presence. We did not speak unless spoken to. A fine preacher and a strict disciplinarian, the bishop was much given to issuing rigorous episcopal directives to his clergy. He insisted, for instance, on correct attire at all times, dark suit, clerical collar and a hat. Some of us wore hats under great protest, but any of his clergy seen walking along the street without one was promptly hauled over the coals. When I became senior curate of Christ Church, Noel McKittrick, my junior for a while, a highly intelligent young maverick with an original turn of phrase, often ignored the bishop's ruling on hats and was consequently summoned to the episcopal presence on more than one occasion.

Noel uttered a memorable observation one day as he and I and another priest were walking with the bishop a short distance to lunch during the course of a clerical gathering. As the footpath was very narrow, Noel and I kept abreast of the other two by walking along the road.

'You and Griffin had better get off that road,' the bishop advised, whereupon Noel turned to him and posed the question: 'I wonder which would be the greater loss to the Church, my lord. Two curates or one bishop?' The bishop, like Queen Victoria, was not amused.

Bishop Boyd often asked me to drive with him to his preaching engagements in various parts of the diocese where roads were not as well surfaced as they are today. Punctures occurred occasionally, and I remember the two of us changing a wheel at ten o'clock one night on top of the Glenshane Pass near Dungiven on the homeward route from Maghera. During these journeys, puffing his pipe, he sometimes asked me where I thought my future lay and I would reply that I had come to Derry to gain experience and intended eventually returning to a parish in the South. He would pooh-pooh the idea. 'You're needed here in the North,' he insisted. 'This is where the challenge is.' Bishop Boyd also advised me to give up cigarettes and smoke a pipe; advice which I have consistently followed. 'And make sure,' said he, 'when you start the pipe don't choose a light tobacco. It'll only burn your tongue.'

In late 1956, when Edwin Parke was about to leave for a parish in Belfast, some of the parishioners approached me with the unorthodox suggestion that I should succeed him as rector. Appointing a curate to rector in the same parish, not to mention to the largest parish in the diocese, was a rare occurrence. Knowing that this was a potentially embarrassing situation for the bishop and the diocesan representatives, who together with the parochial nominators constituted the Board of Nomination (lay and clerical) to a parish, I called on the bishop and told him that I would not allow my name to go forward for election against his wishes. He insisted that my name, if proposed, should be placed on the list of candidates.

I was elected and two months later I was duly instituted as rector.

St Eugene's Roman Catholic Cathedral stands across the road from Christ Church. Bishop Neil Farren and I would greet each other when we chanced to meet. On my institution he wrote to me welcoming me as rector. Some time earlier he had noticed a group of Christ Church parishioners, all volunteers, laying tarmacadam in the church grounds. Concerned about the poor state of the tarmacadam around his cathedral he asked my advice. I put him in touch with the leader of the volunteers, a loyalist called Robert Jackson, and, in the true traditional spirit of friendly cooperation between the two communities which persisted in Derry despite the rhetoric, drum banging and gerrymandering, Robert organised the tarmacadaming round St Eugene's.

One Sunday morning the bishop, a Donegal man, short and stout of build, emerged from his cathedral as I was leaving Christ Church to take another service in a daughter church in Argyll Street, about half a mile away. 'I'm going for a stroll,' he told me. 'Could I join you?' It was late morning, another Mass in St Eugene's and another service in Christ Church were about to begin, and people were still making their separate ways towards their devotions. Many of them looked more than once at the sight of the Roman Catholic bishop and the Church of Ireland rector walking up the Northland Road together. The church-warden standing at the porch of the little Mission Church where I was going to must have wondered whether his eyes were deceiving him when, peering into the distance he spied Bishop Farren descending on a Protestant church, an unheard-of thing in those pre-ecumenical days.

Not that I received any criticism from my own flock because of my friendship with the Roman Catholic bishop, but elsewhere in the North such might not have been the case. I might well have had the Scriptures quoted at me by those who believed the Pope was the anti-Christ.

I was nevertheless subjected to anonymous persecution by letter and, especially at night, by phone from extremist members of the wider Protestant community whenever I took issue with the Stormont administration or advocated the abolition of party politics in the Corporation, or closer links between the Churches. As I was chaplain to two hospitals and therefore on call at night I could not leave the phone off the hook in order to avoid the abuse. Some Ulster Protestants did not like what I was saying. I was accused of being a Fenian, a Lundy: a traitor to everything Protestantism held dear.

But I was by no means the only clergyman to receive abusive and sometimes threatening messages. All of us who tried to work for change in Derry came under fire. Bishop Tyndall, who succeeded Bishop Boyd and with whom I enjoyed a close relationship, was very forthright in his condemnation of extremism and suffered dreadfully as a result, so much so that he was occasionally forced to retreat to the peace of Donegal to escape the vitriolic phone calls. We were all tarred with the same brush in the eyes of the extremists. Not only were we a risk to civilised society, Nationalist sympathisers undermining the Union, we were theologically and scripturally wrong as well. 'Ulster is not for sale, no surrender,' they growled.

During the Forties and Fifties it was still possible to live one's life in a totally Protestant environment in Northern Ireland. We read the newspapers and periodicals which conformed to our religious and political views, Protestants taking the *Belfast Newsletter* or *Northern Whig*, the local *Londonderry Sentinel and Standard*, and Roman Catholics the *Irish News* and *Derry Journal*. The *Belfast Telegraph*, commonly called the 'Tele' or 'Tally', an evening publication, had a cross community readership and, although broadly Unionist in attitude, it did not hesitate to take an independent line and criticise the Unionist administration when it deemed it necessary to do so. As well as being the only daily evening paper, the 'Tele' in its obituary column covered both communities. If they did not meet in life they at least did so in death in the columns of the *Belfast Telegraph*.

Protestants who had come from the South or had family or business connections with the 'Free State' as it was called, also bought the *Irish Times*, while Roman Catholics with Southern interests bought the *Irish Independent* or *Irish Press*. Today few people in Northern Ireland, outside the professions and business interests, buy any Southern Irish newspapers. They are twice the price of the UK papers and, since the 'troubles' began in 1969, North and South have grown further apart.

The Provos by their campaign of murder, bombing and burning have tarnished their United Ireland 'cause'. The end has been corrupted by the means. The majority in both communities appear to have lost interest in the idea of a United Ireland, espoused by those so insensitive to human suffering and so dismissive of human rights as the Provos. They, in their warped thinking, have discarded any Republican ideals they may once have had and chosen instead the way of Fascism. For the average Northern Irelander, Protestant or Roman Catholic, the Republic beckons as a place to spend a relaxing holiday or weekend or as a venue for sporting or cultural events — Lansdowne Road, Croke Park, the Curragh, the Point Theatre. Nothing more.

The Protestant community in 1947 felt under threat and the old siege mentality of 1689 was ever present. Protestants if pressed would admit to discrimination against Roman Catholics, particularly in employment, but they would justify it on the grounds that the Church of Rome was intent on destroying the State and having a United Ireland under Rome rule. Therefore giving influential jobs, especially in the Corporation, to followers of the Pope would mean placing potential traitors in positions of power.

Protestants pointed out that Roman Catholic bishops had opted out of the political and social life of the Province, refusing to appoint chaplains to Stormont or to accept invitations to State functions. They contrasted this with the loyalty, indeed subservience, of Southern Protestants to the Republic in spite of having to submit to Roman Catholic moral teaching there. They looked on the Southern Protestants as a dying breed; nice, respectable, quiet people who, having lost the instinct for survival, gracefully awaited the undertaker. Northern Protestants had no intention of joining their Southern co-religionists on the annihilation road. They would be vigilant. 'You can't trust Roman Catholics. All they want is a United Ireland, Rome rule with not a Protestant left.' Discrimination was really on political grounds. Religion was the indicator of political allegiance, but since religion and politics coincided to the extent that Protestant was synonymous with Unionist and Roman Catholic with Nationalist, when discrimination occurred, it was usually seen as discrimination purely on the grounds of religion. 'Religious discrimination' was highlighted by the media, not political discrimination. In truth the core issue was political, where one stood on the Union, not on divisive theological questions.

Protestants saw the Roman Catholic position, to say the least, as inconsistent. In their eyes Roman Catholics seemed quite prepared to enjoy the advantages of living in the United Kingdom while at the same time giving no loyalty to the State. They were infuriated by Republican propaganda which depicted Roman Catholics in the North as an oppressed and persecuted minority, ground into the dust by the jackboot of Protestantism. 'Why', they asked, 'if there is such oppression, do Roman Catholics remain and multiply in Northern Ireland? Why are they not fleeing from the land of tyranny as persecuted minorities in other countries have had to do? If they are so fond of the South why don't they go and live there?' This was the general Protestant reaction to criticism of Northern Ireland.

To be fair it must be stated that health, social welfare and educational facilities were freely accessible without distinction. I saw school buildings of both communities extended with public funding, and impressive educational facilities up to and including third level were provided for all irrespective of community. Roman Catholic children rightly enjoyed the same benefits as Protestant children. There was no obvious poverty in the sense of barefooted children begging in the streets. Roman Catholics had large families, especially in areas like the Creggan Estate and the Bogside, and were entitled to exactly the same scale of allowances as Protestants, which in the case of a large family amounted to a considerable sum.

Male unemployment was widespread not only among Roman Catholics but also among Protestants. I was frequently approached by parishioners for help in getting a job. 'I hear there's a job going in the gas yard. Any chance of putting in a word for me?' Derry was a working women's town. The women went out to the shirt factories while the men stayed at home and looked after the house. The dole queues had both Protestants and Roman Catholics.

When I returned to the Republic I discovered a widely held notion that all the Corporation houses were allocated to Protestants and a Roman Catholic stood no chance of being housed in Derry. This was not true. Large numbers of Roman Catholic families were housed in the Creggan Estate and the Bogside (indeed statistically, I believe, more Roman Catholics were housed by the Corporation than Protestants), though it is fair to say that not enough houses were being built for either community to meet the demand. As Roman Catholics tended to have more children, their need was more acute. I was frequently approached by a Protestant couple with the following, typical, request: 'We're living with my mother who's not too well and it's getting us all down. There's one wain and another on the way. I see the new houses on the Waterside are nearly finished. We've had our name down for two years. Can you do anything for us? It's our only hope.' If they did happen to be allocated a house on the Protestant Waterside, especially over the heads of a Roman Catholic family with four or five children — although both families may have been as long on the waiting list — the media moved in and highlighted the plight of the unfortunate Roman Catholic family, living in appalling conditions but denied a house. The Protestant family were made to feel guilty although the usual defence was, 'Why should we be penalised for having fewer children?' The real problem was that there were not sufficient houses to satisfy the demand.

A second misconception, still quoted in the Republic from time to time, is that Roman Catholics were denied voting rights in Northern Ireland. In parliamentary elections the franchise was always open to all. However, in local elections successive Unionist governments continued the practice of the company vote, long abolished in the rest of the United Kingdom. This limited franchise, whereby members of local councils were elected only by ratepayers or householders and those with a business stake in the community (the latter group being thus entitled to additional corporate votes), guaranteed a Unionist majority on the Corporation in places like Derry. When the Civil Rights Movement later demanded 'one man, one vote' they were referring to local government elections, not to parliamentary elections where universal franchise had always been the case.

Generally Protestants employed Protestants and Roman Catholics also favoured their co-religionists. However, the success of the business always took precedence, and if this entailed employing some from the opposite camp for reason of their skills and reliability so be it. In such a mixed work force Protestants and Roman Catholics worked harmoniously together and friendships were formed across the religious divide.

While Roman Catholics were concerned about discrimination in local government and housing, Protestants often complained about the Post Office, convinced that in that institution Rome was in complete control and had taken the whole apparatus over, lock, stock and barrel! Nor was discrimination an issue solely between Roman Catholics and Protestants. Where Presbyterians were in the majority on education and other committees, and they often were, Church of Ireland members at times felt that well-qualified Church of Ireland candidates were turned down in favour of Presbyterians.

I remember an occasion where Church of Ireland and Roman Catholic members of the Londonderry Education Committee united to ensure the appointment of a Church of Ireland teacher and the defeat of the Presbyterian candidate. Nepotism, political and religious, was always a significant factor, especially in local government in Northern Ireland.

The Protestants who joined Orange Lodges or Apprentice Boys of Derry Clubs in the vast majority of cases were not fanatics imbued with hatred of their Roman Catholic neighbours. The Orange Order arranged social evenings, dances and band practices. This social and community role encouraged many Protestants, particularly in rural areas, to join the Order. James Galway learned to play the flute in an Orange band.

Roman Catholics came out to watch the parades and traders brought their stalls to sell refreshments to the Orangemen or Apprentice Boys along the parade route. Roman Catholic pubs were also kept busy after the parade. Parades were generally regarded as folk occasions.

Indeed, it was not unknown for the lending of instruments to take place between Green and Orange bands before a parade of either community. I have heard of the appropriate insignia being painted on a borrowed drum and the original repainted when it was returned, and there were occasions, I am told, when bandsmen were also borrowed across the divide to stand in for those prevented by illness from parading.

This lending a hand to all and sundry in times of need irrespective of religion or politics was second nature to the Derry people. A prominent parishioner of mine described an incident which took place during the Troubles around 1921 or 1922. He was an officer in what were known as the 'B Specials', a constabulary organised on a part-time basis to assist the RUC, and one evening came across a leading IRA man from Derry endeavouring to drill a squad of volunteers on the strand near Fahan, Co. Donegal, and making a very poor fist of it. Becoming suddenly aware of the Specials officer surveying the scene from the cliff above and knowing he was an expert in military drill, the IRA man shouted up, 'For God's sake will you come down here and lick this crowd into shape.' So down went the 'B' man and drilled the IRA volunteers on Fahan strand. Politics were temporarily forotten. All that mattered was to extend a helping hand to a fellow Derry man in difficulties and to take pride in a job well done.

Looking back it is sad to think that clergy of all denominations working in Derry, although serving the same Lord Jesus and entrusted with proclaiming the Gospel message of reconciliation, made no attempt to get to know each other. We remained in our own little ghettos and it never once occurred to us that by failing to reach out to our fellow Christian priests or ministers we were falling short of the teaching and example of the One Lord whom we all professed to serve. Church of Ireland clergy occasionally met Presbyterian and Methodist ministers at weddings and funerals and from time to time might exchange a greeting on the streets, but, since marriages between Protestants and Roman Catholics were frowned on by both sides and funerals were single-denominational affairs, no such opportunities were available for even a brief encounter with Roman Catholic priests. Among the Roman Catholic clergy I knew only Bishop Farren, Monsignor Doherty, whom I met on the Education Committee, and Father Jim Coulter, later Head of St Columb's, a large Roman Catholic college in Derry. In those days he was Roman Catholic chaplain to Magee University College where I lectured part-time in philosophy. Jim Coulter was a light-hearted man with a choice sense of humour, about the same age and build as myself. During long discussions which we had in the hostelries of Donegal and in the rectory we discovered we had much in common, in particular the vision of a united community in Derry, free of sectarian bitterness and sterile political strife, with all working together to realise the full potential of our historic city.

Shortly before I left Derry he invited Daphne and myself to a farewell meal in Roneragh House Hotel, on the shores of Lough Swilly, to recall past times together and to wish us well as we set out for Dublin and St Patrick's. Being a pipe smoker himself and no doubt thinking it would make a suitable gift for another contented pipe addict, he presented me with a very large, most unusual reddish-amber pipe ashtray. As it sits on my table that ashtray is a daily reminder of a genial companion and a very good man who has since died, tragically, of cancer.

It was Jim Coulter who introduced me to a young teacher who shared our hopes for change in Derry and with whom I have remained on friendly terms ever since. His name was John Hume. A moderate socialist with no tincture of sectarianism, John was happy to work within the prevailing political structure in the North to achieve a fair deal for all. Latterly it has been said he has become more Nationalist in his thinking, doubtless in view of the failure of the power-sharing executive which seemed to rule out the possibility of an internal solution. He felt there must be an all-Ireland dimension and this was later enshrined in the Anglo-Irish Agreement. Although always convinced that his position was reasonable and realistic he was perfectly willing to listen to another point of view and, where possible, accommodate it if he thought it had some validity. I found him an earnest, cerebral man, totally immersed in politics, his great obsession, at times appearing a little aloof with little time for small talk or mere tittle tattle, but in company always worth listening to and not averse to telling and enjoying the occasional joke, or seeing the comic side of Northern politics and politicians. His great love was, and remains, Derry, for which he will spare no effort to promote the wellbeing of all its citizens.

John Hume and I and some liberal Unionists wanted to break away from the traditional stagnant Nationalist-Unionist party politics and engage in joint action which would benefit all the citizens of Derry, particularly in the area of unemployment which afflicted the whole community, Protestant as well as Catholic. It seemed to us that Stormont was pursuing a deliberate low key policy in order not to threaten the status quo. The lion's share of new industries seemed to be concentrated in the North East. No infrastructural developments such as motorways were being planned for the North West. Instead a new town, Craigavon, was built not very far from Belfast. Derry's increasing isolation was made more acute by the closure of the Great Northern Railway line which ran via Strabane, Omagh and Portadown to Belfast and Dublin and served the interior of the province. The Derry Corporation refused to consider extending the city boundaries, a move which would have allowed more space for much needed new housing. The Unionist line was that to upgrade Derry significantly would result in an influx of more Nationalists from across the nearby Co. Donegal border and this in time would mean the end of Protestant and Unionist rule in the city. I actually heard a prominent Derry Unionist declare, 'We don't want any more industry here because if we upset the apple cart the RCs will come in and swamp us.' Everything was nicely arranged. The Unionist majority was assured. So why upset the status quo? Change spelt danger.

In my sermons I tried to bring the Christian Gospel to bear on the situation in Derry. What was wrong? Why was it wrong and what changes should be made? Not long after the decision to close the GNR railway I preached a Christmas sermon in Christ Church, on the lines from the carol:

The star drew nigh to the north west,
O'er Bethlehem it took its rest.

'The star never draws nigh to the north west in this benighted province,' I said. 'We are the forgotten people. The star in Ulster is always drawing nigh to the north east.' The sermon received a fair amount of media coverage and, while I received some very critical letters from extreme Protestants who told me not to preach politics from the pulpit, the majority of messages which I received were favourable and encouraging.

A further blow came when Derry was not chosen as the site for Northern Ireland's second university, though common sense pointed to developing what was already there and centred on Magee University College. But the university went to Coleraine, a decision which at least in the early years of the university's life proved no more enlightened than the disastrous choice of Craigavon as a new centre for population and industry. These actions not only sharpened Nationalist discontent but also annoyed many moderate Unionists. Before the decision in favour of Coleraine was announced we held a great public meeting in the Guildhall, attended by people and political representatives from both sides of the community, whose enthusiasm to work together for the good of Derry was wonderful to behold. Roman Catholics and Protestants together drove in a long motorcade through Strabane and Omagh to Stormont to lobby the government in Derry's cause, a government which included our MP, Mr E.C. Jones, Attorney General of Northern Ireland.

Unknown to us the decision had already been taken. Although most Unionist leaders in Derry were outwardly in favour of a university for the city, some of them had reservations, and it was widely accepted that the confidential message to Stormont from a group of influential Unionists was, 'Don't bring the university to Derry.' Word got round that certain 'faceless men of Derry' had stabbed the city in the back. Teddy Jones, the

Unionist MP for Derry, well aware that feelings were running high in Derry in support of the university, nevertheless submitted to the Stormont Whip and voted against the city. Some diehard Unionists in the city defended Jones, saying he had no choice because his political career was at stake!

I wrote an article at the time for the Christ Church parish magazine, which was subsequently taken up by the local press. I pointed out that according to Holy Scripture the high priest said of Our Lord's crucifixion that it was 'expedient that one man should die for the people'. But nowhere in Holy Writ was it ever recorded that all the people should die for one man, yet this was what we were being asked by some to accept, to let Derry and its people die, in order to ensure Mr Jones' political survival!

John Hume and I shared a mounting frustration at the lack of interest Westminster was showing in Northern Ireland affairs. We felt that if only Westminster instead of Stormont were in charge constructive and progressive changes would take place. I believe that had the Nationalist community been given a choice in the early Sixties between Stormont and rule from Westminster, the majority of them would have chosen Westminster. They did not trust Stormont and were convinced that Westminster would certainly not tolerate sectarianism or discrimination of any sort from any quarter. John and I were in contact with Westminster MPs such as Paul Rose (Labour) who asked questions in the House of Commons on key issues. Invariably they received the same reply. This was solely a matter for the Government of Northern Ireland. The Westminster Government does not interfere with the policies and decisions of the government of Northern Ireland.

One evening we were sitting in a car outside the GPO in Derry when John said to me, 'We'll have to break the old Nationalist-Unionist mould here. If I took on Eddie McAteer and stood for the Foyle Division (Nationalist seat) would you take on Teddy Jones in the Unionist seat? What about fighting the two Derry Stormont seats together?'

'Whatever about you, John,' I replied, 'I'm ruled out. Look what happened to Godfrey MacManaway.'

A colourful, jovial, former rector of Christ Church and army chaplain in World War II, MacManaway was well known in Derry for having set up the Fighting Fund, a weekly collection from Protestant households to enable Protestants with limited means to purchase houses for sale in Protestant areas, thus ensuring that the accommodation did not fall into Roman Catholic hands. He had stood as Unionist candidate and was elected to Stormont representing Londonderry and later to Westminster, representing West Belfast. One Geoffrey Bing then entered the arena, insisting that MacManaway had no legal right to sit in Parliament because he was episcopally ordained. Bing's contention was received with disbelief and indeed amusement by the Unionist hierarchy. Bing was a Labour MP, doubtless a lawyer of some distinction — he later became Attorney General of Ghana under Nkrumah — but in this case his Unionist opponents were certain that he had misunderstood the situation and was talking through his hat or his wig. After all, they argued, the Church of Ireland was disestablished. There was no link with the State. Welsh Methodist ministers, Presbyterian and Congregationalist clergy could, and did, sit in Westminster. Why not a Church of Ireland clergyman? Even the Attorney General, Sir David Maxwell-Fyffe, gave his considered legal opinion that there was no obstacle to MacManaway sitting in Westminster and Stormont. Then came the bombshell when a judicial committee of the Privy Council ruled in favour of Bing. The crucial point was episcopal ordination, not establishment or disestablishment. There was no question of my standing for election with that precedent, and it was the only time I seriously considered entering politics.

I sometimes travelled to meetings in Belfast by train in the company of Eddie McAteer, Nationalist MP for Derry's Foyle Division. During the course of one of our long conversations he said to me, 'I've been going up here for years. I've seen young fellows join the Unionist Party and standing for election. Before you can say Jack Robinson they've become junior secretaries then Ministers in Stormont, with all the trappings of ministerial office. But I go on year after year with never a hope of getting into Government. It's all so frustrating and unjust.' I could well understand Eddie's point of view. The normal democratic process did not really apply in Northern Ireland. For democracy to function properly there must be the possibility that the party in opposition will one day gain power. This was not so in Northern Ireland, and Nationalists opted out of constructive politics, using Stormont simply as a venue for airing grievances or blowing the anti-partitionist trumpet. Unionists could not see that condemning Nationalists to a second-class role of perpetual opposition was bound to lead to discontent, increased alienation and a lack of confidence in the parliamentary process. The only hope lay in some form of power-sharing with joint responsibility for government but this was completely unacceptable to the Unionists. They would have seen this as doing a deal with Republicanism, consorting with the enemy, akin to making a pact with the devil himself.

Several RUC officers and their families were parishioners of mine. Doubtless there are rotten apples in every barrel, but for the most part the RUC exercised great restraint when placed in the invidious position of policing hostile demonstrations. I was always infuriated later when I returned to the South and, at times, heard the RUC described as thugs or Fascists. I know these people. Most of them were the salt of the earth, doing a difficult job well, always ready to help anyone, of whatever creed or class, in every possible way.

One of them, Paul Kerr, was County Inspector and a member of my congregation. Son of a former bishop of Down and Dromore, with family roots near Tinahely in Co. Wicklow, a tolerant, liberal man for whom I had great respect, he found himself with the unenviable duty, during the early days of the Civil Rights Movement in 1968, of having to enforce a ban imposed on demonstrators by William Craig, then Northern Ireland Minister for Home Affairs. As part of their march the Civil Rights leaders planned a route through the old city centre into the Diamond, the sacred shrine of Derry Protestantism. The order came to prevent the marchers reaching the city centre by stopping them at the foot of Carlisle Road. Since the

Civil Rights leaders announced their intention to disregard the ban, there was a threat of bloody confrontation at the police cordon.

On the eve of the march Christians of all denominations, including the Civil Rights leaders, prayed for peace and reconciliation during a vigil begun in St Columb's Cathedral (Church of Ireland) and continued in St Eugene's Cathedral (Roman Catholic). In the event, the situation was defused when a symbolic breaking of the ban, by the leaders only, was allowed and honour thereby satisfied.

But as time went on, a violent confrontation seemed inevitable. I remember returning from Belfast one Sunday afternoon and experiencing an almost palpable atmosphere of tension and sullenness as I drove through the city, following a baton charge on marchers at a cordon in Duke Street the day before. Gerry Fitt, one of the marchers, had been struck by a baton and taken to Altnagelvin Hospital with a cut on his head. The story went the rounds that when the hospital orderly asked him his name he replied, 'Ian Paisley', which the orderly accepted without question. Thus humour was not entirely absent even in those dark and cruel days.

My attack on what I felt to be unjust in Derry and the North West was carried out primarily in the pulpit and media and most of my congregation supported me. This encouraged me. The die-hards will never be swayed, they survive on slogans, but it *is* possible to convince the majority of moderate Protestants that they just cannot continue in the same old way. They will never respect authority for its own sake, either religious or political, but they will always respond to someone who they feel shows conviction. Reason must be combined with passionate conviction if it is to be taken seriously in Northern Ireland. Paisley's success with his followers lies in an inner conviction and passionate commitment to the symbols of the past.

The leaders of moderate opinion so often speak with reason but without such passionate conviction. The Northern Ireland people like passion, emotion, feeling, in their politics and religion. Hence the success of the Protestant Gospel halls and political demagogues. Emotion in speech and song compensates for the austerity of puritanism in art and religious ritual. Terence O'Neill failed, for although he came over as a decent, reasonable man, he was perceived as aloof, frosty, lacking burning conviction, devoid of passion. He had no chance against Paisley.

All efforts to persuade the Westminster Parliament to accept greater responsibility for Northern Irish affairs and thereby ensure fair treatment for both sides of the community fell on deaf ears. I remember addressing a large and representative gathering in the Embassy Ballroom in 1967 where the BBC were filming a programme on Derry. I was invited by the BBC to introduce the programme and highlight what I felt about the city. The BBC told me that I had been chosen because from their soundings I was the only one acceptable to both communities, or at least to the moderates in both communities. I advocated the extension of the city boundary and long overdue liberal changes in local government, for example, the putting aside of party labels and the working together of both traditions to make Derry a proud and confident city. I criticised Stormont's neglect of Derry and the North West: 'Time is not on our side,' I warned. 'It doesn't take a wise man to see that we are rapidly approaching flashpoint. If nothing is done, and done soon, the whole thing will very soon blow up in our faces.' I was supported by various members of liberal views in the audience, including Stephen McGonagle, who later became a senator in the Republic and was at that time a prominent labour leader in Derry. And, of course, by John Hume.

But I was attacked by, amongst others, a government minister who accused me of scaremongering, of arousing fear where no fear was. He informed me that having come from the South I would never understand the North and that it was presumptuous of me to dictate to those born and bred in the Province. I replied, 'I sincerely hope I am proved wrong, but one doesn't have to be a genius to detect the signs of doom approaching.'

As I was leaving the ballroom that night I was accosted by a fanatical Unionist bitterly opposed to what I had said. She caught me by the lapel and shouted as she shook me violently.

'You're nothing but a Fenian. Go back to the South. Go back to your Republic. How dare you come here to lecture us.' I looked her straight in the eye.

'You'll live to see a terrible desolation overtaking this Province if something is not done very quickly,' I replied. She ripped my lapel in her fury. When I got home I showed it to Daphne and added, 'That was torn by a rabid so-called Unionist tonight. God help them and God help this city.'

Together with local government arrangements to produce a Unionist majority on the Corporation (commonly referred to as gerrymandering), the rejection of Derry as the site of the second University of Ulster and the closure of the GNR railway link, there was another factor adding to discontent in the North West. Mr Geoffrey Copcutt produced a plan for the development of the Province which recommended large-scale development in Derry, concentrating expansion in the North West instead of creating a new city, Craigavon, in the already favoured North East. One of the reasons given by Stormont for accepting the report of Sir John Lockwood on the siting of the university in Coleraine was that as they had employed an expert it was entirely reasonable to accept his decision. Trust the expert. But Copcutt was also seen in Derry as an expert, and when *his* report was rejected Derry citizens naturally concluded that in Northern Ireland an expert's advice was only followed if it conformed to political interests. In the final analysis, Unionist party politics ruled the roost, they concluded.

8

Northern Divisions

THE Protestant community had a problem with identity. If Irishness meant being Roman Catholic, Nationalist and supporting all things Gaelic, a definition which it appeared was accepted without question in the Republic, then they were definitely not Irish. 'We are British,' they would say. When put to them that British was really only a blanket term to denote membership in the United Kingdom of the three nationalities, the English, Welsh and Scots, each proud of its national identity while sharing a common British citizenship, some Protestants might admit to being Irish or Northern Irish and British in this sense. But there was always a certain hesitancy for, in the Republic, Irish and British were seen as being mutually exclusive and one could not be both. This Southern attitude confused the Northern Protestants. If the stark choice was either Irish or British, then they were British. 'Ulster is British' was a popular slogan. If pressed further to define their identity within the British context they might say, 'We are Ulster people, British and Ulster,' or occasionally, 'We are Northern Irish and British.' Protestant children were not taught Irish history. They knew of the Norman invasion of England (1066 and all that) but were unaware of the Anglo-Norman invasion of Ireland under Henry II. The Ulster flag had the 'red hand' superimposed on the cross of St George of England!

Members of the Church of Ireland, I think, had less difficulty with the Irish dimension. They were members of the Church of *Ireland*, not the Church of Britain. They celebrated St Patrick's Day, wore the shamrock, made pilgrimages to St Patrick's reputed burial place in Downpatrick and observed in the

Church calendar the Irish Saints' Days such as St Columba and St Brigid. They were less inclined to see any contradiction in being Irish and British. Indeed, Patrick himself could reasonably have claimed to be both. But Irishness for the Northern Church of Ireland people was not to be equated with the narrow exclusive religious and political connotation so often tacitly accepted in the Republic and reinforced by Taoiseach Costello's pledge of loyalty to the Pope. Such a concept of Irishness made their Southern co-religionists into second-class citizens not truly and authentically Irish, since to be Irish meant to be Roman Catholic.

For the Northern Protestant there was nothing foreign in being British. The British army was their army in which so many of their ancestors had proudly fought and died, particularly at the Somme in 1916. The memory of their glorious dead gripped them. To weaken in their allegiance to the Crown was tantamount to dishonouring the hallowed memory of the dead. Loyalty to the Crown was symbolic of this memory and the National Anthem and Union flag, or Union Jack, always evoked a patriotic emotional fervour, an unmistakable assertion of their British identity, the more resolutely proclaimed in the face of a constant threat from those who would seek to deprive them of their British inheritance. 'Brits out' meant for the Northern Protestant 'Protestants out', since *they* were the British in Northern Ireland.

Then there was the financial advantage of the British connection, a factor which weighed heavily not only with Protestants but also with many Roman Catholics. This ensured access to all the benefits enjoyed by all other United Kingdom citizens. Could they be assured of a better financial deal in a United Ireland? Doubtful. So, 'beware of letting go of nurse, for fear of finding something worse'!

Protestants also saw the Union as the protector of their civil and religious liberties, the guarantee that they would not be absorbed into a Roman Catholic State. This was especially the case amongst the more fervent and enthusiastic Protestants. The Union defended their civil and religious liberties. Protestants cried liberty. Roman Catholics cried freedom. To defend their liberty the Protestants felt justified in taking whatever measures they felt were necessary to keep the Roman Catholics in their place. Repression was always justified on the grounds that it was undertaken solely to protect Protestant liberty. For Protestant liberty to be maintained Protestantism had to be in the ascendancy. Roman Catholics naturally saw this as the very denial of the true nature of liberty, as indeed it was. On the other hand, when Roman Catholics talked of freedom Protestants saw this as freedom *from* Britain but also freedom *for* Rome to impose its moral disciplines on all in a United Ireland. Brits out, but Rome in!

Protestant liberty and Roman Catholic freedom were both qualified: Protestant liberty by fear of Rome and Roman Catholic freedom by acceptance of Rome. The Churches, both Protestant and Roman Catholic, went hand in glove with their respective political allies, Unionist and Nationalist. The politicians in their turn used religion to serve their political ends. It was a vicious circle, religion using politics and politics using religion, an unholy mixture, in which eventually both religion and politics were to be the losers.

In retrospect I sometimes think I could and should have made a more public stand against discrimination, gerrymandering and sectarianism. My failure to do so showed a lack of courage. On the other hand, we must appreciate the difficult situation facing every moderate Protestant clergyman in Derry. If we had taken to the streets we would have undoubtedly alienated large numbers of moderate Protestants. We would have been written off, accused of being sympathisers with the Republicans, enemies of the State. Although many Protestants felt that there was need for change and were unhappy at the neglect of the North West by Stormont, yet, for all their defects, the authorities were seen by the Protestants as the protectors of Protestantism against a Nationalist/Roman Catholic conspiracy which would, if successful, obliterate Protestantism from the face of Ireland, North and South.

The Roman Catholic Church was identified with the Nationalists. The Protestant Churches were identified with the Unionists.

Roman Catholicism was Nationalism at prayer for a united Ireland. Protestantism was Unionism at prayer in defence of the Union. Therefore to take to the streets alongside Nationalists and Roman Catholics was tantamount, in the eyes of Protestants, to a betrayal of the Protestant faith, to be written off as a 'Lundy' with no possibility thereafter of influencing Protestant opinion to move in a more progressive direction. We were in a historical strait-jacket, the victim of the centuries-old alliance of God and Caesar, the Protestant God with the Unionist Caesar, the Roman Catholic God with the Nationalist Caesar, and, to our shame as Christians allegedly serving the same God, the Churches, both Protestant and Roman Catholic, did nothing to break that political stranglehold which served so effectively their respective denominational interests. I was often asked, on my return to Dublin, why Protestants, particularly clergy, did not protest at the unjust treatment of Roman Catholics in Northern Ireland. While I do not wish to defend or try to justify Protestant complacency, two things must be said. First, Protestants in the North, for the most part, did not believe that Roman Catholics were unjustly treated. With their large families they (the Romans) seemed to be doing rather well on State benefits, etc! Such was the immediate reaction to any question about unjust treatment of the minority. Second, let us put the boot on the other foot, as Conor Cruise O'Brien might say. Imagine in the Republic a 40 per cent Protestant minority who wished the Republic to be part of the United Kingdom under the Crown, believing that the natural geographic and political unit was the two islands taken together. The majority Roman Catholic community would certainly feel threatened and most likely would adopt what they believed to be the necessary policy to preserve the Republic, such as giving preferential treatment to those loyal to the State and discriminating against those who professed loyalty to Britain, a foreign State. If some moderate Roman Catholic priests felt that such discrimination, say in housing and jobs, was unjust and were prepared to say so to their congregations in sermons and parish magazines, would they also have joined Protestants in street demonstrations, perhaps with Union Jacks and 'God save the Queen' as an accompaniment to their legitimate protests against the unjust treatment of Protestants? If these good priests had done so, would not their parishioners have regarded them as fellow travellers with the Unionists, traitors to the honoured Republican dead and the faith of their fathers? Would these priests not have felt that they might achieve more by gentle persuasion inside their own community than by participating in a political demonstration on the streets? It is easy for outsiders to criticise and condemn, but when we put ourselves into the shoes of those who were involved then perhaps we become more understanding and sympathetic towards Northern Protestant clergy who found themselves in a situation where social issues such as housing and jobs were set in the context of religion and politics, and where every word and action to relieve social injustice was at the same time taken as an indicator of that person's political allegiance, where he stood on the Union, was he sound? In Ireland, said Swift, we have enough religion to make us hate, but not enough to make us love. Too often our religion has simply been the making of a political statement, not the sincere worship of God and obedience to Christ and his Gospel of love, even love of our enemies.

For when we replace the worship of the God of Love by worship of our own ideas, or dogmas or tribal prejudices, we are well down the road to hatred and conflict. As idolators we fashion a God to suit ourselves, making God in our image. We then claim divine sanction for our attitudes and aspirations. To recapture our Christianity, I believe we have first to go through a period of scepticism and secularism in our society, North and South, where increasing numbers will continue to desert the institutional religion of the Churches, becoming hostile or indifferent or 'humanist', or looking for religious or mystical experience in other forms. While the vast majority will still believe in God and reverence Jesus of Nazareth, the Churches will lose out numerically. As a result, they will become slimmer and fitter until eventually after a period of critical and constructive self-examination they will be in a healthier condition to witness more effectively by word and deed to the unifying power of the Gospel of love.

We judge the strength and influence of the Gospel too much by ecclesiastical statistics. This was inherited from Constantine who made Christianity the official religion of the Roman Empire, and thereafter its success was measured in worldly or quantitaive terms, the greater the number who professed Christianity in its State-established form, the greater the success of the Gospel. But this is not the teaching of the New Testament. God's work is not done by the big battalions. Jesus talks about the little flock, the grain of mustard seed, the pinch of salt, as descriptions of how the Gospel operates in the world. (Incidentally, an official State religion, Roman Catholic, Orthodox or some form of Protestantism, was the norm throughout the Christian world until the latter part of the eighteenth century. It survives today in the Church of England, many would say as an anachronism.)

Leaders of our institutional Churches, especially in Northern Ireland, fearful of a decline in their Church membership, have been too ready to trim their ecclesiastical sails to the political wind. In so doing we are all guilty of turning our backs on Christ and the pain of the cross through which alone can come resurrection to a new way of thinking and acting towards our fellow men. It might be said that whereas in the Republic the Roman Catholic Church dominated politics, in the North politics dominated the Churches.

It will be clear to the reader that my time in Derry enlarged and clarified my thoughts on politics and religion. Let me now try to summarise what I gleaned. It is difficult enough to get 'the feel' of the situation even after twenty-two years immersion. We should beware of 'experts', especially from outside, peddling simple solutions.

1. Unionists never accepted what may be described as 'the map image' with its implication that Irish political unity is dictated by geography and a God-made boundary, the sea, which divides Ireland from its neighbouring island. The sea is primarily a means of communication as in the link between

Ulster and Scotland from the earliest times. Columba in AD 563 when he set sail for Iona certainly did not regard the sea as a delineating factor, defining separate national identities, Irish and Scots. Indeed the word 'Scot' originally meant a native either of Ireland or of the country we now call Scotland. Thus the Unionist saw Irish Nationalism with its separatist policy as responsible for the partition of Ireland. When the natural political arrangement of a United Ireland in a United Kingdom was broken, the partition of Ireland was inevitable. Partition was not caused by Unionists but by Nationalists. Such was the Unionist viewpoint on the union of the two islands.

2. The Unionist siege mentality stemming from a sense of vulnerability and insecurity led to discrimination in jobs and housing against the Nationalist community, particularly at local level. Not all discrimination was of the Unionist variety. Nationalist-controlled councils were also guilty, but as they were in a minority Nationalist discrimination was never so apparent or widespread as Unionist.

3. In the sphere of education the Stormont government had a good record which compared favourably with any other part of the United Kingdom. It should also be noted that Catholic schools in Northern Ireland under the Stormont administration were treated more generously than Roman Catholic schools in the Republic. Grants for all Northern Ireland schools, irrespective of denomination, for heating, lighting, cleaning, school meals, books, etc., were far in excess of anything in the Republic, not to mention the fact that all tuition fees for third-level education were paid by the Government.

4. The Nationalist and Roman Catholic attitude to the RUC was ambivalent, seeking its protection while at the same time accusing it of being a sectarian force. The Nationalists and the Roman Catholic Church failed to encourage Roman Catholics to join and take up their share of the available places. The Garda Síochána in the Republic might similarly be termed a Roman Catholic police force, statistically speaking. But Southern Protestants would rightly never refer to it as a sectarian force. On the contrary, Protestants, although a tiny

minority, are continually encouraged by their Church leaders to join the gardaí and Irish army. They have a positive and supportive attitude to the organs of law enforcement, always cooperative, appreciative and well disposed.

5. The Stormont administration was foolish in not following Westminster in 1945 by abolishing the property vote and extending the franchise in local government to all adults instead of confining it to householders and their spouses. The slogan 'one man, one vote' conveyed the false impression that the franchise in all Northern Ireland elections was restricted, even for Stormont and Westminster. Indeed, many believed that Roman Catholics were totally disenfranchised in Northern Ireland. How often was it said to me, 'Roman Catholics were not allowed to vote in Northern Ireland.' As I have already mentioned, in Derry, in particular, where the Nationalist population of 62 per cent was represented by 40 per of the Corporation (eight Nationalists to twelve Unionists) the restriction of the franchise and the political manipulation of local electoral wards gave great offence, and rightly so. Stormont presented a bad image to the outside world.

6. Successive Unionist administrations, although solidly entrenched, showed no generosity and made no reconciliatory overtures to the Nationalist population. Perhaps such advances had they been made would have been rejected. The stark fact nevertheless remains that the Unionists never had the will to encourage the Nationalists to participate in constructive politics in Northern Ireland. The cry was always 'no surrender . . . what we have we hold . . . not an inch . . . them or us' instead of 'them *and* us' — both joining together in some form of joint responsibility for the better government and welfare of all the people. The Unionists lacked the generosity which would have invited the Nationalists to share in constructive politics.

7. The Unionists lost a great opportunity by not participating in the New Ireland Forum in 1983. There they could have effectively presented their case and demanded that certain vital matters be spelt out, such as the financial cost of unity, the claim by the Republic to exercise jurisdiction over Northern

Ireland, the concept of nationhood with due recognition of all traditions, the formidable question of Church and State relationships — particularly in the Republic. These issues were let go by default by the refusal of Unionists to participate.

8. On the Anglo-Irish Agreement, while the Unionists had legitimate grounds for complaint at not being consulted, they from the outset adopted a negative attitude: 'Ulster says No.' They had an opportunity to react in a positive manner by offering to work the agreement only on the condition that a referendum would be held in the Irish Republic on a proposal to delete from its Constitution any claim to jurisdiction over Northern Ireland. The Dublin Government would not in all probability have agreed to this, but at least they would have had to face up to the issue and the Unionist demand, I believe, would have attracted substantial support in the Republic. Unionism would have appeared in a more favourable light. Unionists also could have insisted on Unionist representation in the Anglo-Irish Conference, the more so since Nationalists had representation through the Government of the Republic. Dublin was let off the hook by a negative Unionist response. The Unionists were seen as totally intransigent and unreasonable, not only in the Republic but in the UK and on the international scene, while the Nationalists, in spite of their ambivalence on issues such as security, were regarded as reasonable and constructive. It always seemed to me that the Unionists were politically naive. As someone once said to me, 'Give them a hand of trumps and they will somehow manage to lose every trick.' They appeared to be unaware of, or insensitive to, the great world outside their six counties of Ulster. 'Let the rest of the world go by. It matters not to us.' They did not know how to present their case in the international forum and seemed to have no wish to learn. 'What right have others to poke their noses into our business?' was their parrot-like response as they failed to realise the powerful international impact of the TV camera. Again, their response was negative and hostile to the non-Unionist media, which, they held, should not meddle in the internal affairs of the province.

9. In spite of the innate goodness and kindness and the simple desire to live and let live, characteristic of the vast majority of the 'common' people of Northern Ireland of all creeds, the Protestants are perceived throughout Europe and the USA as backward looking, negative, fanatical and sectarian. Instead of leading their people along a more constructive and progressive path to the future, leaders of Protestant and Unionist opinion for the most part chose to remain in the fortress of the past, feeding off memories of battles long ago, rattling off old divisive slogans. Doom for all, they insisted, would be inevitable should any choose to venture forth and leave the fortress: 'not an inch . . . Ulster is not for sale . . . what we have we hold . . . no surrender . . . Ulster says no' — a proliferation of negatives.

10. The Orange Order saw the Unionist party as an exclusively Protestant political organisation. The road to a political career was through membership of the Order. It was necessary to don the sash, go through the rituals and be seen on parade on the twelfth of July, whether or not any deep commitment existed behind those outward observances. The Order frowned on any suggestion that Roman Catholics might be encouraged to join the Unionist party, believing that no Roman Catholic could be a sincere Unionist. This fallacy deprived the Unionist party of many influential Roman Catholics, among whom were some with a long family tradition of loyalty to Crown and the Union. The Unionist party consequently became the Protestant party. Carson would never have wished it so, for although, like Randolph Churchill, he 'played the Orange card' in an effort to preserve the union of the two islands, he was above all a political Unionist, and his opposition to the idea of a Northern Ireland Parliament stemmed from his conviction that the Union should have only one Parliament, Prime Minister and Government. He may also have had in mind the ominous probability that a local administration at Stormont would fall into the hands of religion and sectarianism and be found wanting in dealing with the proper business of politics. Northern Ireland's affairs should be seen and dealt with in the wider context of the United Kingdom and its Government in Westminster. Such was Carson's credo.

The other political parties, Nationalist, Labour, Republican, had no such 'hang-up' on religion. Although most of their supporters were Roman Catholics, Protestants were always welcome as members. There was no Catholic Nationalist party as such, and, although the Roman Catholic Church's point of view on certain issues such as education was naturally reflected by committed Catholics in the party, there was no official link with the Roman Catholic Church or any other Roman Catholic organisation, such as the Hibernians, to compare with the link between Unionism and the Orange Order.

9

Daphne

I FIRST met my future wife, Daphne, a schoolgirl of seventeen, at a social evening run by Presbyterian students at Magee College. I was fond of ballroom dancing and assumed that the social evening to which I was invited would be a dance as in any Church of Ireland parish hall. However, to my dismay I soon discovered that in strict Presbyterian circles dancing was not encouraged. The evening's entertainment consisted of party games and perhaps a military two-step, but nothing more provocative. I was disappointed and bored. Two other fellows from my digs were with me and we decided to move on and end the evening in a dance-hall near the Diamond. Then I caught sight of a tall, elegantly dressed girl with a stunning smile. Any young man would have cast his eyes hungrily in her direction, and I was instantly ensnared. 'This is very dull,' I said. 'There's no dancing. We'll go up to the Corinthian. Will you come with us?' She declined — although I afterwards discovered that she adored dancing — because she had been invited to the social by one of the Presbyterian students and felt duty bound to see the evening out.

I didn't lay eyes on Daphne again until years later, when I had moved to Christ Church as senior curate. I heard that she had been to Trinity and was now teaching history in Limavady. The curate of Clooney (Daphne's parish on the Waterside), Cecil Bradley, later to become Dean's Vicar during my Deanery at St Patrick's, brought us together. He invited me to join him on a visit to her parents, and by chance Daphne was home from Limavady.

By that time I had bought a car (Standard 8) in which Cecil Bradley and I often drove into Donegal, becoming well acquainted not only with the scenery but also with several hostelries. One night we went into Jackson's Hotel in Ballybofey and ordered a sumptuous meal, each under the impression that the other had sufficient money. When the bill arrived we had only half the amount between us. How fortunate, as it transpired, that we were wearing our clerical collars! Before we had a chance to explain our predicament to the waiter he remarked: 'You needn't worry about the bill because that cattle buyer who sat over there said he'd settle up for you.'

'That man we waved at coming in?' I asked.

'Yes. He had a good day selling cattle and told me, "I'll take care of the priests' bill."'

'Be not anxious for the morrow,' said I. 'The Lord will provide.'

Daphne's reappearance put an end to our adventuring in Donegal. I started to spend my free time visiting her in Limavady, sometimes taking her out to the summer theatre in Portrush or Portstewart. She was by no means the first girl to turn my head, though these contacts never became serious attachments. Some of my girl friends were teachers at the Londonderry High School (for girls), one of whom, being English, criticised my uncouth Irish pronunciation when I asked her, 'What *filim* will we go to?' She insisted I say '*film*', which is why I am careful to pronounce that word properly to this day. I am very conscious of those who say 'filim' or 'filum', and always feel like shouting out, 'No, no, it's film!' My institution as rector of Christ Church took place in April 1957 and I invited Daphne. She wore a glorious pink wide-brimmed hat and I knew instinctively that she was the one for me. I like wide-brimmed hats.

We were married the following year, in May, in All Saints, Clooney. A protracted stag party in Donegal caused me to sleep the sleep of the just on my wedding morning but I managed to arrive in good time for the two o'clock ceremony. The guests were received in the Old City Hotel, now, alas, destroyed by IRA bombs, and Daphne and I set off in my car to drive to Belfast where we were to take the ferry to Heysham en route for the Scarborough hotel we had selected for our honeymoon. We stopped for a cup of tea in Antrim. Having other things on my mind, I recklessly parked in a prohibited area near a pedestrian crossing and received a summons as a result. Presenting myself at the RUC barracks and explaining that I was on my honeymoon, I was greeted with smiles and a waiving of the summons in view of mitigating circumstances.

Around half-past six the following morning we arrived in Heysham famished, for no breakfast had been available on the ferry. The dockside station was deserted, the cafe closed. Eventually we discovered two fellow humans, signalmen, having breakfast in their cabin. 'Where can we get something to eat?' we enquired. Taking pity on us, they invited us inside the signal box to share their sandwiches, washed down with tea in enamel mugs. Thus our first day of married life began with strong tea and thick sandwiches in the signal box in Heysham.

We journeyed to York by the slow Sunday train and had a long wait after lunch for the train to Scarborough where, exhausted, we were welcomed by a hotelier who was the soul of kindness and commiseration, being all too familiar with the shortcomings of the local train service.

Two weeks of blissful freedom stretched ahead, after which, with happy hearts and a few souvenirs in our luggage, we travelled home to Derry to begin our new ministry as husband and wife.

Daphne had resigned from teaching before we married, for in those days a clergyman's wife was expected to be a full-time helpmate. She threw herself into parish activities with great enthusiasm and efficiency. Having delayed marriage until I was nearly thirty-four, and sensing that the older a man is on becoming a father the more difficult for him to relate to his children, I was delighted when Daphne told me there was a baby on the way. Had we known then that she was expecting twins I certainly would have felt unequal to the responsibility.

She continued working, apparently tirelessly, through her pregnancy, when she should have been resting. The baby seemed to be growing very large. The presence of twins was only revealed by an X-ray on the day before they were born! Though we later discovered that there had been twins in previous generations on both sides of the family, neither of us was aware of it at the time. I kept asking myself, 'Where on earth did these come from?' This was a very urgent matter. Everything had to be duplicated.

The following morning, a Friday, I was visiting patients in the old City and County Hospital, having driven Daphne in the early hours to the nursing home, when the phone rang for me in the hospital office. The matron of the nursing home congratulated me and passed on the welcome news that twin boys had been born. She also gave me a message from Daphne that I was to finish my rounds before coming up to see her, a message typical of Daphne's unruffled, matter-of-fact attitude to life. I must confess that I rushed the last few visits and was in the nursing home by noon.

Recovering from the initial shock of the previous evening I began to experience a certain satisfaction in becoming the father of twins. I felt quite proud of being able to ring up my parents and friends and announce that Daphne had given birth not only to twins and to twin boys at that. 'You're making up for lost time. You should have been married years ago,' was the general reaction.

Bringing up twins was no easy task. Daphne, who should not have taxed her energies so much during her pregnancy, became exhausted, possibly a factor which contributed to the onset of her illness two years later. Kevin and Timothy cried a lot at first. We were feeding them strictly according to the amount indicated on the tin of powdered baby milk, but their requirements far exceeded those of the average infant. When we realised they were protesting at the insufficiency of their diet and fed them as much as they demanded, the crying stopped. I have vivid memories of the two of us sitting up in bed, each holding a bottle and a hungrily sucking baby.

Daphne never fully recovered her strength after Timothy and Kevin were born. She always seemed tired. One winter day I came home for lunch to find that she had collapsed in the kitchen earlier that morning. She told me she had been looking through the window and the snow outside seemed to dazzle her. Her head began to spin and she felt she was losing control of her body. She slumped to the floor, unable to move. By the time I returned she was a little better. Our doctor called in a consultant who said, 'We'll keep an eye on her. See that she takes it easy.' Useless advice for someone who has twin babies to look after! But she appeared to be recovering, nevertheless.

The following spring we took a short holiday together in Dublin, where we stayed in the old Standard Hotel in Harcourt Street. We had a very frosty spell before Easter that year. I noticed when we were out walking that Daphne seemed to be dragging her feet as if they were leaden. The condition deteriorated and by the time we returned to Derry she could hardly put one foot before the other. A week later she was in Altnagelvin Hospital, paralysis spreading within a few days from her toes to her waist.

There were fears that her breathing might be affected and because Altnagelvin had no iron lung, should one be needed, the consultant decided to send her without delay to the Royal Victoria Hospital in Belfast. I drove behind the ambulance, not knowing whether she would still be alive when we reached the Royal. I saw her safely settled in and then had to drive back to the twins and get ready for Whit Sunday services the next day.

During those weeks, seeing Daphne, an athletic, fun-loving, extrovert woman of twenty-eight with so much to give, lying helpless in a hospital bed, I often asked God, 'What does all this mean? God, I suppose you know what you're doing, for I certainly don't.' When frustration, rage and self-pity take over I'm sure God smiles and says, 'He's at it again. It'll blow over.'

I don't think I ever lost my faith. I never gave up praying. I may have got angry with God, and not understanding what He was up to infuriated me. At times I wished I could be an atheist, for atheists have no problem with suffering, since it results solely from the mechanical impersonal fixed laws of cause and effect. Therefore one can only grin and bear it, without ever asking 'Why?... for what purpose?' But I could never be an atheist for although I might question God, lose my temper with God, yet for me He was always there and I was aware of His presence.

When I went to Belfast to visit Daphne on Whit Monday I was told that the paralysis had, mercifully, spread no further. I found her calm and practical as ever. The neurologist, Dr Alison, a cheerful, optimistic man to whom she had warmed instantly, had examined her. His diagnosis was that she had an unusual type of multiple sclerosis, a disease of the nervous system which can take many forms and the cause of which remains a mystery to medical science.

'This may look bad,' he said to me, 'but if you are unfortunate enough to get one of these neurological complaints, sometimes it is better if the disease knocks you for six straight away rather than causing a slow and gradual creeping paralysis. I'm going to give her something which may help to bring back movement. How well she'll recover I don't know, but I'll try to get some movement back into her legs.'

A new form of cortisone, ACTH, was then being tested. With a stoical determination to make the best of things and to return to a life of near normality as soon as possible, Daphne gave Dr Alison her wholehearted consent for the drug to be tried on her, and as soon as treatment began she started to improve. She was radiant one day when I visited her. 'Great news. I can move my toes.' Little by little, the movement returned until about a year after her admission she came out of the Royal walking on hand crutches and I brought her home.

Timothy and Kevin were by now about three years old, bursting with mischief and initiative. Daphne's mother had been looking after them and came to the rectory daily to help out, stepping in again fulltime whenever Daphne had to be hospitalised for further spells. From her wheelchair, which she preferred to hand crutches because of its speed and mobility, Daphne cared for the twins, cooked, entertained and ran the house.

From the time we were married, she has been unshakeable in her conviction that my calling should always come first, never allowing domestic problems or her own needs to interfere with my work. She was — and is — utterly unselfish. Looking back I often wish that she had insisted on my easing off on parochial duties to spend more time with her and our sons. She did not do this. It would have been out of character, and I blame myself for having made so little time available to spend with my family, especially when the twins were growing up.

Shortly after my ordination I chanced to meet a retired clergyman, Canon MacQuaide, a paternal figure and in his day a popular dramatic preacher who took me aside and offered a memorable piece of advice. 'You will need three books,' he said, 'a bible, a prayer book and a visiting book. Read your bible, say your prayers and visit your people. This is the threefold cord which must never be broken. Put not your trust in committees or conferences for at best they are secondary. What is primary is your personal relationship to God and to your people.' I have tried to follow his advice through the years. Indeed, I'm sure I overdid the visiting to the neglect of my family. I remember one day on a pastoral round I was told that a retired army Colonel and his wife had recently come to reside in the area. I called and rang the doorbell, only to be confronted by a tall, lean, sallow-complexioned man who briskly demanded what I wanted. When I replied that I was the rector and had called to welcome him to the parish he gruffly dismissed me with the admonition, 'If I want you I'll send for you' and promptly closed the door in my face. Discouraged but not defeated, I made a point of always calling on my rounds in that area and always receiving a similarly curt reply. One day, on hearing that his wife had suffered a stroke, I presented myself as usual and was admitted to see her while the Colonel, pleading atheism, removed himself to another room. Thereafter I visited his wife frequently until the time of her death, about two years later. The Colonel then took to religion with a vengeance, became a regular church-goer, read the lessons, borrowed my theological books and phoned me at all hours to come and discuss the Incarnation, Atonement or the Resurrection. Arriving at the rectory late in the evening after attending a parochial meeting or activity, Daphne would greet me with the refrain, 'The Colonel was on the phone again, he'd like to see you immediately,' and at times I had the irreverent thought that if only he'd remained an atheist, I would have been spared all this. Visiting can have unforeseen and demanding consequences!

The boys became well known in Derry for their frequent escapades. They were dubbed 'the terrible twins'. Raiding their money boxes, they would set off for the railway station and buy themselves excursion tickets to any place that took their fancy. At first we were extremely worried when they disappeared and phoned the police, but as they always returned eventually, safe and sound, often with an understanding police escort, we took to waiting calmly until they turned up again.

One night, when they were five or six, a taxi drew up and out stepped the two of them from the back, having managed to convince the driver somewhere in Donegal that daddy would pay the fare. Another night they arrived in a squad car after spending the day in Coleraine and missing the last train home. Instead, they had boarded a returning football special bound for Derry. They were subsequently met at the station by a police car manned by officers to whom they were, no doubt, old acquaintances.

There were incidents during church services which caused not a little embarrassment to Daphne and myself. One Sunday morning, for instance, the twins and I had gone to church during holidays in Portstewart. While the congregation was at prayer one of them, clearly bored with the proceedings, reached for the handbag which the woman in front had left lying on the seat beside her and emptied out the entire contents. I had to replace them rather hastily, hoping that the prayers would continue long enough for a cleric not to be discovered red-handed, and indeed red-faced, apparently rummaging in a lady's handbag.

On another occasion, when the rector announced that the service the following Sunday would begin at ten fifteen, one of the twins jumped up, faced the congregation and repeated emphatically, 'Ten fifteen.'

And then there was the time I preached in Christ Church after a visit to America, relating to the congregation my experience of meeting some Mormons in Utah. The boys were sitting with Daphne as usual, and when my sermon drew to a close one of them commented in a loud voice, 'Very good, wasn't it?'

Like many small boys they had very clear ideas about what they were going to do when they grew up. Kevin wanted to be a policeman, Timothy a soldier, and their favourite games revolved around dressing up in the respective uniforms. But, unlike most boys' early intentions, their determination to pursue their chosen careers never wavered.

They went through the usual cowboy phase and expected my mother-in-law to be as much a devotee of cowboy films as they were. Once they persuaded her to bring them to a violent Western, a torment which she sat through, enduring patiently. In the middle of the epic one of them turned to her and shouted above the din of a pitched gun battle, 'Aren't you glad you came, Granny?'

Daphne's long stays in hospital caused her to miss much of the twins' early life and deprived her, to an extent, of the special relationship which developing children normally enjoy with their mother. Having been a talented sportswoman she would especially have loved to have been able to teach them to swim and to play cricket. It was hard for me too, having to accept that Daphne could not always assume her rightful position as pivot of the family.

Her mother willingly took on the responsibility of bringing up Timothy and Kevin and we shall always be deeply grateful to her for such loving care, but a grandmother cannot replace a mother. Youngsters tend to regard grannies as dispensing machines, always good for a touch, and our sons were no exception.

As a direct result of Daphne's illness, however, the pair of them became extraordinarily self-reliant and resourceful from a tender age. And they grew up regarding disability as an unembarrassing fact of life.

In the early days of her illness I was approached by some well-meaning clergy committed to the Church's Ministry of

Healing. One of them, a dedicated and sincere priest but rather emotional, came and ministered to Daphne by celebrating the Eucharist, with the laying on of hands and anointing with oil. There was, alas, no improvement in her condition, indeed for a time it got steadily worse. She had been given to understand that faith could move mountains and when there was no improvement she began to question whether this was due to her lack of faith. It is essential to recognise that the Ministry of Healing is exercised primarily by the medical profession. Of course, the Church has an important role in ministering to the sick, but we must avoid giving the impression that it is some-how offering an alternative way of healing. The Church's ministry to the sick must never be dramatised or emotionalised but always exercised in a normal pastoral manner, administering the sacrament, laying on of hands, anointing, bringing comfort and consolation to the sufferer. It must never build up false hopes which can so often end in bitter disappointment, self-reproach and a guilt complex. Every priest is a minister of healing and every prayer, every Eucharist, is part of that ministry. The actual forms which healing may take, whether spiritual or mental or physical, is for God alone to decide. While the physical condition may not improve, indeed may deteriorate, the healing process directed at the whole person continues and brings to the sufferer inward strength, serenity and peace. Broadly speaking, I suppose there are three ways in which we may react to suffering. We may resent it and blame God: 'What have I done to deserve this?' Or we may grin and bear it in a resigned stoical sense. 'Nothing I can do about it, just too bad it's happened to me. I'll have to put up with it until death releases me.' Or we can take the positive approach and use it to draw nearer to fellow sufferers, to understand common needs, to work together in various ways to encourage the community to recognise such needs and address them. This approach gives the sufferer a wider vision and takes the mind away from exclusive and introspective obsession with the self and its many problems. Of course, the problems still remain but they are seen in a wider context. There is a ministry of suffering as well as a ministry of healing. Resentment or stoic resignation leads to isolation and looks backwards to what has been, whereas the third approach, which is the Christian one, leads to participation and looks forward to what might be. And God is also suffering with the sufferer, bearing the pain and heartache and turning Good Friday sorrow into Easter joy.

In chronic illness it is a case of living one day at a time. There were the ups and downs, joys and tears, frayed nerves and quick tempers, hopes and fears for the future, resignation and resolve to make the best of our lot, gratitude for the support of so many friends. 'I do not ask to see the distant scene, one step enough for me,' as Newman put it. So Daphne and I with our twin sons lived in the rectory in Northland Road, thankful for each day together and relieved that her condition showed no sign of further deterioration.

10

St Patrick's Cathedral

IN 1968 the Dean of St Patrick's Cathedral in Dublin, the Very Rev. John Armstrong, later to become Archbishop of Armagh, was elected Bishop of Cashel and Waterford, and a new Dean had to be appointed. The Dean of the Church of Ireland's National Cathedral is also the Ordinary, which means in effect that he is his own boss. His position is unique in the Church of Ireland. As Ordinary 'he gives the orders', is not in any way inhibited in his preaching and may invite anyone he chooses, of any creed or none, to the pulpit of St Patrick's. Free from episcopal control and subject to no ecclesiastical authority except the General Synod of the Church of Ireland (an assembly of lay persons as well as bishops and clergy), to all intents and purposes, he has a free hand in St Patrick's.

It is sometimes said that since the Church of Ireland has two Cathedrals in Dublin we should be satisfied with one and hand the other over to the Roman Catholic Church. But the fact is that the Church of Ireland has not got two diocesan Cathedrals in Dublin. Christ Church is the Dublin Diocesan Cathedral, the seat of the Archbishop who appoints the Dean of Christ Church and to whom that Dean is subject. St Patrick's, although physically located in the diocese of Dublin, does not belong exclusively to the diocese. In the Constitution of the Church of Ireland it is described as a National Cathedral, having a common relation to all the dioceses, North and South of the border. Each diocese, or united diocese, is represented by a Prebendary or Canon on the Chapter and the Chapter elects the Dean from among their number. The Constitution of the Church of Ireland in 1870 removed St Patrick's completely from any particular diocesan or local context.

It is today the Cathedral for the whole Church of Ireland, North and South, and hence it is incorrect and misleading to speak of St Patrick's as owned exclusively by the Church of Ireland people in Dublin. Indeed, the Cathedral depends very largely on the financial help received from the Northern dioceses. This setting of St Patrick's in a national context is a good and wise thing for it affords a point of meeting and unity between North and South. It is the outward and visible sign that the Church of Ireland recognises no border between her people.

I was the Canon or Prebendary representing the Diocese of Derry and Raphoe on the Cathedral Chapter, and was duly summoned to Dublin on 18 November 1968 to elect a new Dean. Having to perform this electoral duty on that particular day was, to say the least, inconvenient, for I had a parish dinner arranged the same evening to launch a Christian Stewardship parochial appeal. However, I assured Daphne that I would be back before the function started at eight o'clock. 'It should be over by early afternoon, and I'll leave immediately,' I promised.

The election, a most solemn occasion, begins with Eucharist in the Cathedral's Lady Chapel behind the high altar, after which the members of the Chapter process, robed, to St Peter's Chapel where the procedure of choosing a Dean takes place. There are no proposers or seconders. The ballots are taken in silence, each member at first writing down a number of names, some of which will be subsequently short-listed. The voting continues with names being eliminated at the end of each round until one emerges as the majority choice. From the early stages I could see my name coming through on the lists and the possibility that I might be elected suddenly dawned on me. What was I to do? I was happy with my family in a large parish in Derry and there was the important issue of Daphne's illness and the indispensable help of her mother, especially with the twins, now in Foyle College Prep School. I felt somewhat guilty about leaving Northern Ireland, abandoning my parishioners, especially as the dark, ominous storm clouds began to burst. I was on the point of withdrawing my name from the final round but was physically restrained by two members of the

Chapter, who reminded me that the Chapter had prayed for the guidance of the Holy Spirit and who was I to resist their choice? Put like that, I reluctantly accepted, muttering inwardly to myself, 'I suppose God knows what He is doing.' Now this has taught me a lesson. Sometimes one cannot decide on purely rational or intellectual considerations alone. Another dimension to decision comes into play. Plato called it the inner sense (the diamonian). Come to think of it, if the builders of St Patrick's Cathedral had made a scientific study of the possibility of placing a majestic building like that, the largest church in Ireland, on such boggy, marshy ground, they would certainly have concluded that such a project, judged solely on engineering and architectural standards, was completely out of the question. But because St Patrick had baptised his converts on that site, because a little church had stood there from the fifth century, they felt compelled to go forward in faith, indeed to achieve the scientifically impossible. And so they built, and 800 years later this great monument to their faith still stands secure.

There was no possibility of my leaving immediately to return to Derry as I had intended. The choir was called in to sing the *Te Deum* and the Cathedral bells were rung to celebrate the election of a new Dean. The press appeared, asking for interviews and photographs. The fact that I had come from Derry seemed particularly newsworthy.

All the time I was wondering what Daphne would make of it. I tried to phone her but making a trunk call in the sixties was not as trouble-free as it is today. When at last I succeeded I announced, 'A dreadful thing has happened. They've elected me Dean.' But she knew already. I could hardly believe it.

'Bishop Farren rang me,' she explained. 'He was listening to the Irish news and heard you'd been elected. He wanted to congratulate you and said how much he would miss the two of us.' And so the first person in Derry to offer congratulations, indeed the one who broke the news to my wife, was the Roman Catholic bishop.

I need not have been apprehensive about Daphne's reaction. Having happy memories of her student years at Trinity during which she had made many friends in Dublin, she confided that if we had to leave Derry she would rather move there than anywhere else.

The parish dinner, held in the Embassy Ballroom in the Strand, had to start without me. When I made my very belated appearance I received a standing ovation from the diners! 'Is this' I said, 'because you are all glad to be rid of me — no more begging bowls from Griffin!' The speeches which followed stressed the importance of having someone in Dublin with twenty-two years experience of the Northern situation.

While I enjoyed the support of my parishioners during my time in Derry, and we parted with mutual regret, there were others who were delighted to see me go. 'Good riddance to the Fenian . . . you always were a Lundy . . . no surrender.' I was the recipient of these and many similar messages by letter, telegram and phone, together with articles in extremist Protestant publications on ecumenists like myself alleged to have betrayed the Protestant and Unionist cause. But, I hasten to add, an avalanche of good wishes and 'Sorry to see you go' also descended on us, and this confirmed my faith in the innate goodness of the Northern people of all creeds and classes.

My clerical friends said to me, 'Well, you're on the launching pad now. All you need to do is keep your nose clean and you'll be a bishop.' Deans of St Patrick's will normally be approached to let their names go forward for a bishopric, and many Deans of St Patrick's have left on record their regret at having to leave St Patrick's on being made bishops. I decided when I came to St Patrick's that there I would stay.

Indeed, I had only been in Dublin nine months when the bishopric of Derry fell vacant and I received an urgent phone message from the Electoral College meeting in Armagh asking me if I would consider returning as bishop. The reply I sent was to the effect that having been persuaded by the Chapter 'to put my hand to the plough' in Dublin I did not believe it was in the providence of God or the will of the Holy Spirit to send me straight back to Derry again, like the Grand Old Duke of York.

I was installed as Dean on 19 January 1969 and lived with Cecil Bradley, who had preceded me to St Patrick's from Derry and was now my Dean's Vicar. The Christ Church incumbency remained vacant for some time after my installation so fortunately there was no immediate pressure on Daphne to vacate the Derry rectory.

In tune with the thinking prevalent during the sixties and early seventies, when the planners' dream was to rid the city centre of 'outdated' housing by re-settling the occupants in leafy suburbs and transforming the heart of the metropolis into a network of highways leading to towering office blocks surrounded by parking lots, the Deanery had been allowed to deteriorate over a period of years. Money was not spent on the building for it was generally assumed that a new Dean would wish to join the general exodus and live in fashionable Ballsbridge or Foxrock.

The Deanery is steeped in history. For as long as there has been a Cathedral, a house belonging to St Patrick's has always stood on that site. The present basement dates from Tudor times, and a kitchen of the period, with its old fireplace, is preserved there unaltered. In 1702, eleven years before Jonathan Swift became Dean, the upper stories were rebuilt by Dean Stearne. When Daphne and I first visited the house as prospective occupants we found the external fabric in good condition except for the roof, which was letting in rain. Wallpaper was peeling off damp wall patches inside and there was the institutional brown paint, once considered both serviceable and fashionable, but which gave the whole interior a gloomy and sullen air. At the same time we were both drawn to the Deanery and we felt a sense of peace and contentment within its walls — evidence, we believed, that during its long and eventful history it had been cherished as a haven of calm and comfort.

When we made it known that we intended living in the Deanery some people thought we were out of our minds. Daphne, to her eternal credit, was undeterred. 'I'm not going to live in the suburbs,' she insisted. 'I want to live here, in this old house. We're going to restore it.'

Repairs were still in progress in May when we moved in. At first we had to squat in Swift's dining room while carpenters, electricians, plumbers, central heating engineers, plasterers and painters worked around us. The rest of 1969 passed in a gradually receding state of chaos until, by the end of the year, substantial renovations had been completed, a lift installed and ramps built to facilitate Daphne. The large Georgian rooms and wide doorways and corridors were already well suited to a wheelchair user. A history graduate, Daphne relished the opportunity of living in a house which had such tangible links with the past and of bringing it back to its former state, making suggestions as the work went on. She was convinced there must be an Adam ceiling in the entrance hall and was vindicated when workmen uncovered one hidden under layers of paint. In the basement we found marble busts dumped there when the Deanery was unoccupied. Most of them were of past Deans but there was also one of Wesley and one of Sir Benjamin Guinness, all of which we rescued, brushed, scrubbed and placed on display once again.

When a new Dean of St Patrick's is elected many of the congratulatory messages he receives refer to him as Swift's successor. I must confess that I knew very little about Jonathan Swift except that he had written *Gulliver's Travels* and had been a pupil in my old school, Kilkenny College. I felt I must do something urgently to repair this omission so I began to read Swift and what had been written by so many literati about this enigmatic character, by A.L. Rowse, Denis Johnston and Michael Foot, not to mention Thackeray, Dr Johnson and many others who were captivated by his uniqueness. The more I read, the more fascinated I became with this literary and political colossus, the complexity of his character and the relevance of his satirical thought for us today. I found the eternal Swift speaking to every age his words of wisdom.

And there were those domestic touches concerning his life in the Deanery: his servants and his horses, his groom stacking damp hay in the stables until it smoked like a chimney; how he would run up and down the stairs from the basement to the attic to keep fit when bad weather prevented him taking exercise outside; how carpenters were still hammering away at library shelves a fortnight after they had promised to complete the work.

Records show that he ate very simply when dining alone. Meals served to guests were more elaborate, and he took pride in offering them a selection of good wines, comparing himself as host with his predecessor, John Stearne, who, he maintained in verse, provided a better choice of meat than of wine.

> In the days of Good John if you came here to dine
> you had choice of good food but no choice of good wine.
> In Jonathan's day if you came here to eat
> you had choice of good wine but no choice of good meat.

The accounts which survive for a Chapter dinner during Swift's time, on St Patrick's Day 1715, bear witness to such an assertion. Twice as much was spent on wine as on food on that occasion (food in an abundance of great variety cost £4.11.5 and wine and beer £8.12.11½). The wine bill for a typical canons' dinner when Daphne and I were responsible amounted to approximately one-sixth the cost of the food.

Swift, a somewhat maverick Tory, was vexed about an old cat which wandered about the Deanery, an unwelcome legacy from his predecessor Stearne. He complained that she whined so much she must be a Whig like her former master. She was probably not as quick-witted as our cat who once managed to snatch two chicken legs from a basket left unattended by caterers in the process of setting up a typical Swiftian dinner. (Beneath the venerable portrait of Swift by Binden the food was to be photographed on the dining table adorned with heavy Georgian silver lent by Sybil Connolly.) The Deanery and its Swiftian meal were to feature in a book on meals in historic houses around the world entitled *Tiffany Taste*, commissioned by Tiffany's restaurant in New York. Daphne witnessed the cat making off with his booty but decided to keep silent on the matter. The chicken legs were not missed. I trust Swift would have been glad to partake of the meal, and had Stearne's cat stolen the legs we would certainly have been regaled with some Swiftian satirical displeasure in an apt and well-turned phrase.

There is a tradition that his ghost haunts the Deanery. Soon after we moved in we were asked, 'Did you see Swift's ghost?'

We did not and expressed ourselves thoroughly sceptical about the whole notion. But in time we became aware of a benevolent presence in the building. Daphne, often alone on long winter evenings, never felt the house lonely or creepy. Someone else seemed to be with her, gently keeping her company. Sometimes she had the impression that this presence was standing behind her in the kitchen, lovingly bending over her in her wheelchair. Once or twice she actually thought it was Kevin or Timothy and turned round to speak to them, only to find no one there.

Although always sceptical about ghosts and preferring natural explanations to supernatural, I had nevertheless what might be described as a ghostly experience in the Deanery, when late one evening, in the dim light of the hall, I saw what appeared to be the figure of a man going up the stairs and disappearing into the large bedroom on the landing. I assumed it was my brother-in-law who was staying with us at that time and had spent the evening out on the town with friends from his Trinity days. I called to say 'Goodnight', but there was no reply.

'That's strange,' I remarked to Daphne, 'Brian came in just now and he never spoke.'

'I wonder is he all right?' she said. I went into the bedroom and switched on the light. There was no one there. About six months later there was a repeat performance, same figure, same hour, same room.

'I'm sure there's someone in this house. He must have got hold of a key and he's hiding somewhere,' I suggested. I began a thorough search from basement to attic while Daphne, not in the slightest perturbed, assured me, 'You'll find nobody. Don't worry — there's no intruder.' She was right. It later occurred to me that the figure had entered the bedroom where Swift spent his declining years. I conjectured that this mysterious figure might have been the ghost of some old retainer seeing his master comfortably settled for the night before he himself retired to bed. And may I say for the benefit of those who might be tempted to attribute these apparitions to the after-effects of a good dinner, that I was perfectly sober on both occasions! Daphne, always practical and down-to-earth, was convinced that the presence welcomed us and approved of our living in the Deanery. If she of all people felt that presence in an almost tangible way, it was certainly no figment of her imagination.

Not long after I arrived in Dublin, however, I made the momentous discovery that for some, at least, Swift was alive and well and still in St Patrick's. Lying on my desk in the Cathedral office was a letter addressed to Dr Jonathan Swift, St Patrick's Cathedral, Dublin, Ireland. Someone's idea of a practical joke, I thought, but I opened it nevertheless. The letter was dated 29 June 1969, and purported to be from a Professor in the North Texas State University. It read:

Dear Dr Swift,

I request permission to use the material specified below from your publication in a book which my colleague and I are preparing entitled *Compensation Theory Practice*, and in future editions or revisions thereof, to be published by the McGraw-Hill Book Company, Inc.

'And he gave it for his opinion that whoever could make two ears of corn or two blades of grass to grow upon a spot of ground where only one grew before: would deserve better of mankind, and do more essential service to his country: than the whole race of politicians put together.'

It is understood, of course, that full credit will be given to your publication. The acknowledgement of the source will be printed on the page where the material appears as follows, or in accordance to your suggestions:

Jonathan Swift, *Gulliver's Travels*, The Heritage Press, New York, 1965, p.146.

Your prompt consideration of this request will be greatly appreciated. A release form is given below for your convenience. The duplicate is for your files.

I crumpled the thing up, threw it in the wastepaper basket, being convinced it was the work of a crackpot or hoaxer, and forgot all about it. A month later another similar letter was awaiting Dr Swift which expressed the fear that the first might have gone astray and politely reiterated the request. Would he be kind enough to sign the form? 'These fellows really are serious,' I said to myself. There and then I took out a postcard and penned the following reply:

My dear Professor,

I have a letter here from you addressed to Dr Jonathan Swift. Dr Swift left St Patrick's on 19 October 1745. Unfortunately he did not leave a forwarding address. Where he is now God only knows. However, in his name I accede to your request and should he return in the near future I shall doubtless experience his savage indignation on informing him that I have had the audacity to give you permission to quote his Gulliver — without even negotiating a fee!

I signed it, sent it off and heard no more. But there followed a remarkable sequel to the story. About a year or so later, after early service one Sunday morning in the Cathedral, an American approached, me asking if I was Dean Griffin.

'Let me shake your hand,' he insisted.

'Whatever for?' I asked.

'I'm on a world tour,' he explained. 'When I was in Athens having a glass of wine outside one of those little cafes two obviously cultured Greeks sitting opposite me, reading a newspaper, suddenly burst out laughing. They proceeded to tell me in very good English what they had found so hilarious. They'd just read a story about an American professor having written to Jonathan Swift in St Patrick's Cathedral and the reply that the present Dean, a man called Griffin, had sent. I told them I would be visiting Dublin and they asked me to seek out Dean Griffin and shake his hand, with the compliments of two Greeks.'

I had mentioned the correspondence to a number of people and the Dublin papers got hold of the story. From there it resurfaced in the European press some months later.

A Dean of St Patrick's is surrounded by Swiftiana. When he brings visitors into the dining room of the Deanery, Swift's huge portrait on the far wall — which the great man gave orders should never be removed on pain of his curse descending on whoever did so — dominates the room and the conversation.

One is drawn to the humanity of this man who could not bring himself to attend the funeral of his dear and trusted friend, Stella; who could not even bear to see from the Deanery window the lights burning in the Cathedral for her burial service. Or that touching tribute to Alexander McGee in St Patrick's:

> Here lieth the body of Alexander McGee, servant to Dr Swift, Dean of St Patrick's. His grateful master caused this monument to be erected in memory of his discretion, fidelity and diligence in that humble station — OB March 24 1722/1 Aetat 29.

Swift had great passion but also great compassion. He was a mixture of savage indignation and tenderness, a Vanessa and Stella rolled into one.

By the sheer force of his personality he held his beloved Dubliners in the hollow of his hand. To them he was the great Dean or 'Dane' who, when a large, noisy crowd gathered in the Deanery yard to get a better view of a predicted eclipse of the sun, made them disperse quietly by sending a message through his servant that he, Swift, had postponed the eclipse for twenty-four hours; who, with a substantial price on his head and known by everyone in Dublin to be the anonymous writer of pamphlets which railed with 'savage indignation' against the English government's iniquitous treatment of the Irish nation, was never betrayed; and to whom the populace of Dublin came to pay their last respects when his body was laid out in the Deanery entrance hall, prior to being buried in St Patrick's in accordance with his wishes — in the south west of the nave under the second pillar.

I find myself irresistibly drawn to Swift in his emphatic concern for the poor and exploited, his distrust of any establishment, State or Church, which treated persons as pawns, his rejection of war as a means of solving political disputes and his utter detestation of cruelty, especially the suffering inflicted on the poor and innocent by war or civil conflict. 'Utopias' in whatever sphere of human endeavour were mere chimeras. Perfection can never be attained. We have to be content with trying to achieve what we believe to be the least imperfect, thus Swift.

I have often been asked why, with my interest in politics and social issues, I did not enter the political arena. My answer is that I have always felt that I could serve God and my fellow men better in the Church. While I am interested in politics, and believe all Christians should be, for politics is concerned with human relationships, I would never have made a successful politician. We must distinguish between politics and party politics. I could never have been a good party man and to achieve anything of significance a politician has to be a loyal party member and be prepared at times to put loyalty to the party above his private convictions. But I have always liked doing and saying my own thing in my own way without relying on the approbation of others. As Dean of St Patrick's I had the privilege of being able to speak my mind freely and a national platform on which to do so.

Canon McKegney, my first rector, wrote to me from Derry when I became Dean of St Patrick's. 'That position is tailor-made for you. The office may lead to a bishopric but don't be tempted. Stay there.'

In Ireland the bishops, whether Church of Ireland or Roman Catholic, act together and exercise collective responsibility. This is not so in, for example, the Church of England, where the bishops in public often express conflicting views on political, social and moral questions. It has been said that it is unfair and inconsistent to criticise the alleged influence of the Roman Catholic hierarchy on Irish politics, when bishops of the Church of England sit in the House of Lords apparently immune from such criticism. But this is to miss the point. The bishops of the Church of England do not form a solid, monolithic voting block, exercising a collective pressure on the political system. They form no party. Their votes are cast in accordance with how they as individuals decide the issue in debate. Some bishops will be found in the Conservative lobby, others in the Labour or Liberal.

Bishops of the Church of Ireland, unlike their Roman Catholic counterparts, exercise constitutional episcopacy, which means they are bound by decisions of Synod or Council or Committee, and in the Church of Ireland such bodies at diocesan or national level consist of clergy and laity as well as bishops. The General Synod of the Church of Ireland includes all the diocesan bishops, with elected clergy and laity from each diocese or united diocese in the proportion of two members of the laity for every clerical member.

The fact that a bishop in the Church of Ireland has to keep in step with clergy and laity in Synod, Council or Committee is frequently not understood, particularly in the Republic where the media, so accustomed to Roman Catholic bishops speaking on behalf of their Church without reference to any Synod or Council, naturally conclude that the Church of Ireland bishops can do likewise. Church of Ireland bishops are subject to the decisions of General Synod, as are the clergy and laity. Outside this restraint they are free to act individually or collectively as they choose. They invariably choose to act collectively and, like the Roman Catholic hierarchy, to present a united front on important controversial issues. Unlike the Church of England bishops, the bishops of the Church of Ireland will not disagree in public on doctrinal and moral questions. In private, perhaps. In public, definitely not. In the General Synod the bishops take their exalted places, 'high and lifted up' on a platform. There they sit together, separated from their brothers and sisters in Christ, the clergy and laity, who occupy the body of the hall. I am told this does not happen elsewhere in the Anglican communion. We appear to be unique in the Church of Ireland in having this outward and visible sign of bishops as *apart from* the Church rather than as *part of* the Church. On enquiring from a bishop the reason for such episcopal segregation he replied: 'to allow us to consult together quickly and reach a common mind on any thorny unexpected matter which might crop up in the course of the debate.'

In the North of Ireland, where the Presbyterian Church is the largest Protestant denomination, bishops are treated with less deference than in the Republic, especially in the Republic's rural areas where traditional respect for episcopal office still survives. Presbyterians reject the hierarchical principle. All clergy as presbyters are equal and one of their number is elected yearly to hold office as Moderator or Chairman, presiding over General Assembly or local Synod.

This 'levelling down' or 'levelling up' process which also obtains in the Methodist Church helps to deprive high ecclesiastical office, *per se*, of any distinctive mystique. The ready access of every Tom, Dick and Harry to the media and participation, especially in radio and TV discussions, has also diminished the aura of high office in both North and South. All are equal and equally vulnerable on the TV screen. Leaders, whether religious or political, are respected only if they show conviction, commitment, have a positive and courageous message, not long but lean, and are not given to platitudes or to vain repetition of things said so often by so many and so obvious to all. Office itself fails to excite.

In the Presbyterian Church the reports of various Church committees are subjected to detailed scrutiny. Each member of Assembly or Synod is intensely aware of his or her democratic right actively to participate in the formation of Church policy. In the Church of Ireland there is a tendency to accept reports and recommendations without similar intense scrutiny. Committees representative of the bishops, clergy and laity, elected or appointed to deal with doctrinal, social, political, educational or liturgical matters, are on the whole credited with the wisdom to make the right decisions which are therefore not lightly to be rejected. In some cases the General Synod may decide to leave a particular issue solely in the hands of the bishops. This certainly expedites the business of the General Synod. Protracted debates are a rarity.

Looking back I find there has been a dramatic change on the question of authority, particularly Church authority today. No longer is authority obeyed simply because it is an authority. It is now generally accepted that the decisions of authority must always commend themselves to reasonable people and not fly in the face of science and the facts of contemporary knowledge and experience. Authority must be credible and be seen to be credible. This means that theology must never be isolated from the findings of other disciplines, such as psychology and sociology. In seeking the answers to moral issues in such matters as family planning, contraception, AIDS, sterilisation, divorce, abortion, homosexuality, nuclear weapons and so on, Christians must have regard, not only to Holy Scripture and Christian tradition, but to the whole body of relevant scientific and empirical knowledge. God expects us to use our intellect, to have vision and foresight and to take the appropriate humane measures to cure or prevent our ills. Answers to complicated moral problems must be arrived at by patient and informed discussion and debate under, as Christians believe, the guidance of the Holy Spirit. There is no short cut. There is no immediate, simple and final answer supplied by the ready application of such concepts as 'divine' or 'natural' or 'moral' law. The moral law is not something self evident, ready to hand, which can be applied to give a prompt and conclusive answer to every complex moral problem. It is not something imposed on the situation, as it were, from the outside. It emerges from the inside, from the ever-deepening insight into a complex moral issue arrived at by the collective and informed experience of Christians who use their heads as well as their hearts, their intellects as well as their emotional attachment to any particular theological position.

The idea of authority in the Christian Church as a sort of oracle, dispensing infallible and satisfactory answers to every doctrinal or moral problem, is a fiction. We have to work hard, think hard, pray hard to find the answer. Even then we may be mistaken. We cannot be certain. But we can be sure of one thing. If a mistake is made, in all good conscience, God in his own time and in His own way will eventually 'correct what is amiss and supply what is lacking', provided we persevere in faith as pilgrims and seekers of the truth.

On the authority of the Christian ministry it is sometimes said, though not as often today as in the past, that true or valid Christian ministers have to be ordained by bishops, and Roman Catholic bishops at that. Theologians through the centuries have debated the question: 'What constitutes valid ordination?' But most Christians today are not really interested in this matter. Especially in this ecumenical age it is becoming increasingly evident that, judged by Our Lord's criterion, 'By their fruits shall ye know them', non-episcopal as well as episcopal ministries have been effectively used by Our Lord in His service. Ministry is service, and an ordained ministry which is to serve the needs of whatever kind of Christian unity may in time emerge to replace our unhappy divisions will, I believe, embody the valuable insights possessed by different Christian traditions, Episcopal, Presbyterian, Congregational and so on. Each has something to contribute to the total enrichment and effectiveness of the work and witness of the Church. Indeed, it may well be that instead of one form of ministry accepted everywhere and by all, there will be different forms, some more suitable than others depending on the circumstances, historic, cultural and racial, of particular countries or regions.

The ministry is there to serve the Church, the people of God, and true 'apostolic succession', whether episcopal or non-episcopal, is in the people of God. The only criterion of a valid ministry is how effective it is in doing Christ's work in the world.

The theory of the divine right of kings resulted in the popular acceptance of a hereditary monarchy as the only valid form of government, the very 'esse' or being of the State: no monarch, no State. Similarly, belief in the 'divine right' of popes or bishops resulted in the popular acceptance of apostolic succession through episcopacy as the only valid form of Church order and government, the very 'esse' or being of the Church: no bishop, no Church. But no one doubts today the validity of a Republican constitution for any State which so chooses. Equally 'apostolic succession episcopacy' should be reluctant to question the validity of non-episcopal ministries and thereby to limit catholicity to Roman Catholics, Orthodox and Anglicans, indeed, to limit it further by a refusal to ordain women to the priesthood. Catholic consensus is the consensus of the whole people of God throughout the whole world who can affirm their common faith by reciting together the Creeds and Lord's Prayer.

As I looked round the Cathedral when I was installed as Dean on Sunday, 19 January 1969, I could not help noticing that all the great traditions which had fashioned our Irish history and heritage were enshrined within these walls: the Celtic, the Anglo-Norman, the medieval, the Anglo-Irish, the Gaelic, and the Huguenots who worshipped here from 1666 until 1816. Here in St Patrick's Wesley had ministered. All the great traditions co-exist and the Cathedral is an object lesson in reconciliation. The whole concept of Irishness is made more inclusive by each tradition enriching the others. St Patrick's in its very fabric and history seemed to articulate the message that instead of one particular tradition claiming to be the only authentic Irish tradition and regarding the others as imposters or aliens, there must be a tolerance of all in a pluralism of traditions. If we were to implement the Christian Gospel of reconciliation here in Ireland I felt we must move towards a more open, tolerant and pluralist society.

Might the Cathedral be used to that end. In 1970 I wrote:

I am convinced that the most effective witness which St Patrick's can give is by ceasing to be used exclusively by any one denomination, for in a very real sense it is greater and nobler than any of us. I feel it should be shared by all. I would like to see the Cathedral regularly being available by mutual agreement for worship according to the rites of the main Christian traditions, and further I would like to see in St Patrick's Christians of each tradition joining frequently in the worship of other traditions. In this way I believe we can learn from each other, contribute to each other and help to bring nearer the day when all shall be visibly and organically one. St Patrick's can be a powerful force to heal the wounds of division and at the same time to witness to our common underlying unity, brotherhood and reconciliation in Christ.

I also wrote to the leaders of the other main Churches, Roman Catholic, Presbyterian and Methodist putting forward my suggestion that St Patrick's be shared by all. Only the Methodists displayed any interest. I think the Roman Catholics and

Presbyterians imagined that there was some 'catch', a hidden motive, to entice them into supporting the Cathedral financially!

Is it not rather presumptuous for a Church with only 3 per cent of the population in the Republic and about 18 per cent in Northern Ireland, to lay claim to being the Church of Ireland? Certainly on purely numerical grounds there can be no justification for such a claim. But when we consider the wide spectrum of political opinion from extreme shades of Republicanism to extreme shades of Unionism which the Church of Ireland embraces, I believe there is some justification for its title on the grounds that it represents more than any other an 'Irishness' which is all inclusive. Of the two other major Churches the Roman Catholic identity is with the Nationalist community and the Presbyterian mostly with the Unionist community in Northern Ireland. The Church of Ireland also claims to be both Catholic and Reformed, or Catholic and Protestant. There is the commitment to Holy Scripture as the standard of her faith, to the ancient creeds, sacraments and ministry, combined with a respect for responsible individual freedom and a concern for credibility in the light of modern knowledge and experience. The Church of Ireland, being unashamedly Catholic and Protestant, is well placed to act as a 'bridge Church', bridging the gap between Protestantism and Roman Catholicism, helping to promote mutual understanding and reconciliation since she has so much in common with both.

The Church of Ireland is Anglican and Irish. Anglicanism when true to itself at its best is very open, very patient, on the surface showing a certain hesitancy and untidiness, to the world presenting sometimes a disconcerting picture of weakness and indecision, of internal stresses and divisions; but in a paradoxical way these very features constitute its inner strength, the strength of honesty in admitting that we do not always have a ready and final answer, tolerance of those who see things from different viewpoints, openness in the face of complexity. This is the Anglican ideal, however we may at times fall short of it. The faith cannot change, for Jesus Christ and the Gospel is the same, yesterday, today and forever. But the interpretation, the understanding of the faith, can change and indeed, if it is to be a living faith, must change under the guidance of the Holy Spirit in the light of changing circumstances. To seek to discern this guidance takes time, prayer, patience, waiting on God. God is never in a hurry, and He in His own good time and in His own good way will, Christians believe, lead us to a deeper insight into the meaning and relevance for our age and its complexities, of the one eternal truth as it is revealed in Jesus Christ. To live is to change. To stagnate is to die. True, in religion and politics as in biology. The future can never be a stereotyped repetition of the past. Any attempt to imprint the past on the future is sterile and will come to naught. The past exists to enrich the future, not to dominate it.

Jesus said: 'You shall love God' and 'You shall love your neighbour.' In the final analysis there are only two absolutes, love of God and love of my neighbour. There are different interpretations and applications of these absolutes, and there is the ever-present temptation to absolutise the interpretation, to assert that my view or my Church's view is the only valid and true Christian one. In this way lies intolerance and strife.

11

Appeal

Having been assured that I would have plenty of time to read and perhaps write something while Dean of St Patrick's, I came to Dublin expecting some sort of ecclesiastical sinecure offering at last a degree of leisure which I had previously never enjoyed. I was in for a rude awakening. I found instead a vast amount of work awaiting me, including, alas, yet more building programmes. In Derry I had been responsible for building a new church, St Peter's, on the Culmore Road, and a new primary school attached to Christ Church. Now I began unconsciously to walk in the footsteps of Jonathan Swift, who had been so meticulous in his care of the Cathedral fabric and grounds.

St Patrick's was nearly eight hundred years old when I became Dean and had been, incidentally, the first university in Ireland (hence the title 'Collegiate' church). It needed extensive repairs and renovation both inside and out. In particular, the great west Minot Tower (so called after Archbishop Minot who erected it in 1370) had to be saved from further deterioration. Its eleven-feet-thick walls were taking water which was running down the spiral staircase.

I launched an appeal in 1972 for a quarter of a million pounds, a considerable sum in those days, which met with a generally sympathetic response from the public at large but which also subjected me to some harsh criticism in letters to the press. I was accused of falling short of my Christian vocation in having the temerity to seek money for a building which had had its day when there were starving masses throughout the world in need of every penny that the hard-pressed public could afford to give. 'People are more important than things' was the slogan voiced abroad in the early seventies. It took the Wood Quay controversy to make us aware as a nation of the importance of preserving our heritage, to realise that the urban environment consists of old familiar buildings which have embodied and nourished communal life for generations.

I had also to try and raise funds for the rebuilding of the Choir and Grammar Schools, the oldest schools in Ireland, founded in 1432. The Grammar School, in particular, had fallen into an alarming state of decay. It was too late for repairs to be undertaken. New buildings were essential. When I arrived the Grammar School teachers issued me with an ultimatum! Something must be done immediately or the school would have to be closed. Teaching posts elsewhere were easier to obtain at that time than they are now.

Prefabricated buildings were an obvious temporary measure, but a supplier I knew, a Derry man then in Dublin, informed me that I would have to wait eighteen months at least. When I insisted this would be too late to save the school, he promised to see if he could expedite matters on the condition that I paid him 'on the nail'. I agreed, taking a chance on being able to raise the more than twenty thousand pounds required. I went out to Church House in Rathmines, put my case as forcibly as I could, and borrowed the money from the central Church of Ireland authorities, commonly known as the Representative Church Body.

But my troubles were by no means over. The school architect insisted on having planning permission before he would erect the buildings. My application had just been submitted and was likely to take many months before being granted. Eventually he agreed to erect them on condition that I gave an undertaking in writing before a solicitor that I would undertake personal responsibility in law for any repercussions arising from an action which contravened official regulations.

About a year later the planning authorities requested me to visit them as they had then got round to considering my application. I went down to their offices, then in Dame Street, and told them the school buildings were already in place.

'What? You can't do that,' they said.

'I had no choice.' I replied. 'I couldn't allow children to be educated in unsafe buildings with archaic toilet facilities and rain pouring in through the roof. Time was not on my side. I had to act quickly. The staff refused to work there and were bent on resigning *en masse*.'

The authorities decided to review the position. I did not have to go to court or jail, and planning permission was eventually granted retrospectively in view of the urgent and extenuating circumstances. Permanent accommodation for both schools was a necessity so I launched a second, separate, appeal for an educational fund to supplement the grants which we anticipated and in time received from the Department of Education. I decided to take my begging bowl to America on a three-week tour in search of money to help restore the Cathedral's fabric and save the schools.

Having to leave Daphne at home, knowing how she would love to have travelled with me, I felt a little guilty. But in her practical, positive and non-sentimental way, she always insisted I go, assuring me that she would find it much more difficult to cope with my staying at home on her account. 'Well, I hope you get what will at least pay your fare,' were her parting words as I set out from Dublin airport to cross the Atlantic.

My thoughts as I began my journey centred wryly on its purpose. 'You never seem to be able to escape from administration and fund-raising,' I told myself. However, I was convinced that an ancient, historic Cathedral such as St Patrick's must be preserved at all costs and its schools retained as an essential part of its work and witness. I had committed myself heart and soul to this task.

The Irish diplomatic corps, very sympathetic to my mission, arranged meetings for me with influential, moneyed Americans, as did contacts in organisations both private and commercial. The Bank of Ireland was particularly helpful through its American associates. The idea of a Protestant clergyman going cap-in-hand to the cream of the largely Roman Catholic Irish-American élite did not, apparently, strike anyone as particularly strange. My connection with St Patrick's gave me an immediate entrée to their circles. I told them, as I had been trying to make clear in Dublin ever since my arrival, that I wanted the Cathedral — embodying as it does so much of Ireland's history and heritage — to be used on a regular basis by all the main denominations for their own distinctive forms of worship, thus making St Patrick's a focal point of unity in a much-divided land.

While my suggestion did not receive a positive response on the part of the churches in Ireland, it certainly appealed to Irish Americans, who wished me well in such endeavours.

One of the functions I spoke at was a luncheon in a Boston hotel arranged by Ted Kennedy through the good offices of the Irish Consul. Ted was not available that day to host the meal but asked his cousin, one of the Fitzgerald family, to do the honours instead. However, Ted sent me a substantial cheque and wished me well.

In New York I preached in Holy Trinity Church, Wall Street, late on a Friday afternoon, before the weekend exodus leaves America's financial centre deserted. I also met Paul O'Dwyer, a leading New York lawyer and we had lunch together. A Democrat with strong socialist leanings, well known for his defence of the underprivileged and his outspoken criticism of the nation's wealth controllers, he is *persona non grata* in certain quarters. His family came originally from Mayo. I found him, on Irish politics, unashamedly Republican in his desire for a united Ireland but in no sense a narrow Roman Catholic Nationalist. He would not for a moment countenance the domination by one religion — Roman or Protestant — of a nation's affairs. Some have criticised him for having a rather abrasive manner, but I warmed to Paul. He and I got along well together.

Ten years later, when I was active in the abortion referendum campaign, he read a speech of mine which had been quoted extensively in the *Irish Times* and wrote to congratulate me on my stand for pluralism and against Church interference in the affairs of State.

While fund-raising in Philadelphia I enjoyed the company of Henry McElhinney and his sister, descendants of a Ramelton, Co. Donegal, Presbyterian family. A man who had amassed many fortunes, the owner of a castle in Glenveagh, Co. Donegal, he invited me to lunch in his home, a gracious, opulently but tastefully furnished house and a showcase for his renowned collection of art and antiques. He was a generous host who showed great interest in and knowledge of the Celtic tradition. He also had a high regard for Swift, and much of our conversation centred on Swiftiana and St Patrick's.

Everywhere I was entertained lavishly and received a sympathetic hearing, but the cheques, when they began to arrive, were not as large as I had hoped for — a common experience, I have since discovered, among the many who go begging to the United States under the illusion that the country is full of wealthy individuals only too willing to shell out their dollars to help the Irish.

The one sad note was when the Roman Catholic authorities in New York turned down a suggestion that, as a gesture to ecumenism and an Ireland inclusive of all traditions, I should be invited to review the St Patrick's Day parade standing on the steps of St Patrick's Cathedral in the company of the Cardinal and the other Roman Catholic dignitaries. This was refused. Probably the hierarchy and the AOH could not conceive it possible that an Irish Protestant would dare to lay claim to being a true Irishman and follower of St Patrick! So thanks to Kevin Rush from the Irish Consulate I witnessed the parade from a VIP stand with senators and diplomats as lofty banners demanded 'Brits out of Ireland'. I wondered about St Patrick, surely a most distinguished Brit. Would he be the first candidate for expulsion and ethnic cleansing? St Patrick, son of a deacon, grandson of a priest, a simple uncomplicated Christian who knew nothing about papal infallibility or the Immaculate Conception or the Assumption of the Blessed Virgin Mary, was being hijacked before my eyes and portrayed as anti-British, anti-Protestant, the very embodiment of narrow Roman Catholic confessionalism and negative Republican triumphalism.

Fund-raising events were, of course, taking place at home. Concerts were given by the Cathedral choir. I travelled around Ireland making my plea on behalf of St Patrick's and its schools at various luncheons arranged by local businessmen in key cities North and South. A set of special commemorative silver plates depicting St Patrick's was minted to help the Cathedral renovation appeal.

We decided that it would be a fitting and incidentally rewarding gesture, in view of the publicity it was likely to generate, to present a plate to each of the candidates for the 1973 Presidential election. We planned also to honour Mícheál Mac Liammóir in like manner at the same ceremony in appreciation of the many occasions on which he had given readings in the Cathedral. He had also played Swift in Eugene McCabe's play in the Abbey.

A reception to present the plates was duly arranged for Marsh's Library, beside St Patrick's. Erskine Childers and Mícheál and the press arrived but there was no sign of Tom O'Higgins, the Fine Gael candidate. The unfortunate Mr O'Higgins had, alas, mixed up the dates in his diary. He had to run the gauntlet of the journalistic fraternity who were having a field day with the missing man in the photos — the man who never was! I tried to make light of the affair. We arranged for his plate to be presented on another day, but it was open season for the media. In the event the election was won by Erskine Childers. Whether the 'plates' put paid to the Presidential pretensions of Tom O'Higgins is a speculation best left to the historians!

In June 1973 the service to mark the inauguration as President of Ireland of Erskine Childers was held in the Cathedral. This followed the precedent of a similar inauguration service which Douglas Hyde had requested on his appointment as first President of Ireland in 1938.

My Vicar, Cecil Bradley, and I were invited by Mrs Childers to dinner to discuss the form of service. Erskine Childers made it clear that he wished the service to take place within the context of the Eucharist, the central act of Christian worship.

From an ecumenical point of view this presented a problem for some Roman Catholics because in those days the Roman Catholic hierarchy felt uneasy about attending the celebration of the Eucharist or Holy Communion in Protestant churches.

The hierarchy would have preferred an ecumenical service drawn up by representatives from all the Churches. But the President elect was adamant, the service must be the Eucharist on this solemn occasion. I totally supported his view and even consulted Archbishop Buchanan who agreed that Mr Childers' wish should be paramount. The matter was also raised in the House of Bishops, where the Bishop of Ossory and later Archbishop of Dublin, Dr H.R. McAdoo, won the support of the Church of Ireland episcopate for my decision to have the Eucharist.

As the President is President of all the people of Ireland, I decided to invite leaders of the various denominations to participate in the Eucharist, by assisting in the readings and prayers at the service. Presbyterians, Methodists, Salvation Army, Society of Friends, Moravians, Baptists and others all gladly accepted my invitation. I asked Archbishop Ryan, the Roman Catholic Archbishop of Dublin, if he would give an address or say prayers or read a lesson either before or after the service of Holy Communion or give a special blessing should he feel unable to join the other Church leaders in the actual service. I stressed how very much I would like him to participate in the ceremony in whatever way he felt he could, and I assured him that two places in the Sanctuary with the Church of Ireland bishops would be reserved for himself and Cardinal Conway of Armagh.

To my great disappointment Archbishop Ryan was not willing to cooperate. The media was, I believe, to a certain extent responsible for the misunderstanding. When it was announced that I intended inviting representatives of other denominations to participate, the media described it as an ecumenical service. As I was well aware of the strictly technical and restrictive nature of the term as perceived by the hierarchy, I deliberately refrained from using it. So Archbishop Ryan was under the impression that I had advertised an ecumenical service and was trying to slip in the Eucharist under the cloak of ecumenism. The fact of the matter is, I had emphasised that the service would be the Eucharist according to the Order of the Church of Ireland but I was also inviting other denominations to participate.

It should be noted that previous Presidents who were Roman Catholics had their Service in the Pro-Cathedral and this was invariably the Mass. Representatives of other Churches were present but were not invited to take part. President Childers and I felt that the Eucharist according to the rites of the Church of Ireland would certainly be in keeping with established precedent, but in our case we wished those from other Churches not only to attend but to participate in conducting the service.

The Archbishop's reply to my invitation was cool, stating that he and the Cardinal would attend the service but would sit in the nave. They would take no part in the proceedings. I was told by those sitting near them that the Archbishop was as good as his word and appeared to take no interest whatever in the Order of Service. But the incident was soon forgotten and the Archbishop and I, on subsequent occasions when we met, never mentioned it, nor was it allowed to impair a happy and friendly relationship which I enjoyed not only with Archbishop Ryan, but with his successors, Archbishops MacNamara and Connell. We had our disagreements on theological issues, but differences of conviction should never be allowed to destroy Christian charity. We must speak the truth, as we see it, always in love.

An ecumenical service in the technical sense, particularly for the Roman Catholic Church is one drawn up by representatives of the various Churches and agreed by the bishops and other Church leaders. Such a service, reflecting of necessity the lowest common denominator and without any recognised or recognisable liturgical form, generally fails to impress, edify or inspire. I believe all Christian worship, of whatever denomination, must be ecumenical, for Jesus Christ is Lord of all, Saviour of all. Because of this, Christians who profess to worship Him as Lord and Saviour must always welcome, indeed invite, fellow Christians of different traditions to join with them in what really

Dissenting voices: with John de Courcy Ireland, Tomás Mac Giolla and Jim Kemmy at a meeting to highlight issues of equality at a commemoration of the French Revolution in April 1989, and at a meeting to protest about road-widening outside St Patrick's Cathedral at City Hall in 1987. *(Irish Times)*

Receiving an Honorary Doctorate of Divinity at Trinity College in July 1992 with Jennifer Johnston and, in the background, George Kurkjian of Aid Armenia. *(Irish Times)*

With Pastor Kurt Pressman, St Finian's Lutheran Church and Reverend Gabriel Daly, OSA at the 500th anniversary of the birth of Martin Luther at St Patrick's Cathedral in November 1983. *(Irish Times)*

With Daphne outside St Patrick's Cathedral in June 1987 and *(below)* at my Farewell Sermon in September 1991. *(Irish Times)*

Celebrating Kevin passing out at Templemore Garda Training Centre in August 1984. *(Irish Times)*

Kevin and Timothy in June 1993. *(Bill Doyle)*

matters, the worship of their common Lord and Saviour Jesus Christ. Jesus Christ is the true ecumenist, the Saviour of the world, the Catholic Christ, having the whole Gospel for the whole world. Catholicism must be as wide and inclusive as the love of God.

Ecumenism, thank God, has moved on since 1973. Today Roman Catholic bishops are present in the Sanctuary during the celebration of the Eucharist on such occasions as the ordination of a Church of Ireland bishop. Twenty years ago the attitude of the Roman Catholic hierarchy was that ecumenism should only stretch as far as a jointly agreed service.

It was a source of great sadness to President Childers that he had to go forward alone in that service to receive Communion because his Roman Catholic wife was forbidden by her Church to join him. And he was, of course, similarly excluded from receiving the sacrament with Mrs Childers at official functions where Mass was celebrated. On a number of occasions he told me how he could not understand why individuals who wished to partake of Holy Communion should be prohibited by ecclesiastical regulations and decrees from doing so. He felt this could not be in accordance with the mind of Christ.

Of course he was right. We must never lose sight of the fact that it is the Lord's service and the Lord's table, that the invitation to sup with Him comes from Him alone and not from any priest or any denomination. He is Lord of the Sacrament as he is Lord of the Church. As I see it, it is the height of presumption for priest or minister to decide who shall be allowed to come and who shall not. All denominations should extend an invitation to every Christian present, and it is a matter for the individual whether he or she accepts or not according to their conscience. Barring people from coming forward because they do not hold a particular theological or philosophical belief as to how exactly Christ is present in the sacrament is, I believe, usurping the place of God and becoming a judge of the worthiness or unworthiness of individuals. Religious legalism is then in command. 'We have a law and by that law he ought to die,' howled the mob crying out for Christ to be crucified. They believed it was God's law, divine law, the divine imprimatur. How often is Christ crucified with his love and compassion in the name of the law of the Church. We have a law. . . .

But God is not in our hands. We are in his.

Less than eighteen months after his inauguration President Childers was to have preached at the Thanksgiving Service in November 1974 to celebrate the completion of repairs to St Patrick's, but he died unexpectedly the week before. I visited Mrs Childers in Aras an Uachtarain to express my sympathy and personal sense of loss and we found the sermon he had written for the occasion. I read it at the Thanksgiving Service which she attended with members of the family.

In 1979 I was nominated for a People of the Year Award. My campaign to preserve St Patrick's, to defend the surrounding community in the Liberties and to keep the Choir School in existence — the only school of its kind in Ireland — was perceived as meriting the award citation 'For an outstanding contribution to society in Ireland'. The Cathedral was fast becoming a landmark on the international tourist trail, attracting up to a quarter of a million visitors a year, and I was credited with indirectly helping to boost the country's tourist industry.

The award was a recognition of the importance of preserving the ancient Cathedral and the Liberties and my efforts to that end. It was presented by Charles Haughey, then Minister for Health, who has always taken a keen and supportive interest in St Patrick's, its Deanery and Schools, and with whom over a number of years I may be said to have enjoyed a close and helpful relationship.

John de Courcy Ireland was another recipient that year, as were Monsignor Horan and Willie Bermingham. A tireless campaigner for seafarers and for the need to protect the sea and its resources from pollution, John de Courcy was at one time a teacher in St Patrick's Cathedral Grammar School — indeed, he began his teaching career there — and has maintained a particularly warm and generous association with the Cathedral since then.

I remember suggesting to the Monsignor that if ever I got into grave financial difficulties with St Patrick's, perhaps he would be willing to send me one of his apparitions from Knock. He took this in very good part. We used to joke about it when we met. 'Any spare apparitions?' I would ask him. I admired his courageous pragmatism, his ability to achieve against the odds what he believed to be right and I was very saddened by his unexpected death. In many ways we were kindred spirits.

Willie Bermingham's already legendary work for the lonely and destitute elderly gave rise to a deep level of friendship and communication between us. It was very important to Willie that these rejects of society should have a decent Christian burial. He would ring me up to arrange the funerals and I always made sure that the Choir or portion of it would be present. Willie saw to it that these unfortunates were at least accorded in death the dignity which they had been denied in life. Always the boy choristers, and sometimes the whole Cathedral choir, would attend and sing the full choral Burial Service.

Alas, Willie himself was taken from us in April 1990 after a long and painful illness during which he continued his caring and concern for others, retaining to the end his good cheer and sense of fun, with never a word of complaint. He sent for me to visit him in hospital and asked if I would grant his request that his funeral service be ecumenical and in St Patrick's Cathedral. This I readily acceded to. A vast concourse of people of all walks, creeds and classes, lecturers and lawyers, paupers and professors, poured into the Liberties from all over the city, filling St Patrick's to overflowing, standing in their hundreds in Street and Park and Close, as the services on Friday evening and Saturday morning were relayed over the loudspeakers. They bore testimony to one who so freely gave so much of himself to help so many whom the world had passed by on the other side. Willie the Good Samaritan.

12

Croke Park and Lansdowne Road

WHEN I opened the appeal to restore and preserve the Cathedral fabric, I was pleasantly surprised in January 1973 to receive a message from Seán O Siocháin, Director General of the GAA, saying that he and the President, Patrick Fanning, together with Tom Loftus, Chairman of Leinster County Board, wished to call at the Deanery to present me with a cheque from the GAA in aid of the Cathedral restoration. It was a generous cheque for one thousand pounds, and in my words of thanks I mentioned that St Patrick's and the GAA were two institutions which embraced all Ireland and both had a unique opportunity to promote reconciliation based on mutual respect and understanding throughout the island. So began my friendly association with the GAA and my presence at Croke Park as their guest whenever I was free to attend the All Ireland Football or Hurling Finals.

The first occasion was the Football Final between Armagh and Dublin in 1977. The news that, for the first time ever, a Protestant Dean — and the Dean of St Patrick's, the National Cathedral at that — would attend a football match in Croke Park on a Sunday caused quite a stir. The mixture of a Protestant clergyman, the GAA and the Sabbath was too much for some staunchly Protestant stomachs. Phone calls and letters informed me that I was a traitor to my Protestant faith, a consortor with the IRA, a disgrace to my family. But there were supportive messages also. One, I remember, came from the Select Vestry of the Church of Ireland parish in which Sam Maguire, who presented the All Ireland Football Cup, had been a member in Co. Cork. I felt I was doing the right thing by going to Croke Park. I had been involved in so many controversies and taken so much criticism that by now I was pretty immune. I lost no sleep. My advice to critics is: if they think an organisation like the GAA needs to change its image or policy, then far better to get involved, to attend matches, to meet the officials, to listen, learn, talk and contribute.

On my first appearance in Croke Park in the Ard Comhairle box I was greeted with TV cameras, press photographers and journalists eager to explore the possible effect on the GAA or the Church of Ireland of my attendance on Sunday in Croke Park. Thankfully the novelty soon wore off. It is no longer news that 'Dean Griffin was present in Croke Park'. I am now free to go unnoticed by the media and to enjoy the match and the reception generously hosted by the GAA afterwards.

The *Irish Times* asked the question 'How is the Dean doing good?' and went on: 'Just by being there on an occasion which warms the heart of so many fellow Irishmen. . . . It is not that one group, be it in religion or politics or sport, wishes to sink its identity entirely in that of another or to bow down entirely to the other, it is that we should learn to rejoice in our real strength which is the strength of diversity. . . . There are so many, so simple gestures still to be made before the country drags itself out of the miasma of mixed-up identity that has clung so long to us.'

The Croke Park episode had an interesting and happy sequel. I had been approached on many occasions to allow my name to be considered by episcopal electoral colleges for a bishopric but had always steadfastly refused. I felt I could serve the Church best as Dean of St Patrick's and had no desire to move elsewhere. However, it was put to me by one of the more senior bishops that such continual refusals meant that I was placing my own interests before those of the Church at large which I professed to serve. Reluctantly, I agreed to let my name be proposed for the bishopric of a certain diocese whose

Church members could hardly be described as ardent supporters of the GAA with a propensity for attending Sunday Gaelic games in Croke Park, Dublin! I hope I am not so naive or presumptuous as to believe that had it not been for Croke Park I would have been episcopally home and dry. But I like to think that Croke Park and the GAA played some part in keeping me in St Patrick's with a clear conscience, by helping to produce the desired result in my one and only outing in the episcopal stakes. Truly God moves in a mysterious way.

In the early seventies I was approached with others to put my name to a letter of protest against the Irish Rugby Football Union for inviting the South African Springboks to play Ireland in Lansdowne Road. At that time apartheid in sport as in other areas was rampant in South Africa. We felt that politics and racism should have no part in sporting activities, and that the action of the IRFU appeared to condone, if not approve, the apartheid policy of the South African Government. The then Archbishop of Dublin, Alan Buchanan, also signed, as did well-known people like Conor Cruise O'Brien, and others prominent in political life and in the anti-apartheid movement. We all processed from O'Connell Street to Lansdowne Road with placards denouncing apartheid. For some years it had been customary for the IRFU to send two complimentary tickets to the Dean of St Patrick's for internationals in Lansdowne Road. No tickets arrived for me, and on enquiring the reason for the omission I was curtly informed that in future no tickets would be forthcoming. I appeared to have blotted my copy book with the IRFU and all my pleading about having played rugby in Derry and encouraging it in St Patrick's was of no avail. I assume the anti-apartheid protest was the cause of my unpopularity. Subsequently at a social occasion, on meeting a friendly and well-disposed official, I was given to understand that the IRFU on reflection had come to realise that perhaps there had been an over-reaction to a well-meant protest which, far from harming the game, was really intended to advance it by demanding justice and equality for all engaged in sport. I still go to Lansdowne Road for internationals when I can, but with tickets by courtesy of my friends. How strange, I would sometimes think, free tickets and generous hospitality in Croke Park. No free tickets or generous hospitality in Lansdowne Road!

I first met that stalwart anti-apartheid campaigner Archbishop Trevor Huddleston when he came to address a clerical meeting in Northern Ireland in 1960. Later on as Dean I renewed my acquaintance, and on two occasions he preached for me in St Patrick's. I was also very glad to welcome Archbishop Desmond Tutu to the pulpit and was honoured to be invited by Terence McCaughey and the anti-apartheid movement to take part in an ecumenical service of thanksgiving to celebrate the release from prison of Nelson Mandela. Donald Soper (now Lord Soper), Methodist, Hyde Park orator, committed socialist, also held forth in St Patrick's on the evils of apartheid, discrimination and poverty with a Swiftian 'savage indignation'.

13

Visitors to St Patrick's

THE five million or so visitors who thronged to St Patrick's from all parts of the world during my time as Dean, some in an official capacity, others as tourists with a serious intention to 'do' Dublin in twenty-four hours, brought with them much goodwill and sometimes left behind a smile or two.

I was once asked by an American where St Patrick's grave was. He thought the saint might have been buried beneath the Cathedral as Swift had been. 'He's reputed to be buried in Down-patrick,' I answered. As if sensing his disappointment his wife turned to him.

'Don't worry, dear,' she assured him, 'I just got a lovely photo of St Patrick sitting outside the Cathedral.'

'There's no statue of St Patrick there,' I thought. 'Where did you take the photo?' I enquired, intrigued.

'Just out there,' she replied, pointing to the Close.

Then it dawned on me. It was the statue of Sir Benjamin Lee Guinness she'd snapped, and I hadn't the heart to disillusion her.

During the early seventies the 'venerable' Miss Shaw had charge of the robes used by the clergy and choir. She had been robes mistress for many years. One day she emerged from the robing room as I was chatting to a group of American tourists looking at the brass tablet on the wall beside me bearing the names of all the Deans of St Patrick's.

'Ah, here's Miss Shaw,' I announced. 'She's been here for ages. I wonder how many Deans she remembers,' and I started reading from the list: 'I think she even remembers Dean Swift.'

Out stepped a portly lady from the group. 'Honey, let me shake your hand,' she enthused. 'Well, won't this be something to tell the folks back home that I've shaken the hand of someone who knew Dean Swift.' I'm afraid I remained silent. Sometimes it's kinder not to expose innocent error in public.

The Archbishop of Canterbury, Michael Ramsey, visited Dublin in 1975 and preached in St Patrick's Cathedral. A saintly and scholarly man, a formidable theologian but quite indifferent to such ordinary mundane matters as clothes and domestic minutiae. His chaplain requested a bedroom in the Deanery to allow the Archbishop some rest after an early luncheon engagement before going over to the Cathedral for Evensong at 3.15 p.m. Daphne prepared the guest room, enhancing the decor with a selection of books and periodicals which she thought suitable for episcopal perusal. I took the Archbishop to his room, pointed out the bathroom at the end of the corridor and arranged to collect him at 2.45 p.m. Everything went according to plan until Daphne, having ascended by the lift to get ready for Evensong, was horrified on opening our bedroom door to behold Michael, sleeping the sleep of the just, fully stretched out on our bed. What to do? I was hastily summoned and told to tiptoe to the wardrobe at the other side of the bed and retrieve the necessary garments. The wardrobe door squeaked, and the Archbishop twitched as Daphne, from her wheelchair, frantically signalled to me indicating the requisite hat and dress and other items of feminine refinement. To extract the appropriate garments from a wife's wardrobe is not easy at the best of times, but under such conditions, with Daphne gesticulating, mostly in frustrated disapproval of my amateurish efforts, I was reduced to a nervous wreck. However, the Almighty had blessed the Archbishop with the gift of deep sleep. The mission was eventually accomplished satisfactorily, although I did not presume on the Almighty's continued indulgence and gently tiptoed out leaving that squeaking wardrobe door open. Dumping the garments unceremoniously in her lap I gently closed the bedroom door. Daphne changed in the Archiepiscopal bedroom!

Michael always remembered us at Christmas, when not only did he send a card but enclosed a handwritten letter. He showed particular, fatherly concern for Daphne, once devoting a whole hour at a reception to talk to her during a very busy travelling schedule when he must have been exhausted; he had just flown over to London and back again to Dublin after a meeting of the Privy Council with the Queen before returning to the reception held in his honour. Looking around St Patrick's he commented: 'There is a holy austerity about this place. It reminds me of a great cave cut out of a giant rock.' I can still hear his piping staccato voice as after his characteristic vocal hesitation he finally hit on and emphasised the phrases 'holy austerity, great cave, giant rock'. I'm sure he had in mind the Irish and Celtic vision of the power and presence of God in the things of nature: air, sea, sky, rocks and caves.

Archbishop Coggan, Michael Ramsey's successor, also preached in St Patrick's and insisted, in spite of a busy schedule, on visiting Daphne who was in hospital at that time.

Archbishop Runcie, who had the unenviable task of leading the Church of England during difficult and controversial times, brought Terry Waite with him. Terry was supremely self-confident, efficient, knew exactly what he wanted in planning and organisation, enjoyed publicity, was very much at home in the spotlight and with the VIPs. When talking to him I got the impression he was always two steps ahead, that he was not really listening but had other more important things or people on his mind, as perhaps he had. When I asked him at the reception in the Deanery if it would be in order for me to present the Archbishop with some Malton prints of Dublin to mark his visit, Terry thought it better that he should take the prints and give them informally to the Archbishop. Doubtless this was done, although I must admit I was surprised and annoyed on receiving a letter from the Archbishop on his return to Lambeth to find no mention of the Malton prints. It was simply a case of hurt pride and I soon realised that with so many gifts and tokens presented by so many churches and organisations in any Archiepiscopal visit, some are bound to be overlooked and I hasten to say I blame no one for this omission. Terry as a hostage has been a shining example to us all of Christian faith, fortitude and forgiveness. We prayed constantly for his safe release and rejoiced when we heard the good news of his freedom.

With increasing ecumenical rapprochement there came requests from musical groups and charity organisations for permission to use the Cathedral for fund-raising concerts. Times have indeed changed since Swift's day when it was not considered fitting to perform secular music in the House of God. Swift, ever his own man, was severely censured for organising an annual St Cecilia's Day concert in St Patrick's. With his tongue in his cheek he poked fun at his critics:

> Grave Dean of St Patrick's and how comes it to pass
> that you who know music no more than an ass
> That you who once was found writing of Drapers,
> should lend your Cathedral to players and Scrapers
> To act such an opera once in a year
> is offensive to every true protestant ear.
> With trumpets and fiddles and organs and singing,
> t'will sure the Pretender and Popery bring in.
> No Protestant Prelate, His Lordship or Grace
> should there show his Right or Most Reverend face.
> How would it pollute their Croziers and Rochets
> to listen to minims and quavers and crochets.

Today, both secular music and applause are heard in the Cathedral. Congregations have also occasionally applauded sermons. Brian Hannon, Bishop of Clogher, who preached at the Memorial Service for those killed in the 1987 Enniskillen bombing, received a standing ovation and to my great surprise, and completely out of the blue, the congregation stood and applauded me after my farewell sermon as Dean.

Andrew Lloyd Webber came with Sarah Brightman to attend the Irish premiere of his *Requiem* in the Cathedral, and James Galway gave a recital. James Last and his wife, a charming couple who seemed genuinely pleased to spend time with us in the Deanery, were very popular visitors with Daphne and the boys. The recording the James Last Orchestra made with the Choir of St Patrick's earned the Choir a Golden Disc award. I like to think that Swift would have approved of this achievement by the present-day successors of his Choir from which he demanded the highest musical standards. Writing to Lady Carteret, who had asked for his help in securing a place in the Choir for a protegé, he replied that: 'If her friend had desired a bishopric and it were in his power to grant it, he would readily comply, because in such preferment merit is in no way concerned, but in the situation of a vicar choral merit would be brought to the test every day.'

In July 1972 a grey-haired, rather frail and stooped visitor from the USSR came to St Patrick's to hear a concert of his music played by the New Irish Chamber Orchestra. He was the distinguished composer Shostakovich, whose work was valued more highly abroad than in his homeland, where the Soviet authorities were suspicious and critical of any artistic work which deviated from their narrow inhibiting Marxist canon. I found him a deeply thoughtful man. He was most appreciative of the manner in which his music was performed in the Cathedral but there was a certain sadness, even hopelessness in his manner, and I sensed a longing in his soul that the day might come in the USSR when composers would enjoy the same freedom as their counterparts in western Europe.

Perhaps the most memorable, and certainly the most moving, recital of all for me was that which Mitislav Rostropovitch gave for Daphne in 1977. He had called in the Deanery on the morning of his recital in St Patrick's and regretted that because of her illness and the inclement weather she could not attend. As the recital took place in Lent, Rostropovitch, a devout member of the Russian Orthodox Church, suggested a particular Lenten menu for his customary meal immediately after the performance. While the guests whom we had invited to a reception to meet the maestro after the concert assembled, Daphne served up the Lenten fare in an adjoining room with Rostropovitch protesting that he would have gladly dined in the kitchen to make things easier for her. Such was the calibre of the man, a musical genius but also a great humanitarian, acutely sensitive to the needs of others, whose greatness combined genius with humility. He then brought his 'cello into the large Deanery room, overlooked by portraits of Swift and former Deans, and to the surprise and delight of all, announced that since Daphne had missed the Cathedral recital, he had decided to give another here in the Deanery especially for her. He began by introducing his 'cello which had once belonged to Napoleon, pointing out the scratch made by one of Napoleon's spurs which had accidentally grazed it, an imperial imprimatur! He then placed Daphne in her wheelchair directly in front of him and for half an hour the haunting mellow strains of Napoleon's cello filled the Deanery.

We had arranged the usual 'stand up, chat and drinks' type of reception and had cleared the room of any surplus furniture, including nearly all the chairs. Our guests, including President and Mrs Hillery, the Provost of Trinity, Leland Lyons, and his wife Jennifer, diplomats, music professors, critics and others prominent in arts and literature, promptly dismissed my suggestion to wait for chairs to be provided and the chairless settled themselves on the floor. I am sure past Deans gazing down from their portraits had never witnessed anything like this: what has St Patrick's come to with guests sitting on the floor? We had in our midst a world-renowned cellist and the night when Rostropovitch played in the Deanery shall always remain a treasured memory. Doubtless Swift, and Carolan who played the harp for him in the same Deanery 250 years previously, were also present in spirit and nodding approvingly.

Dame Ruth King, formerly Ruth Railton, who founded the National Youth Orchestra of Great Britain, was responsible for Rostropovitch's visit to Dublin. She had taken him under her wing when he arrived in England, a penniless refugee from Stalinist Russia. Dame Ruth now lives in Dublin and her keen interest in St Patrick's and its music prompted the invitation to the Cathedral which he willingly and gladly accepted.

Internationally famed musicians of a rather different style, the members of U2, attended the Cathedral for the christening of a friend's baby. Their lead singer, Paul Hewson (Bono), had been a pupil at St Patrick's Grammar School for a time. He brought along his movie camera and filmed the whole ceremony.

I once showed the Rev. Ian Paisley round St Patrick's. Not surprisingly, he lingered beside King William's chair in the Lady Chapel behind the High Altar, the chair in which King Billy sat when he came to St Patrick's to give thanks to God for his victory over King James at the Battle of the Boyne. Although I did not see eye to eye with Dr Paisley in Northern Ireland and had been taken to task along with other ecumenists in his *Protestant Telegraph*, he greeted me as a long-lost friend, was interested in my family, especially Kevin the garda, whom he had sought out and spoken to at the Peter Robinson trial in Dublin.

The memorial tablet which Swift erected over Schomberg's tomb intrigued him. Schomberg, who was King William's commander-in-chief, was killed at the Boyne and buried in St Patrick's. Having made numerous unsuccessful approaches by letters and friends to the Schomberg family suggesting the erection of a memorial to their illustrious father, Swift decided to do so himself, adding a Latin inscription to the effect that 'at least you stranger may know where the earthly remains of Schomberg lie buried. The renown of his valour won greater praise from strangers than from his own kith and kin.' On hearing this, the Schomberg family were enraged. Who did the Dean of St Patrick's think he was, not only erecting a memorial without the family's consent but tarnishing the family honour by an acerbic inscription! Legal proceedings were instigated and dragged on and on, to the lawyers' benefit, until finally petering out without a verdict.

Some years ago I chanced to meet in the Cathedral a descendant of Schomberg who was compiling a history of the family and had made the journey to St Patrick's to take a photograph of the memorial. I asked him if he was aware of the altercation with Swift.

'Yes', he replied, 'the prolonged dispute with Swift is well documented.'

'How did it end?'

'I really don't know. I think the jury is still out,' he commented jocularly and added that as a gesture of reconciliation I might like to visit the Schomberg Castle, now a hotel on the Rhine, as his guest.

James Lovell, Jack Swigert and Fred Haise were American astronauts who set off in Apollo 13 in 1970. Space travel was then very much a novelty and their progress made headline news. Suddenly something went wrong with the scheduled mission and the three were marooned in their space capsule with the possibility of not being able to return to earth. I felt we should do something and decided to hold an all-night prayer vigil in the Cathedral for the astronauts' safe return. The American ambassador, together with the Embassy staff, were among the many who attended for periods during the night. On 17 April the Apollo 13 crew landed safely by parachute.

Our prayer vigil, a unique response as far as I know to the astronauts' plight, was reported in the American press, and Lovell, Swigert and Haise came all the way to St Patrick's to show their appreciation. They presented me with a framed photograph of the tiny, fragile-looking capsule descending to earth at dawn between gigantic, dark greenish clouds, buoyed up by three billowing parachutes. The dedication beneath is to Dean Griffin 'who reached for us in the remoteness of space'.

A memorial in the Cathedral to the Rt Hon. George Ogle, an eighteenth-century Member of Parliament, surely must take the prize for eulogy. The man was apparently endowed with every virtue under heaven, the perfect politician held in universal esteem having 'incorruptible integrity, brilliant talents, ardent patriotism, suavity of manners, scrupulous sense of honour, steadiness of friendship . . . the perfect model of that exalted refinement which in the best days of our country characterised the Irish gentleman' and more — much more.

From time to time politicians from the Northern Ireland Office, when in Dublin, came to visit St Patrick's. Nicholas Scott was one of them. Fascinated by the Ogle memorial, he requested a copy of the wording to send to his then most famous con-stituent in Chelsea to whom he thought it might be of particular interest. I presume that Margaret Thatcher kept it somewhere in her files as a stimulus to emulate Ogle's remarkable record.

I first met Tyrone Guthrie in Derry when he spoke at a meeting on Ulster drama. In 1969 he came to Dublin to direct a new play for the Abbey Theatre by Eugene McCabe about Swift, in which Mícheál Mac Liammóir took the leading role. Guthrie, who was well versed in Swift and his times, visited the Deanery with Mícheál to get the feel of the place. He was a towering man mentally as well as physically, a colossus of the theatre, and had also about him 'that exalted refinement which in the best days of our country characterised the Irish gentleman'.

Tyrone was particularly considerate to Daphne in her wheelchair, and had long conversations on the subject of disablement and what needed to be done to facilitate greater participation by disabled persons in the life of the community. Although he invited me to visit him at his home in Annaghmakerrig, Co. Monaghan, I was alas never able to find the time to take up the invitation before his sudden death.

My first opportunity to visit Annaghmakerrig came in 1987 when I had a preaching engagement in Kilmore, Co. Cavan. My good friend, Herbert Cassidy, then Dean of Kilmore, and I drove over to Co. Monaghan and with some difficulty located the isolated house. The warden emerged as we drew up and as soon as I stepped out of the car he recognised me, although I was not wearing a clerical collar.

'You're Dean Griffin from St Patrick's,' he said.

'How did you know?' I enquired.

'I have your photo here in the house with Tyrone Guthrie.' It had been taken while Guthrie was in the Deanery working on the play.

Mícheál Mac Liammóir and Hilton Edwards attended St Patrick's with Tyrone Guthrie, Eugene McCabe and the Abbey cast for a special service on the Sunday preceding the opening of the play. Also present was dear Christine Longford, always so kind and unassuming, with a literary talent which belied her small stature.

Mícheál and Hilton were always happy to come to St Patrick's and give appropriate readings on special occasions such as Advent and Lent. They were passionate defenders of the traditional Anglican liturgy, maintaining that the Book of Common Prayer and the Authorised (King James) Version of the Bible were among the greatest treasures of the English language and should never be tampered with. They inveighed against those who had cheapened and trivialised the liturgy, stripping it of reverence, mystery, poetry and drama. I remember Hilton quoting in rich tones from the burial service: '"Man that is born of a woman hath but a short time to live. He cometh up and is cut down like a flower. He fleeth as it were a shadow and never continueth in one stay . . . " Isn't that wonderful? Imagine being buried to some journalistic concoction of third-rate minds.'

There have been some notable memorial and funeral services in St Patrick's. At the service for Christopher Ewart Biggs, murdered by the IRA a few days after taking up residence as British Ambassador, the address was given by Garret FitzGerald, then the Republic's Foreign Minister.

Erskine Childers' funeral was a major State occasion requiring precise organisation. It was as usual in the capable hands of my Vicar, Canon Cecil Bradley, who I can safely say is without equal in the Church of Ireland, and perhaps wider afield, for meticulously planning processions which start exactly on time. Everyone knows exactly what to do and when to do it and 'all is done reverently and in order'. It all seems so natural and spontaneous that one is never conscious of the many hours of detailed planning which have gone on behind the scenes. Someone has said that nothing is more difficult to organise than a clutch of clergy but Cecil Bradley has found the secret.

Together with the Taoiseach and Government, members of the Oireachtas and judiciary, Church leaders and representatives of every facet of Irish life, urban and rural, social and economic, there was present in St Patrick's for the funeral of President Childers in 1974 the biggest assembly of foreign dignitaries ever to visit the Republic. The royal families of Belgium and Britain were represented by King Baudouin and Earl Mountbatten. Prime Ministers came from Britain, France, Belgium and Luxembourg. Mr Harold Wilson, the British Premier, was accompanied by Mr Edward Heath, leader of the Conservative party. The Lesson was read by the Taoiseach, Mr Liam Cosgrave. How times had changed since 1949 when the government felt unable to be present in the Cathedral for the funeral of President Douglas Hyde because of the Roman Catholic regulations then in force forbidding attendance at Protestant services.

Little did we think that within five years another large and distinguished congregation would be present in St Patrick's for the memorial service for Lord Mountbatten, murdered by the IRA in Mullaghmore, Co. Sligo. The President, Dr Patrick Hillery, the Taoiseach, Mr Jack Lynch, members of the Government, the Council of State, the judiciary and diplomatic corps attended the ecumenical service at which Cardinal O Fiaich and Archbishop Simms, the Church of Ireland Primate, gave a joint blessing.

Cecil King, one time controversial editor of the *Daily Mirror*, worshipped regularly in St Patrick's with his wife, Dame Ruth, when they retired to live in Dublin. Cecil had contacts throughout the entire political spectrum, and I spent many happy and informative evenings in their home, picking Cecil's acute political brain and listening to his incisive comments on politicians past and present. Being interested in every conceivable political point of view, Cecil King knew and indeed developed friendly relationships with people like Ian Paisley and Daithi O'Connell, who were generally regarded as representing politically the two opposite extremes. The wide range of his contacts, internationally and nationally, in journalism and politics was evident at his funeral service in St Patrick's, when amongst the many distinguished people present there were, seated in the front seats, facing the coffin of Cecil King, Ian Paisley of the DUP, Gerard Brady of Fianna Fáil, Nicholas Fenn, the British Ambassador, and Daithi O'Connell of Sinn Féin! Where, I thought, could this happen but in Ireland!

We had our times of sorrow but also times of gladness, when we welcomed amongst others the Grand Duke and Duchess of Luxembourg, the Mayor of Moscow, Metropolitan Philaret of Kiev (who presented St Patrick's with an ikon which is now in the sanctuary), Senator Hubert Humphrey and his wife and, from nearer home, Douglas Hurd, Chris Patten, politicians, diplomats and officials from the countries in the EC.

Probably my most embarrassing moment was when we had invited the French Ambassador and his wife to afternoon tea in the Deanery. Lending a helping hand I laid out all the 'goodies' on a folding-leaf coffee table but unfortunately omitted to secure the clip firmly. On placing another plate on the surface, horror of horrors, the top upended, depositing everything on the carpet. Gulliver, our large crossbred Labrador/Red Setter saved the day. Madame Ambassador adored dogs and, having previously seen and admired Gulliver in the garden, had made me promise that after tea he would be admitted to join the party. He was immediately summoned and while the Ambassador, his good lady and myself, on all fours, merrily fed a delighted tail-wagging Gulliver with mouth-watering delectables, Daphne replenished the table, this time securely fastened. A diplomatic diffusion of a delicate situation.

When the Kirov Ballet from Leningrad, now St Petersburg, came to Dublin in 1986, I received a phone call from the USSR Embassy saying that the Kirov would like to visit St Patrick's. They wished, in particular, to hear the Choir. Accordingly, I arranged a visit to coincide with the singing of Matins by the boy choristers at 9.45 a.m. The conductor and members of the orchestra also came along and our choirboys had a field day collecting autographs after the service. With the aid of an interpreter I gave a short talk on the history of the Cathedral and its place in Irish Christianity today. The following day two complimentary tickets for the performance of *Swan Lake* were delivered to the Deanery, and when Daphne and I arrived at the mammoth canvas arena pitched in the grounds of the RDS we were not only favoured with front centre stage seats but also invited at the interval to go backstage and meet the dancers. They gave us a rousing reception, and presented me with a fine artistic drawing of their prima ballerina in full flight. They also extended a warm invitation to visit the Kirov should I again go to Leningrad.

Some years before, in 1983, I had visited the USSR as a member of the Irish-USSR Friendship Society. While food was basic, with choice sparse in the citizens' restaurants and consumer goods in short supply in the shops, the streets were clean and the people friendly and helpful; so much so, that one evening when I and another member of our party, a Corkman, lost our way and only with great difficulty eventually made the name of our hotel known to some bystanders, they immediately walked with us to the appropriate bus stop about half a mile away, stopped the next bus and told the driver where to let us off. Then with smiles and handshakes all around, we wished each other well. From Leningrad we travelled to Estonia, Latvia and Lithuania. Even then, there was a palpable sense of national identity in these Baltic States and a yearning for independence, with more evidence of western European influence than in Leningrad or Moscow. In Moscow we stayed in the huge Cosmos Hotel, commuted on the marble and marvellous underground, visited Red Square and St Basil's Cathedral. In the Kremlin the three Cathedrals — of the Annunciation, the Assumption and St Michael — had restricted admission by ticket after a long wait. As we were on a tight schedule I and my Cork friend advanced on the door-keeper and by incessant pleading, invoking the name of Patrick and the Irish, tried to explain that we had come from afar and pointed to our watches to indicate that our time was limited. After repeated refusals he relented to the perseverance or obstinacy of the Irish and we were admitted. Three things are immediately obvious on entering a Russian Cathedral.

Firstly, the interior is smaller than its exterior height would suggest, much smaller than comparable cathedrals in western Europe, and surprising too, considering the immense size of the country. The only exception is the Cathedral of St Isaac in Leningrad.

Secondly, there are no seats, and the Ikonostasis or Ikonscreen separating the sanctuary (heaven) from the nave (earth) dominates the building. The Orthodox liturgy behind the screen reflects the unceasing worship of the hosts of heaven in all its majesty, beauty and richness. The worshipper is given a momentary glimpse of heaven and caught up in the celestial adoration of the Triune God.

Thirdly, while the liturgy proceeds, worshippers come and go, standing in adoration, transported to heaven before returning to earth. Orthodox Christians make the Sign of the Cross from right to left, right slightly higher than left, unlike Latin Christians. This, I am told, depicts the triumph of good over evil, of Christ over the devil. The right hand side symbolises for the Orthodox that which is good and the left that which is evil. The essence of the Orthodox liturgy is the foretaste of heaven while still on earth.

My only other excursion behind what was then known as the Iron Curtain was to Hungary in 1985. There, partnered by a luscious Hungarian blonde provided for the event, I won the competition for dancing the chardis in a Budapest night club, one of the items on our tour schedule. As they say: is this a record? While in Hungary I was also introduced to a popular local red wine, Bull's Blood, so called, it was said, by the Turkish invaders whose Islamic faith prohibited alcohol. They fooled their more zealous Mohammedan officers by pretending that the beverage was the blood of bulls and that Hungarian bulls had a unique intoxicating potency!

But to return to Dublin and St Patrick's. I decided that we should have an annual lecture on Swift and wrote to Michael Foot, one of Swift's most fervent admirers. Michael accepted and duly arrived, complete with sturdy walking stick, anorak and an enormous bundle of Sunday papers which he had perused on the flight to Dublin. Speaking without a note, with true Swiftian eloquence and directness, he held forth to a packed Cathedral on the challenge of Swift to statesmen and politicians today, and afterwards confided that he found it a greater ordeal to face the congregation from the pulpit of St Patrick's than to face the House of Commons from the Opposition Front Bench. Michael makes a point of attending the annual Swift Seminar in Celbridge Abbey, home of Vanessa, and we have together taken the floor — or the stage — to perform a 'Swiftian duet', giving voice to the various facets of this enigmatic and inexhaustible genius who still grips the attention of students of politics and human behaviour from all over the world.

It was Denis Johnston who first stimulated my interest in Swift. A tall, impressive, grey-headed and slightly stooped figure, he regularly attended Evensong with his wife, Shelah Richards, on Sundays in St Patrick's. He recommended books, commented on sermons, appreciated the sense of history and the dignified choral worship in St Patrick's. Friendly, constructive, a good listener, Denis was a receptive and humble man in spite of his renowned literary achievements. We laid him to rest in the Cathedral graveyard in the heart of the Dublin Liberties, not far from Swift and on his tombstone, adjacent to that of Lennox Robinson, are inscribed as an appropriate finale some words from his *The Old Lady says No*:

> Strumpet city in the sunset
> So old, so sick with memories
> Old Mother
> Some they say are damned
> But you, I know, will walk the streets of Paradise
> Head high and unashamed.

14

Dublin in Crisis

W HEN I returned to Dublin in 1969, what a change during those twenty-two years absence from the city! Whole streets in the centre had disappeared or were serrated by dilapidated buildings and derelict rubbish-strewn sites. The inner city was being denuded of life and all this, I was informed, in the interests of road widening. The motor car had taken over, and the intention of the planners, as far as I could see, was to create major carriageways, leading to multi-storey office buildings, surrounded by parking areas, an unholy trinity, as I called it, of wide roads, office blocks and car parks.

Before the mid seventies there really was no general awareness of what was taking place or of the need to preserve our heritage. A few brave voices, such as that of Deirdre Kelly, protested at the destruction of Dublin but the property speculators and road engineers were undeterred. There was also a political dimension. Why preserve the relics, the reminders of the Anglo-Irish Establishment, Georgian or Victorian, in this newly created independent State? Better to demolish and replace by something more in keeping with Irish culture. Anglo-Irish must be replaced by Gaelic. There was no question of co-existing or being mutually enriching. Authentic Irishness was exclusive, not inclusive. Brits out!

So until the Wood Quay controversy in 1978 there really was no widespread interest in preserving our architectural or archaeological heritage. Wood Quay was a watershed. Only then did people become alarmed at the destruction of Dublin and decide that it was time to call a halt.

In 1985 a number of us who were concerned at the deteriora-
tion of the city met together and arranged a conference, the
Dublin Crisis Conference, which was held in February 1986 in
the old Synod Hall. We met in Larry Dillon's house in the
Coombe and also present were Frank McDonald, Deirdre and
Aidan Kelly, Mick Rafferty, David Norris and Donal Storey.

The theme was, 'What's wrong with Dublin — why it's wrong
and what can be done about it?' At the conference we had a
large and representative attendance. For the first time people
from interested environmental groups from all over the city
came together and major recommendations emerged. The findings of that conference and the enthusiasm which was apparent
received wide publicity and support. First of all, it was made
very clear that the planners must never again be allowed to
play God. Before putting pencil to paper they should invite the
participation of the local community to consult and discuss. In
other words, first trust the people. No more should the citizens be
confronted with a readymade plan and subsequent objections
steamrolled. There was strong emphasis on the need for a system
of adequate public transport to take precedence over private cars.

At the concluding session, which was addressed by Garret
FitzGerald, then Taoiseach, and Mr Frank Feely, the City Man-
ager, I as Chairperson summed up the main findings: the creation of an attractive urban environment for people to reside,
shop, enjoy their leisure in the city; provision of care and facilities
for minority groups, the disabled, the unemployed, the travelling people; extensive pedestrianisation, suitable and sufficient
play areas for the children. In the inner city there are a number
of attractive garden parks but a dearth of recreation spaces in
which children can kick a ball. This encourages vandalism which
is also prompted by a rash of run-down buildings. Destruction
inculcates a destructive mentality. The Iveagh Baths in the
Liberties, having been denied proper maintenance and allowed
to deteriorate by the Corporation, were eventually closed. Other
points emerged from our discussion groups:

> The place of the juggernaut is not careering along a dual
> carriageway in the inner city belching pollution in all

directions, noise as well as fumes. Its place is on a ring road. To object to dual carriageways in the inner city is not to resist progress. In the inner city there must be roads of a reasonable width, but not dual carriageways, bisecting and destroying communities, sucking in additional traffic, resulting in the end in increased congestion and pollution worsened by the 'stop-go' of numerous traffic lights. People are embodied in buildings, which are part and parcel of themselves. Therefore to uproot people and lay waste their community in the interest of road widening is to deprive them of part of themselves. It is a sin against people. It is a breaking of their hearts. Where we have to demolish let us make sure that what we erect in replacement will be in keeping with the character of the area and not some hideous architectural eyesore. The tragedy is that so much demolition has simply been for the purpose of road widening. The old High Street has now virtually disappeared and it is ironic to find the Vikings who founded the city being commemorated in the High Street (St Audoen's) where visitors to the exhibition are immediately confronted with an intersection of dual carriageways, derelict sites and decaying deserted houses. No High Street, no appearance of a city.

As for the quays, which should have been one of the noblest features of the city, they have been desecrated by bulldozers or uglified by neglect. While some parts of the city are well maintained, there is this insidious idea that we can make up for dereliction and destruction and dual carriageways by planting shrubs and flower beds here and there. Dublin has been the victim of a small-town or suburban mentality in planning — flower beds and offices in the centre with people commuting on dual carriageways in their private cars from their suburban houses.

I believe the Crisis Conference and its subsequent report and follow up made a significant contribution to new thinking on the environment by the authorities.

The proposal to construct a dual carriageway outside the West Front of St Patrick's was first brought to my attention by

Frank McDonald of the *Irish Times*. Whether by accident or design, the proposed scheme was not prominently advertised in the press. I went to the City Hall, where an appeals tribunal was in progress to deal with objections by those who had received Compulsory Purchase Orders for property along the proposed route. I was relieved to find that no such CPO had been served on St Patrick's! However, the matter had grave and frightening implications for the Cathedral. Apparently the planners had never seriously considered the possibility of damage to the Cathedral's foundation and fabric by an increased traffic flow along a 90 feet wide carriageway, or the added risk to the safety of our children and schools by the resultant pollution of the immediate environment, including noise pollution. I drew up a submission to the Corporation setting out in detail these and other relevant points and suggested an alternative 'one-way' traffic system for the area which would facilitate a pedestrianisation of that portion of Patrick Street immediately outside the Cathedral and Choir School. This was promptly rejected by the planners, who assured me that the experts on such matters were completely satisfied that no harm would result to the Cathedral's foundation or fabric by increased traffic flow and vibration. How on earth, I wondered, could any expert predict, be he ever so competent, what might or might not happen to a building which had stood intact for 800 years when suddenly subjected to the incessant pounding of heavy traffic on its perimeter? However, the planners were determined to have their way and the Corporation ready to rubber stamp their recommendations.

I decided we would have to fight this to the bitter end. We held street protest meetings and I took to the soap box and megaphone outside the Cathedral, after which on one Monday evening, led by a Liberties bagpiper, a vast concourse of Liberties dwellers and supporters from all over the city (Ulick O'Connor was present to add his voice and encouragement) and members of the Dublin Crisis Committee, converged on the City Hall to lobby the members of the Corporation. More speeches were made. TV cameras were present and our cause received national publicity. Noel Carroll, the Corporation's PRO, referred to us as 'articulate loudmouths', resisting progress and refusing to face reality. We had some wholehearted supporters in the Corporation, such as Alderman Carmencita Hederman, but the pro dual carriageway faction were in the majority and the Corporation, in spite of protests, letters to the press and local feeling in the Liberties, appeared intent on going ahead with their road plans. The planners were unmoved. They knew better than the citizens. They were the experts. The Corporation believed this and trusted them. At this stage, when all seemed lost, I decided to appeal to Charles Haughey, leader of Fianna Fáil, who had at that time a majority in the Dublin Corporation. I remembered that I had willingly agreed some months before to a suggestion by Mr Haughey that a scene from a TV video production, 'Charles Haughey's Ireland', might feature the historic Deanery as a venue for a conversation between the two of us on the contribution made by Swift and other Protestant patriots to Ireland. The film had a wide circulation and I received some feedback, not all complimentary, for some were critical of my alleged support of Charles Haughey and Fianna Fáil. I might add that I would have been equally willing to appear with any other political leader in conversation in the Deanery had a similar request been made.

On the maxim that 'one good turn deserves another', I picked up the phone and rang Mr Haughey, who listened carefully as I put my case and he promised to try and achieve a mutually acceptable solution. On the following Monday the Corporation, with the support of the Fianna Fáil members, decided to reconsider the question of the dual carriageway. Shortly afterwards I was invited by Mr Haughey to his home in Kinsealy, and when I arrived with Arthur West, our engineer, and Trevor Matthews representing the Cathedral Board, officials of the various planning departments were present, together with Mr Bertie Ahern. Mr Haughey had prepared meticulously for the meeting. An imposing, large-scale, well-constructed and accurate model of Cathedral and dual carriageway occupied centre floor in the spacious room. We all gathered round and the pros and cons were discussed. All were anxious to reach agreement and put an end to public confrontation. Eventually Mr Haughey produced the compromise by removing from the model the section of the dual carriageway outside the Cathedral and Choir School and suggesting a narrower road at a distance of forty-five feet from the existing Cathedral railings, with the intervening space to be pedestrianised or treated in a manner in keeping with the Cathedral's environs. Other related matters, such as limited traffic access to the Close, were agreed. I attempted to raise the question of reducing the width of the Clanbrassil Street carriageway but this was ruled out by Mr Haughey, who insisted we confine our attention to Patrick Street.

However, due to continuing local pressure, the Clanbrassil carriageway was eventually reduced in width from ninety to sixty feet. I was in the Gallery when the amended Patrick Street proposal came before the Corporation. It was a stormy meeting. Feelings ran high. Accusations were flung across the chamber: 'Who does Mr Haughey think he is? Who is running this City, the Corporation or Charlie Haughey and Dean Griffin? Are all future decisions to be made in Kinsealy?' Whatever the procedural rights or wrongs may have been, I shall always be grateful to Mr Haughey for his intervention and his determination to safeguard St Patrick's Cathedral. Were we witnessing the end of the old era when public bodies, corporations and councils, accepted without adequate scrutiny the recommendations of their planning 'experts' and simply applied the rubber stamp? If so, our protest and the efforts of the lone courageous voices crying in the wilderness for many years, such as Deirdre and Aidan Kelly, were not in vain.

15

Inflammatory Words

A s DEAN of St Patrick's, with twenty-two years in Northern Ireland behind me, I had no hesitation in making certain points. For example:

* 'For Christian reconciliation to be achieved in this land, changes will have to be made, not only in the North but in the South. Here in the Republic we must set about cleaning up our own backyard instead of always looking over the wall and in a smug, self-satisfied way pouring scorn on what we find distasteful in our neighbour's.'
* 'We must admit that the Unionists do have a point of view which we must recognise and try to understand. In any new political arrangement the Unionist tradition must be accepted and respected. *Irishness* must be inclusive and transcend religion and politics.'
* 'Simplistic solutions advanced by Southern politicians who have no direct experience of the Northern situation are wide of the mark and can be dangerous.'
* 'We must rid ourselves of the dominant position of the Roman Catholic Church or of any Church in the affairs of State. Home rule must not be Rome rule.'

These were inflammatory words in 1969 and the early seventies. I was immediately in the firing line. Critical and hurtful letters, private and public, were written, the telephone sizzled, threats were made to blow up St Patrick's and anonymous letters informed me that I was on the hit list for assassination! I was accused of being anti-Irish, anti-Republican, anti-Roman Catholic, a Protestant bigot, and told to take myself and my family back to

Northern Ireland where I would be more at home with my Orange friends. Some of the more critical letters were written by members of the Church of Ireland. One I remember from a bank official in the Midlands attacked me viciously as an 'Orange bigot' and accused me of endangering the very existence of Protestantism in the Republic.

But there was also substantial support from right across the religious divide, from Roman Catholics who favoured a more liberal and tolerant approach in matters political and ecclesiastical, from concerned Church of Ireland members (mostly laity), and other Protestants, from members of the Jewish community and those who professed no religion. I must mention sterling support from people like Catherine McGuinness, David Norris, Michael Solomons, Mervyn Taylor, Michael D. Higgins, Seán Mac Réamoinn, Terence McCaughey, Noel Browne, John de Courcy Ireland, Douglas Gageby, Jim Kemmy, Alan Browne, Kevin Nowlan, the late Hubert Butler, Leland Lyons, Theo Moody, Sheehy Skeffington, W.B. Stanford, Charles McCarthy. All felt that we must move to a more open, tolerant and pluralist society with due respect for the many traditions which have made us what we are. We must move away from Irish exclusiveness to Irish inclusiveness.

As I write I am thankful that, although there is still some way to go, there is on the whole a greater recognition of the need to change to new attitudes, not only in the North but also in the Republic. Pluralism is no longer a dirty word, and the New Ireland Forum set forth the concept of an inclusive Irishness with recognition and respect for all traditions.

Shortly after I arrived in St Patrick's I was invited to speak at a meeting organised by a group of people who were anxious to hear at first hand about Northern Ireland and its problems. On the platform with me was a brilliant young lawyer, who was also Professor of Constitutional and Criminal Law in Trinity, one Mary Bourke, later Mary Robinson, and now President of Ireland. She impressed me by her cool, calm and penetrating analysis of the Northern Ireland situation and her knowledge and understanding of the issues involved. It was refreshing to know that here was someone who, unlike most of the so-called party political experts with their simplistic solutions, was aware of the complexities of the situation and realised that the Unionists did have a point of view which deserved our recognition and respect. I kept up my contacts with Mary, and in 1982 when she was a candidate for one of the three Trinity Senate seats, I gave her enthusiastic support, was one of her accessors and sent canvassing letters on her behalf to TCD graduates in Northern Ireland and to those known to me in Britain and further afield. To my great delight Mary not only won a seat but headed the poll.

At a subsequent Senate election in 1987 David Norris, an active campaigner on the Dublin Crisis Conference and supporter of St Patrick's, who had taken to the streets with me to protest against the dual carriageway proposal, was a candidate for a Trinity seat in the Senate. He asked me to second his nomination, proposed by Dr Noel Browne. I was very willing to do this as I knew that David had it in him to make an original, eloquent and much-needed contribution to political debate in the Republic.

Of course, I continued to support Mary Robinson, still acting as one of her accessors, for there were three seats, and lists of supporters printed on election addresses would often show a supporter committed to two or, perhaps, three candidates. I gladly gave Mary permission and approval to make full use of the letter I had written in 1982 in her support. When the media discovered that I had seconded David Norris and that Mary Robinson was using in 1987 the letter written by me in 1982, some reporters thought they smelled a rat and had hit on something which would doubtless cause political embarrassment to Mary Robinson. I was asked if I had *actually* signed my name to the re-issue of the original letter and I replied that, with so many documents for signature almost daily in St Patrick's, unless any matter presented some particular difficulty I would automatically sign. Although I could not really remember having signed the re-issued letter, the question was quite irrelevant since it was identical with the original and I had already given total approval to its contents being re-issued and used in support of Mary Robinson's candidature. The fact that I had said, 'I can't remember having signed,' led to some snide insinuations that Mary had taken unilateral action and indeed was being dishonest. This was quite untrue, and I wrote to the press emphasising that Mary had acted with the utmost integrity, that she had my full approval for what she had done and, while on this occasion I was committed to David Norris as my *first* choice, I still supported her and was confident that she would be re-elected, which indeed she was, together with David Norris and Shane Ross, three worthy representatives of Trinity in the Senate. This has taught me a lesson: a lapse of memory truthfully admitted may be seized on to allege an intention to conceal a damaging fact.

During the controversies of the early seventies I had the complete support of the then Archbishop of Dublin, Alan Buchanan, formerly Bishop of Clogher, who knew and understood the North and repeatedly encouraged me by phone calls and letters. The Church of Ireland clergy, apart from those who were members of the Cathedral Chapter and others who had served in Northern Ireland like the Rev. Billy Gibbons, a former curate of mine, were seemingly indifferent to, or unaware of, the important question of the kind of society we wished to have in the Republic. No mention was made in occasional conversation with me about anything I had said. One felt there was a deliberate attempt to avoid the subject. Some clergy doubtless thought I would make the Church of Ireland unpopular with the Roman Catholics. So the majority of the clergy confined their interests to their parishes, kept their heads down, said neither yea nor nay. They simply did not wish to know.

The parochialism of the Church of Ireland was painfully obvious at the time of the Dublin Crisis Conference. I was shocked to discover that most Church of Ireland members in parishes, especially on the outskirts, were totally unaware of the decay of the inner city and had not the remotest idea of the issues involved in the controversy over the proposed dual carriageway outside St Patrick's Cathedral. The narrow 'I'm all right Jack' attitude reigned supreme. Their vision extended no further than the parish boundary. The Dublin Corporation did not include even one member of the Church of Ireland, a telling indictment of the lack of civic spirit amongst the majority of Church members. Thankfully, there were a few praiseworthy exceptions. At every available opportunity I urged Church of Ireland youth to take a greater interest in politics and public life, instead of opting out like little Jack Horners.

A young man, Trevor Matthews, was a member of the Cathedral Board and also a Fianna Fáil party activist. He was selected as one of the Fianna Fáil candidates in a local government election, and I willingly gave him a character reference and wished him well. Some time later large headlines appeared in the press announcing: 'Dean Griffin supports Fianna Fáil candidate.' True, he was Fianna Fail and a good candidate. But my aim was to encourage young Church of Ireland members to enter the political arena, and it really didn't matter to me to which political party they gave their allegiance. Messages by phone and letter denounced me as being disloyal to the ministry of the Church of Ireland by becoming involved in party politics. A prominent Church of Ireland layman lectured me on the inappropriateness of any clergyman supporting in public any particular candidate in any election. I replied that I trusted he had written in similar vein to bishops and other clergy who seemed to have no hesitation in allowing their names to be printed on lists of supporters of particular candidates in the Senate elections. I received no reply.

At times it seemed to me that the Church of Ireland was scared stiff of controversy. There was an attitude of complacency or resignation. There was one issue, however, which touched the hearts of all Protestants in the Republic — the future of the Adelaide Hospital. The proposal that the 'Protestant' Adelaide should leave Peter Street and become part of a large new hospital planned for Tallaght set the alarm bells ringing. What was to become of the Protestant ethos which respected the privacy and primacy of the doctor-patient relationship, without interference from a hospital ethics committee reflecting the ethical teaching of the Roman Catholic Church? The Protestant position was set out clearly time and time again in Synod, assemblies, committees, by bishops and individuals, lay and clerical.

It was emphasised that on such intimate matters as sterilisation or contraceptive devices and family planning, the person con-erned should have the right to make the decision as to treatment after consultation with medical personnel and, if advisable, with the spouse or immediate family. The Churches, of course, must have the right and opportunity to provide spiritual counselling if sought. Chaplains should be available but the decision must ultimately and conscientiously be taken by the patient.

There was also the question of training Protestant nurses. The Adelaide evokes considerable regard and affection among many who are not members of the Church of Ireland, particularly in the Liberties of Dublin. Its doors are open to all of whatever creed or none. Its emphasis on the direct patient-consultant relationship, with no ethical committee having a veto standing in the wings, has the support and approval of many Roman Catholics who do not see eye to eye with the official teaching of their Church on some sensitive, sex-related matters.

It is sometimes argued that Roman Catholic teaching on sex-related matters is not really sectarian, in that it serves the inter-ests of what is termed 'the common good' of society. At times the concept of 'the common good' is appealed to as a kind of axiom, the truth of which only the morally blind can fail to see, and the notion of the common good in Irish society has strong sexual overtones. But the morality or 'common good' of society cannot be narrowed to the sphere of sexual morality. There is no precise mathematical formula by which to measure the degree of morality in society. No one can logically say that a society which prohibits divorce or sterilisation or abortion under all circumstances has a higher moral tone than one in which such things are permitted with adequate safeguards under certain circumstances. If we are to attempt to make a judgment on the morality of a society or on 'common good', other factors must be taken into account, such as the measure of individual freedom and tolerance, the extent of compassion and caring and the com-mitment to social justice in the community. I believe the primary aims of any society must be to minimise suffering and to max-imise tolerance or, in a word, to exercise compassion and to respect human dignity.

Concentration on questions of sexual morality in Ireland presents a real danger of encouraging in society an attitude in which all morality is reduced to sexual matters, and other vital moral issues such as honesty, business integrity or social justice are regarded as of only secondary importance. The unfortunate result is the general feeling among the populace that there is little to be afraid of or feel guilty about, especially in public life, provided any act of sexual impropriety, as defined by the Church, is avoided or undetected. The credibility of the Christian witness of the Church is undermined by what is seen as an obsession with sexual morality, in that when it seeks to give guidance on other moral and social issues its views may no longer command the respect to which they are entitled.

In the General Synod of 1983 I engaged in some Protestant 'protest' when I launched an attack on the complacency of Dáil Eireann. This resulted in many congratulatory messages and phone calls, not a few highly critical ones from politicians, an editorial in the *Irish Times* and an invitation to lunch in Leinster House with leaders of the Fianna Fáil party — then in opposition — to discuss the whole matter. I had not intended to speak in the Role of the Church debate, but the unsatisfactory economic situation in the country referred to in the report prompted me to advance to the rostrum and hold forth as follows:

The long-suffering people in this Republic are being continually exhorted to make sacrifices and tighten their belts for the common good. But they look in vain for any example of sacrifice in the political leadership of Dáil Eireann. Ample salaries, expense allowances, tax concessions, pensions to sitting TDs, State cars not confined to State purposes but used for party political purposes and for personal and family uses, all this is the order of the day. There is a veritable treasure chest in Dáil Eireann which neither recession nor inflation can diminish. No wonder that parliament is being treated with derision and contempt by a growing number of people, particularly young people. We have in Leinster House too many TDs paid too much for doing too little. . . . The Dáil is a well-paid post for a part-time job. It meets only three days a week and is the most leisurely parliament in Europe today. Until there is a change and a compelling example of leadership and sacrifice at the top, with serious full-time attention given to matters of national interest, all appeals to the hardpressed tax payer for sacrifice and restraint or moderation will fall on deaf ears.

Mrs Gemma Hussey, then Minister for Education, was first into the fray. In a radio interview she described my criticism of politicians as 'ignorant, insensitive and harmful to democracy'. But she was unlucky in the evening newspaper headlines, one of which in large black print announced:

'Hussey says, Dean Griffin is ignorant.'

What Gemma Hussey actually said was that my remarks about the Dáil showed ignorance of the true parliamentary situation but this nuance was entirely lost on the population, particularly in the Liberties, who concluded that the Minister for Education, who should know better, was flinging cheap personal insults at me, and was calling me an ignorant b . . . . . !

Phone calls arrived all that evening from Dublin pubs where the headlines met with such furious and frenzied response that many customers, fortified by alcohol and with a vocabulary to match, insisted on reaching for the phone and telling me in no uncertain terms what they thought of Gemma Hussey. On a few occasions, with abuse reaching new heights — or lows — I tried to cool things down by pointing out that the Minister was not insulting me personally, but was referring only to what I had said, but all to no avail. Gemma was in a 'no win' situation, there was no way of escape. It was the use of the word 'ignorant' which did it: a dangerous word which all politicians should avoid. In the ensuing press correspondence I did not notice even one critical letter: the only time that I received unanimous support from the letter writers!

Fianna Fáil remained silent, except for the invitation to lunch. I enjoyed my lunch with Niall Andrews, Michael Woods and Brian Lenihan. Trevor Matthews came with me and Charles J.

Haughey also joined us for a time. We discussed Dáil reform and I indulged in some political kite-flying. I remember pleading for 'a separation between local government and the Dáil' in the sense that one could choose either but not both. The present duplication whereby TDs can serve as members of county councils or municipal corporations meant that both local and national interests were ill served. There was also the iniquitous situation with the sitting member having to fight not only his political opponents but his own running mate or mates to retain the seat. The sitting deputy was driven to the point of obsession with constituency work with little time for anything else.

I developed my argument. Multi-seater constituencies should be abolished, I said. There should be a smaller Dáil of not more than 100 seats, elected in single seat constituencies on the single transferable vote. Those with political ambitions should have to choose between local and national politics. This would result in both being taken more seriously, would enhance the role of local government and free Dáil deputies from feeling they have always to be involved at parish pump level, right down to the smaller parochial problems. While being of service to their constituents on matters outside the scope of the local councillors, they would have more time to inform themselves on national issues and to make a more constructive contribution to Dáil debates. Of course, there would also have to be an arrangement whereby smaller parties who received a certain percentage of the total national vote, but who failed to have a candidate elected, would be entitled to representation by co-option to the Dáil. This would ensure fair representation for all the electorate.

It was an amicable meeting. They listened sympathetically to what I said and appreciated my remarks to the Synod, doubtless being mindful of the strong support which I had received from all sections of the community. Said the *Irish Times* in an editorial on the 'Uncomfortable Dean':

> . . . all in all, the Dean is doing something that has been enjoined on the Church of Ireland and on Protestants in general in the Republic — that is, speaking up. . . . The Protestants here have been good citizens but mostly not in the

public sphere. They have always been welcome in the Army, in the Gardaí, but have not appeared in numbers proportionate to their representation in the State. In party politics they have almost vanished. It has been said that their talents lie elsewhere but, by and large, they have not said enough and when they have said anything have tended to complain or be mealy-mouthed.

Dean Griffin has spoken up in his own rough-hewn, bantering jocular way. Not all Church of Ireland dignitaries agreed with him. . . . But if the generality of people in the Republic want commitment from — as politicians say now and then — the people of Tone and Emmet and Davis, they are getting it from Dean Griffin.

Perhaps the Adelaide Hospital controversy will arouse Southern Protestants to play a more active part on the political scene, to find a role in the public arena. One thing is certain, Protestant parochialism and indifference, the ostrich-like opting-out of the national scene is the road to extinction. Even if stopping short of total annihilation, the remnant who are left will be irrelevant, without any influence or political clout.

16

Battling for Pluralism

THE Pope arrived in Ireland on 29 September 1979, and we arranged an ecumenical vigil in St Patrick's on that night for peace and reconciliation. It was well attended. We hoped that the Pope would put in an appearance but a crowded and overrun schedule prevented this. However, Cardinal Willebrands, Head of the Vatican Secretariat for Christian Unity, came along, as did Bishop Birch of Ossory and other members of the Irish Roman Catholic hierarchy.

During his visit the Pope condemned the use of violence in Ireland to achieve political ends and also spelt out clearly his opposition to artificial birth control, divorce and abortion. With his conservative Polish background the Pope was concerned about the growing support for change to a more open and pluralist society in the Republic and the increasing readiness to question papal directives on certain moral and theological issues, such as contraception, divorce and the ordination of women. On abortion the Pope had a powerful ally in PLAC, the Pro Life Amendment Campaign founded in April 1981, which ✗ brought together conservative or right-wing Roman Catholics to press for an amendment to the Constitution which would guarantee the right to life of the unborn.

Public opinion was firmly against legalisation of abortion, and no politician had ever suggested such a thing. Yet to rule out the possibility, however remote, of abortion being legalised in certain cases, PLAC demanded a Constitutional amendment completely prohibiting abortion. The instability of government during that period — with three general elections in the space of eighteen months — greatly assisted the efforts of PLAC to ensure

✗ 2 years after the Pope's visit ?

sympathy and support for their proposal from the main political parties, Fianna Fáil and Fine Gael. Labour, while also sympathetic, held that this was not a party matter and should be dealt with by means of a free vote. Dr Michael Woods, Minister for Health in the Haughey administration which was in office from March to December 1982, produced the proposed wording of the Constitutional amendment two days before the collapse of the twenty-third Dáil. Although Dr Garret FitzGerald would have preferred the amendment to be considered with other possible amendments to the Constitution and not taken in isolation, nevertheless the powerful lobby of PLAC extracted a pledge that the new Fine Gael-Labour Coalition Government under the leadership of Garret FitzGerald would introduce legislation to adopt by 31 March 1983 the pro-life amendment published by the outgoing Government. This had the backing of the two largest parties in the Dáil. The Parliamentary Labour Party reserved the right to a free vote on the issue.

The wording of the proposed amendment was:

The State acknowledges the right to life of the unborn and with due regard to the equal right to life of the mother, guarantees in its laws to respect and, as far as practicable by its laws, to defend and vindicate that right.

While the then Minister for Justice, Michael Noonan, said that the Government would consider changes in the wording provided they retained the underlying principle that the practice of abortion should not be permitted to creep into Irish law, Michael Woods for Fianna Fáil defended his party's wording and stated that 'when the amendment was published we were entitled to believe that we had secured the general support and agreement of the Church of Ireland and of the Catholic Church at the highest levels . . . '. Whatever about the agreement of the Church of Ireland 'at the highest levels', I certainly could not agree to the proposed wording, and in a statement to the newspapers in February 1983, I set out my misgivings. This led to an interview with Brian Farrell on the television programme

Today Tonight, innumerable messages by phone and post, mostly congratulatory but some very critical and vindictive, calling me a pro-abortionist, a child of the devil, an angel of death, a Herod advocating the massacre of innocents. I appeared on public platforms as a member of the anti-amendment campaign, including the great concluding rally in Liberty Hall. There were only two Church of Ireland clergy in the anti-amendment campaign, the Rev. Peter Tarleton from Limerick and myself.

Peter was a long-standing friend and admirer of Jim Kemmy, TD, and the three of us occasionally met and lunched together in Dublin during Dáil sittings, for we had many common interests and aspirations. Although some prominent members of the Church of Ireland, such as Catherine McGuinness, Shane Ross, Mary Henry, Trevor West and David Norris, were active in the anti-amendment campaign, many Church of Ireland people were, to say the least, puzzled by statements from Fianna Fáil giving details of three separate meetings involving the Archbishop of Dublin, the Most Rev. Dr McAdoo, with Government representatives while Fianna Fáil was still in office. It was claimed by Fianna Fail that Archbishop McAdoo had accepted the wording but asked for time to consult the Archbishop of Armagh, Most Rev. Dr Armstrong, who was said in turn to have also accepted the wording and expressed gratitude for the efforts made to meet Protestant wishes. Garret FitzGerald, in his autobiography (p. 417), states that 'it has since been confirmed that the draft was shown to and approved by the Church of Ireland Archbishop of Dublin'. Successive Governments, if all this is true, did not understand the workings of the Church of Ireland. Whereas in the Roman Catholic Church, archbishops or the episcopal conference can call the tune and speak on behalf of their Church, in the Church of Ireland the final authority is the General Synod, consisting of the bishops, elected clergy and laity, with its Standing Committee responsible for day-to-day decisions when the Synod is not in session. Knowing the Archbishop very well over the years and having a high regard for his integrity, I can only conclude that he was acting with the full authority and approval of the Standing Committee, and in a laudable effort to avoid unseemly controversy and divisiveness, had approved the wording.

The first public intimation by the Church that any talks on the amendment had taken place was given in a statement by the Standing Committee in November 1982, which said: 'We recognise that an attempt has been made to take account of the complexity of the subject and the views expressed by our own and other Churches.'

Another statement in July 1983 expressed 'appreciation at having been included in the general consultations held by successive governments'. The Archbishop of Armagh further stated in an RTE interview that 'the Church of Ireland had accepted the original wording in the beginning and was very pleased to have been approached by both governments for their opinions'. Meanwhile, there was mounting opposition to the wording, not only by certain committed and loyal members of the Church of Ireland, but by Protestants of other denominations and, more significantly, by a great number of liberal Roman Catholics who were looking to the Church of Ireland and Protestantism in general to give a lead in the anti-amendment campaign.

The Standing Committee, having apparently approved the wording, could only set out certain things to which no one in the Church of Ireland would object, such as repeating the statement made at the Lambeth Conference of 1958 that 'in the strongest terms Christians reject the practice of induced abortion, or infanticide which involves the killing of a life already conceived (as well as a violation of the personality of the mother) save at the dictate of strict and undeniable medical necessity', adding the comments that a Constitutional amendment would not alter the human situation in the country or contribute to its amelioration; and that Constitutional prohibitions were not the way to deal with complex moral and social problems. But there was no examination of the proposed text. Only this morsel of advice: 'given that a referendum is to be held, a responsibility devolves on all citizens to play a full and constructive part in expressing their views on its wording.' Time and time again during the campaign I was accused of being out of step with my own Church. Since my own Church in its Standing Committee was giving no clear lead on the proposed wording, I found it hard to believe that I was out of step. How can one be out of step with a motionless object? On the other hand, from the letters, telegrams and phone calls which I was continually receiving it was obvious that if anyone or any group was out of step with the views of the Church of Ireland it was the Standing Committee. The anti-amendment campaign condemned the proposed wording as sectarian. Indeed, in order to be approved by the Roman Catholic hierarchy, which it was, the wording had to reflect Roman Catholic teaching, so sectarianism was inevitable and inescapable.

It was said by my critics that nowhere did the Standing Committee refer to the wording as sectarian, 'therefore it was not sectarian, according to the Church of Ireland'. This was easily countered by pointing out that nowhere did the Standing Committee examine the wording or pass judgment on it. Silence ruled. It had nothing to say as to whether the wording was sectarian or non-sectarian.

Because of what they had come to believe were dangerous ambiguities in the wording of the amendment, the FitzGerald Government now produced an alternative:

> Nothing in this Constitution shall be invoked to invalidate or to deprive of force or effect a provision of the law on the grounds that it prohibits abortion.

The Standing Committee did say that this was preferable to the original amendment on the grounds that the original wording 'it has been suggested might have to be interpreted by the Courts'. At a time when the possible interpretation of the words was of crucial importance to the Church of Ireland, it grieved me that no clear and explicit lead was forthcoming from the Standing Committee on the ambiguity and implications of the wording. At times during the campaign I felt deserted, shunned, an embarrassment to the Church of Ireland. I remember one letter which stated: 'We all have our crackpots, the RCs have Jeremiah Newman and we have Victor Griffin.' I have developed a thick skin for this sort of thing; so, I'm sure, has Bishop Newman of Limerick.

The Roman Catholic hierarchy opposed the alternative wording, and threw its weight behind the original which was endorsed by the Episcopal Conference in August 1983. Unlike the Church of Ireland, the Roman Catholic leadership did not hesitate to spell out clearly its position and give a lead to its people, as it was perfectly entitled to do. The Church of Ireland was on record throughout the 1970s as advocating a more open, tolerant and pluralist society. Therefore to be true to itself and to the cause it publicly espoused, it should have taken more seriously and more courageously what so many who supported the anti-amendment campaign perceived, and rightly so, to be a threat to the whole idea of pluralism. One Church of Ireland bishop wrote to me giving full support for what I was saying: my good friend Noel Willoughby, Bishop of Cashel and Ossory. A few clergy also wrote in support and one or two in condemnation. They thought I was advocating wholesale abortion on demand! But most backing came from Roman Catholics, priests and people, who wanted our society to move in a more pluralist direction and to have done with any elements of confessionalism in our Constitution. The Church of Ireland laity who took the trouble to inform themselves and examine the situation gave me eager support and encouragement, but sadly it must be admitted that large numbers of Church of Ireland people were totally indifferent, and many were confused by the insidious propaganda labelling all who were against the amendment as pro-abortion, and by the absence of a clear lead from the Standing Committee. The Role of the Church Committee, which dealt with political and social issues, and of which I was a member, congratulated me after one of my TV interviews and expressed unanimous approval of what I had said. This was reported to the media by the Southern Secretary of the Role of the Church Committee, Mr Trevor Matthews, and appeared on RTE news. Within the hour both of us had phone calls from a Church official demanding a withdrawal of the TV report on the grounds that only the Standing Committee had the right to issue reports to the media. This, as we say, was news to me, and since the TV report was simply a statement of what actually happened at a meeting of the Role of the Church Committee and there was no infringement of any pledge of secrecy, we refused point blank to accede to the demand.

The subject was never mentioned again.

Sometimes I think the Church of Ireland is too secretive in its deliberations, unlike the Presbyterian Church where almost everything is open to public knowledge and scrutiny. Doubtless it is necessary for some official body like the Standing Committee to have the authority to issue official statements on behalf of the Church of Ireland, but this policy should in no way inhibit the reporting of views expressed in committees or by committees, particularly if they are intensely relevant to public interest and debate and provided, of course, that secrecy can be resorted to on those rare occasions when it is judged to be in the best interest of all concerned.

In a debate in the Dáil Mr Oliver Flanagan TD referred to me as another Paisley: 'It is enough to have one Paisley in the North without having another down here.' Strange logic, I mused, when Mr Paisley's supporters so often referred to me, while in Derry, as a Fenian, a Lundy, a traitor to the Protestant cause! Other opponents were always on the look out to discredit me, looking for a skeleton in my cupboard. They thought they had found one when a columnist in the *Irish Times* announced that I had been a Unionist member of the Londonderry Corporation! My phone rang incessantly. 'Was this true?' It transpired that the columnist was referring to the Education Committee of the Corporation, on which all the Churches, including the Roman Catholic, were represented. I was one of the two representatives of the Church of Ireland and had decided to propose for the post of Assistant Director of Education a candidate whom I knew was interested, a liberally minded graduate of TCD, athletic, a good sportsman. I was glad that he had applied for I knew he would be well qualified to develop and foster especially the physical side of education, the importance of which was becoming increasingly recognised. I did not know until later that John Hume was also interested in the post, but even had I known it I would not have changed my mind as I was convinced that for this particular post my initial choice was the right one. Incidentally, the candidate was not a member of the Church of Ireland.

The Education Committee incident was seized on as an example of my alleged sectarianism, Orange bigotry and hypocrisy. I was accused of concealing from the public that I had been a Unionist Councillor in the Derry Corporation etc., etc. The *Irish Times* published an apology for getting their facts wrong. I was not after all a Unionist member of the Derry Corporation — indeed I was not a member of the Corporation at all; so much was made clear. Mary Holland then took up the cudgels for me. She wrote to the *Irish Times* telling of a visit to Derry in the sixties when she interviewed one of the young leaders of the Civil Rights Movement 'who was very keen that I should talk to a Church of Ireland clergyman who, he said, had been remarkably outspoken in the early sixties about discrimination in the city and on other contentious issues in a way that was anathema to the Unionist establishment in Derry. The Civil Rights leader was John Hume and the clergyman was Dean Griffin.'

I remember Mary's visit to me in the rectory in Northland Road, my first meeting with her. I have always admired her journalistic skill, integrity and courage. John Hume went on to higher things and the Education Committee episode in no way diminished our friendship.

At the referendum the amendment received the support of 66.45 per cent of those who voted. But only 53.67 per cent of the electorate went to the polls, which meant that of the total electorate in the State only one-third signified their approval of the amendment, and this in spite of the issue being presented as a choice between good and evil, God and Satan. However, the fact that the pro-amendment vote was double the anti-amendment one indicated that there was no intention, at least on the part of the majority, to move in a pluralist direction or to accommodate a minority view. But considering the size of the anti-amendment vote and the very large number of abstentions, in spite of misrepresentation of the anti-amendment case as tantamount to advocating child murder, the result, I wrote, 'is not without some grounds for hope that one day the Republic will move towards a more open and tolerant society affording mutual respect and recognition to all, majority and minority alike'.

Three years later there followed the divorce referendum. While the Church of Ireland has always been committed to the sanctity of marriage, it recognises the fact that in some cases marriages do break down irretrievably and that the State has a duty to recognise and deal with such situations. There are circumstances in which divorce may be the lesser of two evils. The marriage may be dead. The Church of Ireland therefore supported the removal from the Constitution of the prohibition on divorce. In May 1986 the Dáil and Seanad passed the requisite legislation for a referendum to seek an amendment which would remove the Constitutional ban on divorce. Polling day was set for Thursday, 26 June. The Roman Catholic hierarchy came out strongly against divorce. Supporters of the amendment were often accused of advocating divorce 'at the drop of a hat' and there was the scare about property rights, all of which resulted in the rejection of the amendment by a 63 per cent majority. While the Roman Catholic Church gave a clear lead in pastoral letters and episcopal utterances, as it was once more perfectly entitled to do, the Church of Ireland failed to spell out clearly to its members that this, like the abortion referendum, was a crucial issue for the cause of pluralism in society, a cause which the Church of Ireland in Synod and Committees had repeatedly espoused. No pastoral letter was forthcoming from our bishops. Some Church of Ireland members fell victim to the dirty campaign which labelled those who wished to remove the Constitutional prohibition as being in favour of easy and widespread divorce. Indeed, I received letters from two members of the Mothers' Union accusing me of 'advocating a divorce-ridden society completely contrary to the teaching of Christ and the Gospel'.

It was difficult to get across the fact that the removal of the Constitutional prohibition would not interfere with the right of each Church to practise its own moral disciplines and teach its people accordingly. I was condemned as a marriage breaker, wanting divorce to be legally enforced even on unwilling partners!

Seeking provision for divorce in certain circumstances was misrepresented as encouragement of divorce in all circumstances. I believe that the referendum to change the Constitution should have concerned itself solely with the removal of the prohibition instead of spelling out in detail a proposed alternative. Legal arrangements should always be left to the legislature. The Constitution should generalise, the legislature particularise. In sermons and speeches I asserted that the only way forward for Ireland, North and South, was that of a pluralist society based on tolerance.

In 1969, preaching in St Patrick's, I said that:

> In Ireland we have not mastered the art of tolerance, the art of not merely putting up with, perhaps grudgingly, different points of view but positively welcoming the co-existence of different viewpoints, political, religious and cultural, in our land. Unless and until we, the people of Ireland, move towards a pluralist society based on tolerance, on mutual respect and recognition of all traditions, religious and political, there can be no hope of reconciliation. Reconciliation is based on tolerance, tolerance can only come from mutual understanding, and mutual understanding from the removal of ignorance of what others believe and why, an ignorance fuelled by tribal myths, so often masquerading as history, an ignorance which shows itself in bigotry and triumphalism and is the denial of the Christian Gospel of love.

And I went on:

> Christianity is not a collection of doctrinal or theological patterns which are repeated in every detail from age to age. If this were so there would be no need for guidance of the Holy Spirit . . . all the time the situation is changing and we can

render a great disservice to the advance of mutual understanding and charity if we refuse to recognise the reality of
change, if we continue to imprint on this present age ideas and
notions which once may have been relevant and valuable but
which are really out of place and out of date in the complex
dynamic pattern of social, political and religious life of 1969.
The past is a profitable servant but a bad master. The past
exists to enrich the future, not to dominate it.

Time and time again since my installation as Dean in 1969 I
tried to get across the message of pluralism, inclusiveness and
tolerance in sermons, lectures, speeches. In general the main-
stream of both Protestant and Roman Catholic thought has been
hostile to religious liberty and to the idea of a pluralist society.
Liberty has been more often associated with non-Christian influences than with Christian. Religious fanaticism in the case of
Protestants and religious conservatism in the case of Roman
Catholics have produced the most extreme intolerance. Freedom
and toleration have often had to rely on non-dogmatic religion,
for example, the Quakers, or religious indifference or secular
philosophy or anti-clerical politics. We who live in democracies
are pledged to uphold the freedom of the individual and to
promote tolerance and mutual understanding. Tolerance is
recognising and respecting a diversity of views and values based
on the acceptance of human rights and the dignity to be
accorded to every person. True tolerance is not negative but
positive, welcoming the diversity or pluralism in society as mutually enriching and stimulating. Democratic States, of course, have
the right and duty to take whatever steps may be deemed
necessary to curtail the activities of those whose declared intention is to use democracy to destroy democracy.

While there are different types of society there is nevertheless
a large measure of agreement on certain laws, regarded as basic
to any society and finding universal acceptance. Any civilised
form of social life requires that there should be rules governing
the relations between persons in regard to such matters as respect
for life and property, return for services rendered, etc. and that

they should be generally obeyed. And the rules and obligations are in a general way such obvious conditions of individual and social wellbeing that most of them are included in the moral code of most peoples.

Thus there is a common or public morality, recognised and enforced in all societies. This, however, does not constitute the entire morality of any society. For example, the morality of Western society has been largely determined by Jewish and Christian influence. It is thus part of public morality in Christian society that, for example, polygamy is illegal and that women have certain fundamental rights and a higher status than is accorded to them in some non-Christian societies. Social morality is not the result of pure reasoning or logical inference in a vacuum. It is fashioned by the various influences, cultural, religious and economic, which are or have been present in the society.

Love God and love your neighbour is approved and applauded by most religions and, while believers would hold that the principle of love has a divine sanction and an objective and transcendent quality which is universally binding, even Christians disagree among themselves on the interpretation and application of this principle in certain cases. For example, while there is general agreement that such actions as murder, assault, stealing, exploitation of the weak, slander, etc., are inconsistent with love and justice, and should be prohibited and punished by society in its code of public morality, opinions differ on such matters as contraception, divorce, abortion, homosexuality. Some would totally prohibit such practices on the ground that they are morally wrong and offend against the absolute moral principle of love. Others would say that in certain cases such practices as contraception or divorce or abortion may be the morally right course to take under the circumstances or at least may be the lesser of two evils: for example, the use of condoms for family planning or as a guard against AIDS. The principle of love may be served in some cases by such practices as divorce or abortion, or at least it can be argued that it is less offensive to the principle of love to make use of these practices on certain occasions and under certain circumstances than to prohibit them altogether.

Any society pledged to uphold democracy and freedom must be prepared to tolerate different views and practices in relation to certain moral questions. It must avoid being morally legalistic and enforcing a particular view through its legislature and courts in matters of controversy in the moral sphere. It may be described as a pluralist society. A pluralist society, however, does not abstain from making public moral judgments or enforcing certain moral principles. No society can discard its general moral ethos which has been fashioned by various influences, and the moral attitudes of any society are naturally reflected in its concept and implementation of its social or public morality. On the other hand, for legislators merely to reflect the majority opinion can be dangerous. Majority opinion in Tzarist Russia was anti-semitic, and in Hitlerite Germany the policy of anti-semitism may well have had majority support, for educational brainwashing can bend the minds of citizens to suit their political or religious rulers. While legislators should always be concerned with prohibiting what is likely to corrupt society, they should be continually on their guard against organisations or pressure groups who predict social degeneration and decay, not on empirical and factual evidence but on some prior theological, political or racist convictions. Unless there is clear, unmistakable factual evidence that any controversial matter such as contraception or abortion or divorce would never substantially reduce human suffering and injustice, but would on the contrary be a detrimental and corrupting influence on the quality of life in society, the State should refrain from prohibitory legislation, while at the same time taking all reasonable steps towards safeguarding society against abuses or permissiveness.

Laws which are difficult to enforce and which have the effect of turning a 'blind eye' to any section of the community must be avoided. For example, the law restricting the importation of contraceptives into the Republic was a bad law. As a corollary, it follows that help and information on family planning and related matters should not be denied to the citizens of the

Republic or of any State which professes respect for democracy and individual freedom. Also, any age limit on the availability of contraceptives to adults is clearly unenforceable and a bad law. Ultimately questions relating to birth control and contraceptives are a matter for personal conscience acting responsibly in accordance with the individual's religious or moral principles. Laws should not be enacted which are likely to produce a great deal of suffering for some people. The complete prohibition of divorce or abortion may result in causing intense suffering which society has no right to inflict, and such total prohibition is an offence against Christian compassion and concern. Ultimately the wellbeing of the individual person is all important, and that person is deserving always of Christian compassion and concern. There are some actions which are always morally wrong under normal conditions. But that does not rule out the possibility that in highly exceptional circumstances such actions may be morally justifiable. Under normal conditions such behaviour would always be morally wrong, but moral rules are intended to operate against a background of normality, not in conditions which confront us with agonising choices.

Laws, while providing reasonable safeguards for society, should not punish people for what they are. Homosexuality offers an instance of this. Homosexual practices between consenting adults in private should not be a criminal offence. Homosexual conduct in other cases is not only clearly sinful but is rightly a criminal offence. The mark of a free or pluralist society is not that it abstains from making moral judgments or enforcing certain moral principles, but that it is prepared to submit its proposed or actual moral legislation to the most rigorous scientific and informed examination; it must be continually open to serious and constructive views from whatever quarter they may come and must have a willingness to change laws if necessary in the light of experience and reasonable public opinion. A pluralist society will be sceptical of authoritarianism and of pressure groups, whether ecclesiastical, political or racial, and will keep its legislation on moral matters to a minimum.

Within the basic framework of public morality on which there is a general consensus and agreement, each denomination must have the right to preach and practise its own faith and moral disciplines and to offer guidance to its members. Each Church must make its own way and commend itself by its own integrity, without relying on the State to enforce its moral teaching.

The State must never take sides and in a morally controversial issue enforce a particular moral view, even a majority one, on all its citizens. The sole function of the State must be to ensure freedom for all within the context of a generally agreed and accepted public order and morality. It follows that complex moral issues in which there are sincerely held but different points of view or shades of opinion should not be the subject of Constitutional definition. In a pluralist State a Constitution should express a general consensus, setting out basic human rights and responsibilities and steering clear of controversial, complex and divisive moral issues. Such issues, in so far as they have public relevance, should be the affair of the legislature and of the particular Churches, each having the right to exercise its own particular moral disciplines and none having the right to enforce them on others.

17

Ecumenical Needs

THE question of integrated education, understood in Ireland as the education of children of different religions together, should concern all who seek to heal the wounds of a divided community. In a community where religious differences do not run deep (as in Britain or France) denominational schooling will have no effect on the status quo. Whether a pupil attends a Roman Catholic School or a C. of E. school is of no more relevance, as far as the community is concerned, than the game he chooses to play or the club he chooses to join. Where no division exists on political, patriotic or racial grounds, denominational schools will certainly not create one. But the story is different where the community is deeply divided on political and religious lines as in Northern Ireland. Here division is perpetuated by educating children separately in denominational schools. The Christian Churches profess to be committed to reconciliation and the removal of strife and division in society. One would expect them to have taken the lead in promoting the cause of integrated education which, when all is said and done, is the practical expression of the Christian Gospel of one family under one Fatherhood of God. Unfortunately all the Churches have acquiesced in, and sometimes encouraged, the tribalism of their adherents, with resultant tension and divisiveness in the community. At the very outset we implant in young innocent minds a 'them or us' attitude which can rapidly sprout into 'Thank God we are not as the others. We are the elect, the chosen ones.'

Education has a crucial role in ridding our land of intolerance. Only a fool would claim that integrated education is the complete answer. But to meet together, to talk together, to learn together, to play together, *to be* together must surely help to remove ignorance, prejudice and misunderstanding. The teacher of history to a mixed class of Roman Catholics and Protestants will be more alive to the danger of a one-sided presentation and the need to be absolutely fair to all sides than a history teacher in a denominational school. Integrated education helps children to recognise the fact that people do have different points of view and that we must be as tolerant of their point of view as we expect them to be of ours.

Most Protestants and a growing number of Roman Catholics today look on schools primarily as places of secular instruction with provision made for prayers at assembly and some religious biblical teaching. When we analyse that which is often referred to as the 'Protestant ethos' in our schools, we find that what we are describing is a non-Roman Catholic environment, the absence of statues, sacred pictures, decades of the rosary and so on. Ethos has to do with externals and a Protestant ethos is really the absence of Roman Catholic externals and priestly control. In itself it is a negative thing. The aim essentially is to keep Protestant children together and give them a good educa-tion, not primarily to make them better members of the Church of Ireland or better Protestants, but to enable them to pass exams. The idea of segregation was never intended as a means of Protestant indoctrination but to emphasise Protestant identity, to shield the children from Roman Catholic influences which might eventually lead to more mixed marriages and, terrible thought, the loss of more Protestants and/or their children to Rome. A growing number of parents today decide on a school without reference to Church policy, and because there is nothing peculiarly or doctrinally Protestant about Protestant schools, primary or secondary, Roman Catholic parents in many cases have no hesitation in sending their children to such schools for whatever reason: size of school, quality of teaching, liberal and pluralist education.

Mixed marriage has been the scourge of the Protestant community particularly in the Republic. In spite of certain amendments to the *Ne Temere* decree, Roman Catholic teaching still insists that the Roman Catholic partner shall do all in his or her power to have any children of the marriage brought up in the Roman Catholic faith. But this decree is far from being generally obeyed today. Young couples of mixed religion believe that the whole question of family planning, and the bringing up and education of children, should be a private matter. They reason that if they are mature enough to be married, they are also mature enough to make decisions about their children without any external interference. Their attitude is, 'Leave it to ourselves to work out. The clergy can best serve by being available for advice if required but must not intrude into private and personal family matters.'

In Ireland, especially Northern Ireland where there is deeply ingrained religious feeling among Roman Catholics and Protestants, Roman Catholic mixed marriage regulations have serious social and political overtones in that they accentuate the religious divide and the polarisation of communities. Instead of promoting the Christian Gospel of reconciliation and togetherness, these regulations do the very opposite and are seen, not only by Protestants but by many Roman Catholics, as an infringement of the rights of conscience and individual freedom and as a denial of the Gospel message of reconciliation which is at the very heart of Christianity.

Ecumenism which set out with such high hopes has become a disappointment to many in Ireland. It has become bogged down in seemingly endless theological debate without any sign of real progress in the direction of its ultimate aim, Christian unity.

Studying the Bible together, praying and worshipping together on certain occasions such as in the Week of Prayer for Christian Unity, though laudable in themselves, touch only a very small minority of each denomination. The majority are not interested. In the Republic, where most people in all denominations pay lip service to the ecumenical movement, there is no real enthusiasm, partly because there never has been a joint approach, or even joint discussion, by the Churches on important moral issues such as family planning, divorce, abortion, and in the whole field of medical ethics. Neither has there been much practical cooperation in social issues such as unemployment, emigration, drug addiction, etc. When after lengthy discussion by theological experts, joint reports on theological matters such as the nature of Church authority, sacraments and ordination are produced, they are allowed to gather dust on the shelves.

In the North ecumenism has always been a dirty word amongst the fundamentalists and diehards who so often call the tune. For if you believe that you have the whole truth, meeting with others of a different tradition is pointless except to convert them to 'the truth'. Even between the Protestant Churches themselves, ecumenism never generated enthusiasm. Each cosy, complacent congregation was content to plough its own furrow. When the Roman Catholic dimension was added there was the lurking suspicion that ecumenism was being used by Rome in a papist plot to get rid of Protestantism. The Church of Ireland and the Methodists found support at best lukewarm, although both have courageously invited Roman Catholic bishops and priests to their pulpits during the Week of Prayer for Christian Unity. Presbyterian ecumenists are thin on the ground. Roman Catholics are better Church attenders than Protestants, so on ecumenical occasions they are present in greater numbers than Protestants. This, however, does not necessarily signify a greater commitment to ecumenism amongst Roman Catholics, but may be due to bishops and priests encouraging attendance and the willingness of their laity to oblige.

If our ecumenism is to be effective we must first rid ourselves of the old dogmatic position that we each in our particular denomination have the truth, the whole truth and nothing but the truth. We must realise that truth is more than subscribing to creeds or statements. Jesus claimed to be the truth. Therefore to understand truth we have to understand Jesus and be willing and eager to learn from others how they understand him and the relevance of his Gospel for us today.

Thus the whole concept of truth will be enriched by the contributions made by particular insights and points of view. The key idea in ecumenism is enrichment by diversity, and if this is taken seriously it means the end of exclusiveness not only in theology but also in politics, in culture. No longer, for example, can there be a confessional State, whether Protestant or Roman Catholic, based on a collection of Church dogmas, but a State open to the healthy interchange of different points of view, tolerant, willing and eager for the progressive enrichment of its political, social and cultural structures. Nothing must be pushed aside. Protestant, Roman Catholic, Jew, Nationalist, Unionist, all have a part to play, for all have something valuable to contribute to a creative synthesis which will be to the benefit of all the people of Ireland.

We pray for the unity of the Church of Christ, but unity is not of our making. It is the gift of God and will come in God's good time and in God's good way, not in ours. We have our part to play in preparing the ground and sowing the seeds of charity, cooperation and mutual understanding with fellow Christians of other traditions. We must not confuse unity with uniformity, for unity will only be truly unity in diversity, a unity in which nothing of value is lost but in which each tradition will contribute to all and all will learn from each.

Ignorance is the enemy of ecumenism: ignorance of what others really believe and ignorance of what we ourselves really believe. To understand ourselves and others is the first step on the ecumenical road.

Courageous initiatives are called for not only in theology but also in the social, ethical and educational fields. We are all first and foremost Christians, whatever Church we attend. So there is a basic unity already in existence between all who have been baptised into Christ. We are baptised into Christ, not into any denomination. For infants of a mixed marriage, why not a joint baptism with the clergy of both denominations taking part? I can see no good Christian reason against this. The degree of unity by baptism into our common Lord Jesus Christ should surely justify the coming together at the Lord's Table of Christians of different denominations, at least on special occasions, as during the Week of Prayer for Christian Unity.

If I profess to regard my fellow Christians of another Church as my brothers and sisters in Christ do I not make nonsense of my profession if I, at the same time, refuse to share with them or allow them to share with me, the Lord's Supper at the Lord's Table? Can anyone imagine Jesus, who went out of his way to dine with outcasts and sinners, calmly submitting to such restrictions on Communion?

Intercommunion on certain occasions would prove a mighty incentive, encouragement and means of grace to all Christian people to pray more and work more for that unity which is the will of Christ for His Church, particularly at present when there is a large measure of agreement on the Eucharist. There are some who still hold the old conservative view that the Eucharist must be the expression of and seal on a unity already achieved, but there is a growing conviction that it is a fruitful and effective means towards achieving unity in accordance with the will of Christ for his Church.

Church and Bible for us go hand in hand and in the Church of Ireland we have the dictum: 'The Church to teach, the Bible to prove.' In a sense the Church gave us the Scriptures, in that under the guidance of the Holy Spirit it selected these writings from all others and proclaimed them to the world as the inspired Word of God. But the Church was also given the Scriptures by God as the authoritative record of God's revelation to man, for the inspired record had first to be there in order to be selected. The selection was the result of the dawning consciousness of the Church of something already there, unique and authoritative. Therefore the Church also stands under the judgment of Holy Scripture. This has always been the common conviction of the Reformers, however much they may have differed on other theological points.

We must note that the Church which made the selection of sacred books and commended them as the inspired Word of God, was the One, Holy, Catholic, Apostolic Church, and this was many centuries before the rending asunder of the Christian family by controversy and conflict. Thus Christians of different traditions, looking back beyond the later divisive influences, can all identify with the same One, Holy, Catholic and Apostolic Church.

I envisage the united Church of the future as including 'Catholic' and 'Protestant' elements in a healthy synthesis. The Catholic element is essential to emphasise continuity of the faith through the visible community of the Church through the centuries, and to counteract any tendencies amongst Protestantism to subtract from the substance of the faith. The Protestant element is essential to emphasise the necessity of returning to the Holy Scriptures, to keep the distinction between essential and non-essentials, to emphasise freedom of conscience and to warn against any tendency to add to the original deposit of faith. Protestantism and Catholicism need each other. They both belong together and neither can banish the other for they both represent authentic elements within the Gospel. They have a unity made richer by diversity.

On essentials and non-essentials Anglicans make a distinction between what we regard as the essential doctrines of the Catholic faith, held always everywhere and by all, and later additions such as the doctrines of the Immaculate Conception and the Assumption of the Blessed Virgin Mary. Anglicans regard these later additions as optional extras or pious opinions which may or may not be believed but which are in no way essential parts of the Christian and Catholic faith. In essentials unanimity; in non-essentials, freedom to differ; in all things, charity.

The great temptation for all the Churches is to try to bind Christ by the cords of religious dogmatism, to attempt to hold Him captive in the institution, making Him conform to our ideas, creating Him in our image when all the time we should be fashioning and renewing all our Churches and institutional religion to conform to Him, the Jesus of Nazareth whom we discover and meet in the New Testament. The temptation is to worship dogma rather than Christ. No one — no institution — has all the answers, whether religious, political or ethical. As St Paul says: we only know in part. No one has the truth, the whole truth and nothing but the truth. No Church has God in its pocket. We are all pilgrims. We are all seekers, continually exploring and finding new treasures in the inexhaustible riches of the wisdom and knowledge of God, as St Paul reminds us.

I believe that whatever form Christian unity eventually takes, the papacy will have a leading role. The Bishop of Rome, on historical grounds alone, has a claim to be regarded as universal primate and pastor and as a focus or centre of unity, however much Christians may disagree on his claims to universal juris- diction (the ordering of the affairs of local or national Churches by decree from Rome), or the claim to infallibility and the inter- pretation of the Petrine scriptural texts (those referring to Peter). The fact that Rome was the leading city of the world and that the Church of Rome was noted for its charity and generosity gave the Bishop of Rome a position of precedence and influence. Christians in the West looked to the See of Rome as a court of appeal to ensure fair play when disputes arose, as Christians in the East looked to Constantinople. The primacy and precedence of the See of Rome on historical, not theological grounds, was never disputed by Anglicans, and we in the Church of Ireland have no difficulty in accepting the Pope's primacy of honour which was universally recognised in the days of St Patrick and the Celtic Church. But we cannot accept the later papal claim to have the right to interfere in the affairs of local Churches, such as in the appointment of bishops or the claim to infalli- bility. We understand how such claims originated, for the pattern of the Roman Empire with its strong central authority in Rome in the person of the Emperor, enforcing uniformity by his governors and agents throughout his domains with no place for dissent, became the pattern of the Roman Church with its strong central authority in Rome in the person of the Pope, enforcing uniformity by his bishops and clerical agents through- out the whole Church, with no place for dissent or heresy.

Pope John Paul II's finest hour undoubtedly was his cham- pioning the cause of freedom in the face of repressive Com- munist régimes in Eastern Europe. Pope John Paul was seen by millions as a beacon of liberty, giving hope and courage to the enslaved peoples who eventually rose up, cast off their shackles and claimed their right to freedom and justice.

But freedom is infectious and impatient of authoritarianism, whether political or ecclesiastical. Today the Pope is perceived by many — not only outside but also inside the Roman Catholic Church — as a dictator, with an iron fist imposing his will in matters of sexual morality, denouncing and sacking 'wayward' theologians, stifling discussion and debate, refusing even to consider important issues such as clerical celibacy, the ordination of women to the priesthood and the world population explosion; lukewarm towards ecumenism, distrustful of collegiality and participation with others in decision making, consistently filling vacant sees with 'yes' men who can be relied on always to follow the papal line on every issue. 'Freedom is simply freedom to obey without question the decrees and dictates of the papacy.' This in all honesty is how the papacy is perceived by many Christians in all denominations today.

In January 1977 during his visit to Dublin I invited the world-renowned Roman Catholic theologian, Hans Küng, now alas deprived by the Pope of his official status as a Church theologian, to give a lecture in St Patrick's Cathedral to an ecumenical congregation. The Cathedral was packed to overflowing, people stood in the aisles or sat on the floor, and Hans Küng was greeted enthusiastically and loudly applauded by clergy and laity of all denominations. In the course of his lecture, Küng said:

> In the Catholic Church we are undoubtedly in a very critical phase. . . . Today we need inspiring, intellectual-spiritual authority on all levels. But in many dioceses we have merely clerical officials with more of a Roman than of a Catholic mentality . . . there is a dangerous gulf between the bishops and the majority of the priests in regard to more or less every important problem in the Church today.

All this should certainly not be music to Protestant ears or evoke a complacent 'I told you so' response. For the whole world-wide Christian witness in all its traditions is diminished, and other significant papal pronouncements on crucial issues such as war and civil conflict lose their effectiveness, when the occupant of the See of Rome is no longer seen as an apostle of

⊗ See, however.

liberty but as an ecclesiastical dictator, a latter-day Caesar, who will not tolerate or even discuss any theological or moral view which might differ from his own. The credibility of the papacy, and indeed Christianity as a whole, is put at risk by an unyielding totalitarianism.

But we must take heart, for the Christian and true Catholic faith will survive in spite of a dictatorial papacy or fanatical Protestantism, for God never leaves Himself without witness. As Hans Küng put it: 'The crisis of the Church and its leadership today will be overcome by those who, at this decisive moment in the Church's history, despite everything, continue to perform their service in the strength of faith.'

'The dogs may bark but the caravan moves on', and I believe ecumenism eventually will point to a papacy as a primacy of honour which is a focus of unity, expressing the general mind of the whole Church — bishops, clergy and people — subject to Holy Scripture, always eager to listen to and cooperate with fellow bishops, clergy, theologians and informed laity; a papacy which will not see itself in isolation but a papacy inside and a part of the Church with the pastoral role of service to all. This pastoral role will be the mark by which above all else it is recognised and is seen to follow the example of the Good Shepherd, Our Lord Himself.

How better to sum up the ecumenical adventure than in the words of Archbishop William Temple:

> Always the breath — the wind — of the spirit is moving. We know it by its effect. We have no need to ask for its authentication. Is it Protestant? Is it Catholic? Where the fruit of the spirit is apparent, there the spirit is at work. We should place ourselves in its course that we may be carried by its impulse, even though this leads to association with strange comrades.

One final thought: imagine a truly ecumenical council with representatives of the World Council of Churches and the Roman Catholic Church, presided over by the Pope to discuss matters of common Christian concern. A dream? Perhaps for some a nightmare!

18

The Protestant Perspective

Today a great variety of people differing in creed, culture, colour and politics are thrown together in close contact, especially by easy and rapid communication, and all have to share this one planet. To do this with any degree of peace and harmony in such a pluralist world, there must above all be tolerance. Tolerance is the primary need. The greatest thing that the Church of Ireland, and indeed any Church, can do today is to promote tolerance, for there can be no peace or progress in a pluralistic world without it. Tolerance, it cannot be too often emphasised, is positive, not a grudging concession to the other side. The only limit on tolerance is on those who would use tolerance to destroy tolerance; those who would use freedom to destroy freedom; those who would use democracy to destroy democracy.

Tolerance and humility are the ingredients of Christian love which may be defined as always seeing the best in, and doing the best for, those whom we may happen to come into contact with whether we like them or not. To seek to promote the well-being of my neighbour, I must first respect him, understand him, in a word show tolerance and humility, and ecumenism must reach out beyond Christianity to other faiths for we are all children of the one God.

Fundamentalism is the enemy of tolerance: Protestant fundamentalism, Roman Catholic fundamentalism, Islamic and Jewish fundamentalism. It is not surprising that fundamentalism has such a hold on so many people today. We are living in a scientific and technological age. Science seeks certainty, exactness, clear-cut answers. I believe fundamentalism transfers to the religious sphere the categories of science. It looks for absolute certainty, an absolute kind of mathematical certainty in matters of religion. It really seeks to make a science of religion. Therefore it is not uncommon to find scientists who are converted to Christianity taking a fundamentalist or semi-fundamentalist approach. They naturally approach religion with a scientific attitude. They leave their scientific search for truth in the laboratory and enter a different world, the religious one, where they find satisfaction in the certainty offered by fundamentalism or conservative evangelicalism. But faith cannot be treated as science. Faith cannot be vindicated by scientific certainty. It is 'the substance of things hoped for, the evidence of things not seen,' as the Epistle to the Hebrews puts it.

Fundamentalists claim to have a monopoly on truth, to know all the answers and comprehend completely the mind of God. Those who do not see things their way are in darkness and error. But if the finite mind of man could fully grasp the infinite mind of God, man would either cease to be man, or God would cease to be God. If the finite can fully comprehend the infinite, worship and the sense of mystery disappear, and religion becomes a subject for the debating chamber, emotionally hurling Biblical texts around to convince an audience and confound the critics. But St Paul wisely tells us, 'Here we see in a mirror darkly. Here we know in part.'

Faith is taken on trust and tested by experience. Ultimately experience is subjective, mine or yours, or someone else's. Even the collective experience of the Church is at basis personal, the experience of a number of individual persons. This being so, it follows that tolerance of others is a necessary ingredient of faith, for in the end I have only my experience, my point of view. The wise men all saw the same Jesus. But would they have described in exactly the same way to their friends what they had seen? I doubt it. One would have noted one feature, his companion another.

God reveals Himself and His truth to many in many ways. This same truth may be seen from different points of view by different people.

The desire for mathematical certainty to deal with problems, moral, social, political, in an uncertain, strife-ridden and anxious world is understandable. In Islamic fundamentalism there is an attempt to put the clock back to the alleged certainty and simplicity of the past rather than face the uncertainty and complexities of the present, all of which are blamed on Western imperialism. The fundamentalist response to scientific materialism is to conscript the scientific approach in defence of religion; for example, they insist that the Bible is true, literally true and scientifically accurate in every detail. But the reaction to materialism is also seen in the wide appeal of the arts: music, painting, poetry, sculpture, etc. Humans cannot live by bread alone and, as the influence of organised religion declines, the void is filled, or partially filled, by the pursuit of art in some form, offering a spiritual dimension to counteract the current materialism.

Most of our Church of Ireland churches are austere and not of great architectural or artistic merit. We have depended largely on the language of worship, the liturgy, to supply the 'sense of the numinous' the 'other world' dimension and to evoke reverence and adoration. The 'mystery' was in the words. The old language was in itself godly. So at times we hear people complaining that when contemporary language is used, they feel they are missing something. While there are some good features in modern services, the Church of Ireland, where the externals of worship are severely limited by Canon law, must recognise that language assumes an added importance and be careful lest it loses in contemporary liturgical language that sense of mystery, reverence and transcendence which inspired Cranmer. There is the danger of assuming that, in liturgy, theological rectitude expressed in contemporary language is all that is required. The intellect has its place but we neglect at our peril the heart and the imagination.

Worship must keep a sense of proportion between the majesty or mystery of God and the homely love of God, between holiness and homeliness. An obsession with mystery will cause worship to degenerate into magic and superstition, while an exclusive concentration on homeliness to the neglect of mystery will produce a kind of chummy, chatty, 'old pal' attitude to God. God is pulled down to our level. This sense of proportion in worship finds expression for Church of Ireland people in the Book of Common Prayer, which for nearly four and a half centuries has fashioned the character of Anglicanism, with its quiet moderation, tolerant comprehensiveness and rejection of ranting fanaticism and fundamentalism.

The essence of Protestantism is to protest, not in a negative way but positively. Protest means standing *for* something rather than against. Protestants place a high value on freedom of conscience. In the final analysis *I* must choose, *I* must decide, *I* must bear responsibility. No individual, no organisation, no Church has the right to dictate to me. There is for Protestants the emphasis on the direct relationship between the individual and God. The individual has direct access to his Creator. The only intermediary necessary is Jesus Christ. Therefore the Church as an institution in Protestantism has not the same exalted standing as in Roman Catholicism, and there are Protestants who would claim to be good Christians without ever going to church! Institutions whether religious or political, with all their attendant legalism, are subject to continuous critical examination in the Protestant consciousness. The direct encounter with God, and consequently with one's fellow men, dictates that intermediary institutions, whether Church or State, are judged in the light of whether they impede or assist this one-to-one relationship. So Protestantism in its very nature by giving a primacy to the individual is sceptical of absolutes, such as the absolute prohibition of abortion and divorce, which reflect collective thinking and can cause pain and suffering to individuals in certain situations.

It has often been said that broadly speaking in Protestantism the sequence is (1) the individual; (2) the collective or society whose function is to help the individual to realise his or her potential; (3) the individual's duty to contribute to society in order to enrich and improve it.

Whereas in Roman Catholicism the sequence is (1) the collective (Church or society); (2) the individual's duty to be loyal to the collective; (3) in doing so the individual will realise his potential, and improve himself and his fellow men. While Protestantism emphasises the collective serving the individual, Roman Catholicism has the emphasis the other way round: the individual serving the collective.

Roman Catholicism is what has been called 'ontological', that is, it stresses the 'being', the 'existence' of the Church with its wide spectrum visibly embracing all classes and colours, saints and sinners throughout the world. This universal 'given-ness' or 'being there' of the Church has not lacked admirers or converts attracted by its age, universality, inclusiveness and what they perceive as its well-rounded rationality. It has an intellectual and artistic magnetism. Converts like Evelyn Waugh found satisfaction and fulfilment in intellectual contemplation and rational justification of the Catholic idea, in simply 'being a Catholic', warts and all.

Protestantism emphasises inner commitment, conviction and conversion and is more ethical than ontological, more subjective, more internal. The externality of religious observance for the Protestant must be above all else an expression of internality, of the commitment of the heart. If not it becomes empty, form without substance. So true religion must bring about a change in attitude and conduct, a real conversion from the old way to the new.

While Protestantism, with its emphasis on personal commitment, can make Roman Catholicism aware of the danger of religion becoming merely a ritualistic outward observance and of the temptation to make an idol of the institutional Church, regarding it as an end in itself rather than as a means, Roman Catholicism in its turn can warn Protestantism of the danger of assuming the prerogative of God, deciding who are the 'saved and the lost', and of the danger of uninformed private judgment, based on individual 'infallibility', which rejects all Church tradition and collective experience and ends up producing a multiplicity of sects (or individuals), each claiming to have the authentic Gospel — individualism run riot producing religious anarchy.

The philosopher Hegel believed that thought had a triadic movement: thesis, antithesis and synthesis. On this view Roman Catholicism is the thesis, the general statement, the 'being'. Protestantism is the antithesis which questions the thesis, by emphasising the individual, private judgment and conduct. Is there a synthesis which is not merely a piece of ecclesiastical joinery? It has often been claimed that Anglicanism aims at being the synthesis between Roman Catholicism and Protestantism for it claims to be both Catholic and Protestant, holding together the different emphases of the two traditions in a synthesis or tension, often uneasy but always stimulating and enriching, the 'via media', with its appeal to Scripture, tradition and reason. Tradition is not static. It is how the Gospel has been interpreted, understood and applied in the Church. It may be developed or widened in the light of reason and deeper insight into the meaning of the Gospel. In the early Church, tradition was widened to include Gentiles in the Church, against opposition from those who would have limited it to Jewish Christians. Today there is a debate on widening the tradition to include women priests in the ordained ministry. Again there is opposition by those who would restrict the ministry to a male priesthood.

Although the Church of Ireland is part of the Anglican communion it has been identified throughout its history more with the Protestant and evangelical wing of Anglicanism than with the Anglo-Catholic. It was once the established or official State Church of the land and such close association with the ascendancy led to political conformity rather than protest. Indeed, the 'protest', the Protestantism, of the Church of Ireland was limited to anti-Romanism, or anti-ritualism. A few courageous Church of Ireland people like Swift, Molyneux, and later Grattan, Davis, Butt, Parnell, showed their 'savage indignation' at the injustice around them, but the Church of Ireland as a whole in its leadership and councils was unmoved, firmly embedded in the establishment. In Northern Ireland Presbyterians, while showing some protest in 1798 in favour of the United Irishmen and their dedication to the principles of liberty, equality and fraternity, eventually, due to fear of Rome rule, took refuge under the

Unionist wing. Protest ceased, as loyalty to the Crown and conformity to the Union dominated political and social thinking.

Today the Church of Ireland is disestablished, freed from any
official connection with any State. In the North Protestant
protest is largely confined to denouncing the Anglo-Irish Agreement, while in the Republic Protestants are regarded as 'nice'
people who would never take to the streets to protest about
anything. A Protestant street demonstration is seen as a contradiction in terms. The identification of Protestantism with the
British ascendancy has played a large part in the formation of
this negative attitude. 'Better keep your head down and not call
attention to yourself in case you might be accused of disloyalty
to the Republic and an enemy of the State.' From the foundation of the State in 1922 there has really been no strong
Protestant protest — about anything. 'Why should there be?
They have nothing to protest about.' This was the general
reaction to Protestant inactivity. Protestantism might have been
expected to have given a lead in such vital matters as the
removal of Roman Catholic confessional elements from the
Constitution and to campaign actively for a pluralist State.
Protestants, dedicated as they are to the rights of conscience
and personal freedom, should surely have found this a worthy
cause. But we find that the main thrust in the abortion and
divorce debates to move in a pluralist and more tolerant direction
came initially not from a strong united Protestant protest, but
from liberal Roman Catholics, Jews and those of no religion.
As a result Protestants are generally perceived as nice, well-
mannered, inoffensive people in well-dressed and cosy Sunday
church congregations, content to fade away quietly and without
fuss or murmur. Part of the trouble is that most Protestants
have no idea what they really stand for and are simply indifferent to matters of public concern. They know they are not
Roman Catholics or Jews, but can give no positive reason based
on history or Church teaching as to why they are Protestants
and their role, if any, in society. A massive programme of
education is necessary if Protestantism is to survive, especially
in the Republic. If not it will be quietly and gradually absorbed

X But we have had W. B. Stanford, Ivan
McCutcheon, H. R. McAdoo, W. Burrows,
S. McCutcheon, R. O'glaisne ? (see also
next page)

into the Roman Catholic community by mixed marriage, or dissolve into indifference to all religion. True protest has come from people like Yeats, Synge, O'Casey, and Hubert Butler who, in their day, have had to stand alone, largely unsupported by their fellow Protestants and Church leaders.

It was a time of shame on the Protestant community when Hubert Butler was censured by local government bodies, expelled from committees, forced to resign from the Kilkenny Archaeological Society which he had founded, because in the interest of historical accuracy he had dared to mention at a meeting in Dublin in 1952 the forced conversion of 240,000 Orthodox Serbs to Roman Catholicism in Croatia under the dictator Pavelitch during the Hitlerite period.

The Papal Nuncio, of whose presence Butler was unaware, walked out, and accusations resounded throughout the land that Hubert Butler had insulted the Papal Nuncio. In truth he had insulted no one and never intended to do so. He attempted to make a well-informed contribution — for he knew Yugoslavia well — and to give a balanced view of the situation in Croatia under Hitler's puppet, Pavelitch, in 1941. There was no upsurge of Protestant support for Hubert Butler. Protestants were scared. Which tells us something about Protestants but also something about the Roman Catholic community at that time. Had Protestants good reason to be scared? Looking at what happened to Hubert Butler, perhaps they had. I can hear my mother's warning: 'For goodness sake, keep quiet, Victor, or you'll get us all burnt out!'

I was a curate in Derry in 1952 and wrote to Hubert Butler offering my sympathy and support. Many years later when I returned to Dublin we met and lunched together and thereafter he wrote to me frequently expressing approval of what I was saying about the need for a pluralist society. He believed, as I do, that the Irish at heart, both Catholic and Protestant, are a tolerant people. They are made intolerant by religion masquerading as Christianity.

When growing up I never heard a Protestant use a 'four-letter word'. Protestants, although constantly admonished by parents, clergy and teachers against the use of obscene language, might on occasion exclaim 'dammit' or 'blast'. Anything further would offend their puritanical conscience and biblical teaching with its admonition, 'Swear not at all'. Swear words with a sexual connotation were studiously avoided. Why? Is it because Protestants treated sex in a very private, personal and intimate way, not a fit subject for public debate or comment? Unbecoming, indeed shameful to speak of such intimate and private matters. Today the media and the cinema with their highlighting of sex and their spontaneous and unashamed use of four-letter words have brought about a change in the attitude of the younger generation of Protestants who, if they swear at all, appear to use four-letter words without any inhibition. Also Protestants might say, 'For God's sake' but rarely, 'For Christ's sake'. Roman Catholics invoke 'Jesus, Mary and Joseph' or 'Holy Mother of God'. Protestant swearing steers clear of resorting to Biblical names, possibly out of traditional reverence for the Bible as the Word of God. Protestantism is also a Christ or Christo-centred religion with marked emphasis on Jesus as Lord and Saviour: 'Jesus my Lord, my God, my all, my personal Saviour.' Therefore always be careful to treat Christ with respect and reverence. Do not lightly use His name. But the term 'God' is seen as more nebulous, less definite, and so the Protestant psyche feels less guilty with 'For God's sake' than 'For Christ's sake'.

Since I returned to Northern Ireland I feel no less Irish. This set me thinking. What do I mean when I say that I am Irish? First of all being Irish means for me that I was born, or belong to, or feel at home in a particular place: a village, townland, town or city which is situated on the island of Ireland. It is primarily a sense of place where I feel I belong and have my roots. It has little to do with politics or religion or culture. It begins with my being a member of a family, my first loyalty, then a member of the local community with whom I identify. This widens out to the county, the province, the whole country. In my case I cheer for Carnew, or Wicklow or Leinster or Ireland. If born, brought up or living in Northern Ireland my sense of belonging is further widened to include the United

Kingdom or British dimension. So I feel just as Irish in Northern Ireland but I also feel British without any sense of contradiction. Irish and British, nationalist and unionist, are not for me mutually exclusive terms. It is not an *either/or* situation. As I can feel Irish and European at the same time, so there is equally no contradiction in being Irish *and* British and European.

Feeling truly Irish I can stand with pride under the Irish Tricolour for the singing of the Soldiers' Song in Croke Park, and equally feeling truly Irish I can stand with pride under the Union Jack for the singing of 'God Save the Queen' in Northern Ireland. I am but one of many who find no contradiction in this experience. Nationalism and Unionism are both part of our history and heritage and we can experience, appreciate and commend what is valuable in both; Nationalism with its emphasis on our culture and language and the underlying unity in one family of all Irish people, and Unionism with its emphasis on our Anglo-Irish and Scottish-Irish traditions, looking out beyond this island and recognising that history, geography and economics make it necessary for us to have a special relationship of affinity with the inhabitants of the neighbouring island, the English, Welsh and Scots. Apart from our common EC membership, for better or for worse, these two islands have a special togetherness. While Unionism has often been guilty of playing down the all-Ireland dimension to the extent of referring to the Republic as a foreign State, the Republic has also been guilty of what we might call the 'leap frog' syndrome: concentrating on Brussels or Paris or Bonn and playing down the importance of the British dimension to our national wellbeing. The 1992/93 currency crisis is a case in point. When the British had to leave the EMS and sterling was devalued, the Irish Republic gave little or no support to Prime Minister John Major in his efforts to reform the system and discourage speculators, choosing instead to line up with the Germans and French in saying that no change was necessary: there were no faults in the EMS. In spite of our age-old quarrels there are so many family ties between North and South and between Ireland as a whole and Great Britain that these two islands and their inhabitants are closely bound together and can never really be 'foreigners' to each other, whatever the politically correct definition of 'foreign'.

The challenge facing our politicians is to articulate and translate this special relationship of togetherness into an acceptable constitutional structure within the context of our common membership of the European Community.

Meanwhile the idea or ideal of a politically United Ireland has become more remote and no longer figures prominently on the public agenda. Northern interest in the Republic is largely confined to arranging holidays, weekend hotel breaks or attending sporting, musical or theatrical events. While most people know the name of the Taoiseach, very few could name any other member of the Government, and apart from some vague idea of 'scandals' and 'controversies', which even the international media have been eager to report, there is no general interest in the day-to-day political or economic life of the Republic. Mention the Republic to Protestants, and their reaction is cross-border security; to Roman Catholics, and their reaction is sport and holidays.

The truth of the matter is that for the majority of Northerners (and this includes the Roman Catholics), the Republic does not at present offer any sufficient enticement, either economically or socially, to persuade the majority to leave the United Kingdom and join in a united Ireland. They look across the border and are not impressed. Until the Republic can show better prospects of employment, better health, educational and social services, lower taxation and cheaper living costs than currently in Northern Ireland, there will be no general wish to break the link with the UK. Of course there will always be a minority, some put it at around 20 to 25 per cent of the Roman Catholic community, who would choose a United Ireland whatever the cost, 'come hell or high water'. But while most Roman Catholics would favour a United Ireland provided they would not lose out financially, the Republic will have no easy task in convincing the hard-headed Northerner that all will be well, indeed all will be much better, for all in a United Ireland. The Protestants have the added fear of Rome rule in a United Ireland in which they would be a minority.

Protestantism in Northern Ireland has declined in influence over the past twenty years and numerically speaking its majority has also decreased. A lower birth rate, smaller families with emigration of sons and daughters (many of whom because of the troubles and uncertainty about the future have left the province for good), declining church attendance and indifference to religion have lessened the impact of a Protestantism which is becoming proportionally more middle-aged and elderly. The active church-going Protestant, of whatever denomination, is very often a conservative evangelical, and Protestant youth who attend church regularly are more likely to be found in evangelical congregations than in the more middle of the road churches. Roman Catholicism, although outwardly more ecumenically minded than the Protestant conservative evangelicals and increasing numerically (west of the river Bann the school population is in the ratio of three Roman Catholics to one Protestant), also shows no sign of changing its conservative theological stance. Of course, we must be careful not to read too much into denominational statistics, for declared total membership of any denomination will certainly include strange bedfellows. For all that, in third-level education Roman Catholics are in a majority in Queen's and Coleraine universities (vastly so in Coleraine). Increasing numbers of students from the Republic also help to swell the Roman Catholic majority and to promote Roman Catholic influence on educational policies. It has been said that, especially in matters of education, the Roman Catholic authorities in Northern Ireland have more influence with the UK government than their counterparts have with the government in the Republic!

While there is a growing influx of students from the Republic to Northern Ireland, there is also an outflow of students from Northern Ireland to universities on what is usually termed 'the mainland'. In the Republic during the 1940s, 26 per cent of the students in Trinity were from Northern Ireland and nearly all were Protestants. Today the percentage is less than 4 per cent from Northern Ireland most of whom are Roman Catholics.

Protestants have not the same qualms about emigrating as Roman Catholics. They are not as sentimental about 'home' or 'town' or 'native land'. When they venture forth they carry less nostalgic baggage and shake it off more easily, beginning afresh and integrating without much difficulty into a new community and environment. The Ulster Protestants who emigrated to America in the late eighteenth and early nineteenth centuries, and whose descendants account for at least half the alleged 40 million American-Irish today, quickly put the past behind them, adapted to a new country and made a new home.

This may have something to do with the Protestant 'work ethic' which emphasises the 'will' more than the 'feelings' and is embarrassed by the shedding of tears in public. With Roman Catholic numbers and influence waxing and Protestantism waning and the British perceived as at best neutral, many Protestants have concluded that there is no long-term future for them as the preponderate power in Northern Ireland. The mood is one of resignation, dismissive of politicians and politics.

'Take each day as it comes, make the most of it, enjoy your family and friends, your clubs and churches. Don't let anxiety about tomorrow interfere with the normality of today.'

From a purely financial point of view Protestants have less to fear from a British withdrawal from Northern Ireland than Roman Catholics. Protestants tend to be more self reliant, individualistic, less dependent on the State. Those who opted to stay in Northern Ireland after a British withdrawal would soon adapt to any new arrangement provided their civil and religious liberties were guaranteed. But for Roman Catholics, unless there was a cast-iron guarantee that resources would be available from whatever quarter to ensure continuing parity in grants, allowances, etc., with the UK, I cannot see the Roman Catholic community, even with a substantial electoral majority, voting to break the Union. The crucial question as to who will foot the bill for severing the link with Britain remains as yet unanswered, indeed unaddressed.

Society in Northern Ireland has come to rely heavily on the State as a universal provider. The sense of personal responsibility for the environment is usually limited to the home and garden, not forgetting the car, all clean and neat and tidy. If mention is made of the litter, the bottles, cans, discarded cartons and plastic bags which now disfigure the streets, roads and adjacent fields to an extent unthinkable twenty years ago, the invariable reply is: 'The Department of the Environment (DOE) should clean it up, it's their responsibility.' There is an absence of civic pride and a lack of concern for the environment unless the householder or car owner is personally affected, for example, by frostbound roads. Reverence for God's creation of which we are stewards — an essential part of the Gospel — is not emphasised by the Churches and the Christian duty to keep the environment clean and free from pollution and ugliness has few enthusiastic supporters in Northern Ireland today. There is a sort of gnosticism or dualism. Worry about the salvation of your soul, not about despoiling of the environment. On the other hand I have been impressed by the amazing generosity of people of all creeds and classes in support of a wide variety of good causes, local, national and international, for the relief of suffering.

Education in the Republic exists on a financial shoestring compared to Northern Ireland. For all that, I believe the standard is no higher in Northern Ireland. The Republic, in spite of — some would say because of — limited resources achieves excellent results. In spoken English, usages such as 'I done . . . I seen . . . he has went' are more frequently heard in Northern Ireland even among those who have had second-level education, than in the Republic. Having to study grammar to learn Irish may have something to do with this.

In the political field, while Protestants are firmly committed to maintaining the Union, Roman Catholics are not so monolithic in their pursuit of a United Ireland. Consequently there is a greater variety of political allegiance among Roman Catholics, ranging from Sinn Féin, through the SDLP, the Workers' Party and the Alliance, to those who vote Unionist and some who do not vote at all, a significant number who, for whatever reason, have chosen to opt out of the whole political process. Thus while there are Roman Catholics who will vote for those who wish to retain the status quo within the United Kingdom as long as the majority wishes to do so, it is a rarity to find a Protestant, whoever else he might vote for, casting a vote for any individual or party advocating a United Ireland.

When all is said and done, the truth is that for most people in Ireland, North and South, Roman Catholic and Protestant, their heart's desire is simply to live at peace with one another, to be good neighbours, to be treated with justice and tolerance, to have a home and a job, to be able to pay their way, care for their families, feel secure in their homes and walking along the streets. There are deep friendships across the religious and political divide in so many cases. Constitutional niceties, except for political activists, come far down on their agenda. Political leaders do not command unanimous support among their followers for traditional party dogmas. According to a recent survey (*Social Attitudes in Northern Ireland (1991–92)*, QUB) 30 per cent of those who voted SDLP, the main constitutional Nationalist party, believed that Northern Ireland should remain within the United Kingdom. Only 53 per cent of SDLP voters were in favour of a United Ireland. The remainder were 'Don't knows'. On the Unionist side suspicion of all things 'Irish', regarding the Republic as a foreign land, the snubbing of its representatives when on visits to the North, rejection of 'Romeward and United Ireland' ecumenism, so often endorsed by the political leadership, are not shared by a substantial number who vote Unionist. The old ancestral clarion calls rallying the faithful of both traditions to man the barricades are losing their appeal for an electorate increasingly inebriated by TV, foreign travel and membership of the EC. While the formal knee-jerk reaction is still to be found in the polling booth, disillusionment with politicians and politics has meant that the old 'diehard' message, of whatever party, is becoming irrelevant. The majority still vote in the old way — hence the poor showing of new parties such as the Alliance — but without confidence in their politicians. We are, as yet, not witnessing the end of the old order but we have arrived at the beginning of the end. The electorate on both sides will in time push their politicians into compromise. They will demand a solution.

To end on a lighter note. The Church of Ireland is top heavy with dignitaries: deans, archdeacons, canons. While the number of clergy has decreased, titles have not shown a corresponding reduction.

And talking of reduction: is it not time that all the Churches reduced their baggage of confessional formulae by removing statements offensive to fellow Christians? Statements such as: 'The Pope is the anti-Christ' (Calvinism); 'Sacrifice of masses are blasphemous' (Anglican, Article 31); 'Anglican Holy Orders are null and void' (Roman Catholic). Might not the Orange Order remove the prohibition on its members attending services in Roman Catholic churches — hardly an example of Christian charity or good manners when applied even to funerals or marriages?

The eccentric Lord Bristol, Frederick Hervey, who was Bishop of Derry in the eighteenth century and after whom the Hotels Bristol throughout Europe are named to mark his extensive continental tours, built for himself an episcopal palace at Downhill on the Derry coast overlooking the stormy waters of the Atlantic. The palace is today a ruin but a temple on the cliff edge still survives, with lines from Lucretius which appealed to the bishop carved in the architrave: '*Suave mari magno turbantibus aequora ventis, alterius magnum specatare laborem* . . . It is sweet when on the great sea the winds are convulsing the waters to watch another's struggle from the dry land. Not because it delights one that another should be in travail, but because it is a relief to observe what trials you have not to endure.'

However, if Lucretius appealed to Frederick Hervey my conclusions of a lifetime are wonderfully summarised by Louis MacNeice in his poem 'Entirely':

> And if all the world were black and white entirely
> And all the charts were plain
> Instead of a mad weir of tigerish waters
> A prism of delight and pain,
> We might be surer where we wished to go
> Or again we might be merely
> Bored, but in brute reality there is no
> Road that is right entirely.

Amen to that!

✗ What a heartless reflection for a Christian bishop to cherish!

(d) See, however, p. 214.

Index

Supplement to

Mark of Protest

Autobiography of
Victor Griffin
former Dean of St Patrick's

Protestants and the Anti-Abortion Referendum

It all began for me with this statement which I sent to the newspapers on 15 February 1983:

Statement by the Dean of St. Patrick's, The Very Rev. Victor Griffin

Protestants in Ireland are utterly opposed to abortion on demand as a means of birth control or simply to terminate an unwanted pregnancy. But no Protestant Church or Protestant organisation has campaigned for the inclusion of an anti-abortion amendment to the Constitution. Why?

1. Protestants feel that the law governing abortion is really a matter for he Dail. Abortion is already illegal under present legislation (1861 Act which still operates in Northern Ireland). Protestants feel that the Constitution should steer clear of controversial moral questions. It should have wide acceptance, being the expression of a common unity and avoiding divisive issues. Such issues should be a matter for legislation after debate and decision by the Dail and not a matter of the Constitution. To try and encapsulate a complex moral issue such as abortion in a neat and tidy unambiguous form of words for insertion in the Constitution is an impossible undertaking and any such form of words designed to cover every eventuality will prove to be inherently defective.

2. The Amendment, if passed, will do nothing to deal with the social problems underlying abortion. Nor will it prevent those who wish to have abortions from travelling to England, unless we are to have medical examination at the ports of all women of childbearing age.

3. In a time of severe economic recession the country can ill afford to spend nearly one million pounds on a referendum. If such money is available it would be better spent in alleviating distress and helping to improve the quality of life of the deprived and underprivileged sections of our community. (For example, housebound disabled people still do not even have a postal vote in the Republic, yet we appear to be obsessed with the 'rights of the unborn'). We should get our priorities right.

4. The proposed wording of the amendment is ambiguous. It has been framed in such a way as to appear non-sectarian. But if the amendment succeeds and the 'life of the mother' is interpreted by the courts as merely physical life, then abortion for, say, rape or incest of deformity of the foetus would be unconstitutional and a criminal offence. Thus the generally held Protestant ethical view which would allow for abortion as a last resort in certain unfortunate exceptional cases where

there is strict and undeniable medical necessity as the lesser of two evils, would be outlawed by the Constitution.

If the term 'life' is meant to be taken in a wider sense to cover the health and well-being of the mother why is this not made clear in the proposed wording of the amendment? Is it because such wording, allowing for abortion in certain circumstances other that where the physical life of the mother is at risk would be unacceptable to the Roman Catholic Church? Since there is no objection to the wording by even the most conservative Roman Catholics associated with the so called 'Pro-Life' campaign it would appear that they see the proposed form of words as ruling out all abortion as unconstitutional with the sole exception of that which is permitted by the Roman Catholic Church which indeed they refuse to call abortion. They see the amendment as embodying Roman Catholic teaching in the Constitution and they further imply that the Roman Catholic ethical position on this matter is the only true Christian and moral viewpoint and this should be enforced on all citizens, Roman Catholic and non-Roman Catholic alike.

5. No society can discard the ethical ethos which has formed and fashioned it. Irish society cannot discard its Christian ethos - this is part of our public morality and is based on Christian consensus. But where Christians differ sincerely on certain matters of morality such as abortion, the State, if it claims to be democratic and non-confessional, should not enshrine a particular denominational viewpoint, even a majority one, in its constitution, to the outlawing of all others. This is an infringement on human liberty.

6. If an unborn child or 'human being' is equated with a fertilised ovum, even before implantation in the womb (the Roman Catholic view), then certain contraceptive pills and devices such as Inter Uterine Devices could be declared unconstitutional as abortifacients. Herein lurks a danger to family planning clinics which prescribe these methods of contraception as the most suitable in certain circumstances. The Protestant would regard this as an invasion of privacy and a denial of the rights of conscience and individual liberty.

Generally speaking the Protestant would say that a fertilised ovum is a human Life with the potential of becoming a human being or person. There is a gradual development from fertilised ovum and embryo to foetus, right up to the moment of birth. No consensus exists as to at what point exactly there is a 'human being' or 'child' present. You have a right to your opinion and I to mine, but to enshrine one particular denominational opinion in the Constitution is sectarian.

7. How will the courts interpret the Amendment?
If they are guided by what the electorate voted for as seen in the context of the so called 'Pro-Life' campaign which pressed for the amendment, it seems reasonable to assume that since
(1) the so called 'pro-life' campaign people see the wording as conforming to Roman Catholic teaching, and
(2) the vast majority, 95% plus in the State are Roman Catholics, and
(3) The Roman Catholic Bishops have voiced no objection to the wording.
it would be very difficult for the courts to give the amendment a liberal interpretation to take into account the Protestant position. For if these words are susceptible of wider interpretation to allow for abortion, say, if rape or incest where the health of the mother is at stake the courts would be entitled to ask why this was not made clear in the wording. The onus will be on the opposition to prove the exception and the chance of doing so will be remote indeed. A form of words was devised which on first reading may seem non-sectarian and innocuous, but which after further study implies a sectarian point of view. The Amendment is sectarian not so much in what it says but in what it omits to say, what it fails to spell out. Here is the danger for Protestants and for those who object to the rigid view of the Roman Catholic church.

8. This proposed Amendment is one more example of our sex-obsessed society. The idea of sin seems to be confined to the sexual sphere. The moral writ of 'right' and 'wrong' runs only in the domain of sexual morality. Hence far more emphasis is place on so called sexual rectitude than on matters of personal honesty, national righteousness and social justice. It is a sad reflection on our society that for example the career of a politician is more at risk if he is suspected of being out of line with the Roman Catholic teaching on divorce, contraception or abortion than if he is suspected of indulging in dishonest business transactions.

9. We have to ask ourselves the question - What sort of State do we want? Do we want a Roman Catholic confessional State or a pluralist society in the Republican tradition of Tone and Davis? We can't have it both ways.

10. Those who, like myself, are opposed to the proposed Constitutional Amendment should not be labelled as being 'pro-abortion'. I am utterly opposed to abortion on demand, yet I shall have no hesitation in voting against the proposed amendment for the above reasons.

Signed: Victor G. Griffin
         Dean of St. Patrick's   15 February, 1983.

Statement from the Chapter on the Proposed Amendment to the Constitution

We, the members of the Chapter of St. Patrick's National Cathedral, drawn as we are from all the dioceses of the Church of Ireland, both in the Republic and in Northern Ireland, feel, in view of our representative character, that we should add our voice to the many expressions of concern occasioned by the proposed amendment to the Constitution of the Republic.

We desire, first of all, to affirm our opposition to indiscriminate abortion, but at the same time recognise that there can be medical circumstances in which the termination of pregnancy is required.

In common with the vast majority of our fellow-churchmen, we are opposed to the amendment on many counts. We consider it unnecessary. We think it unwise to introduce such a complex moral and social issue into the constitution. We believe that it will be totally ineffective either in helping to solve the problem of abortion as it exists in Ireland today or in improving the moral ethos of the nation. We judge it to be ill-timed and irrelevant in view of the many more urgent problems which at present confront government and people.

Our strongest opposition, however, derives form our position as members of the Church of Ireland in relation to the constitution. The issues involved are clearly controversial, and admit of more than one tenable viewpoint. The wording that has been adopted is excessive, if the intention is to secure a ban only on abortion; it may be interpreted in directions which would gravely offend against our considered moral position. We reaffirm our conviction that the mother has a prior and greater right to life that the foetus, and anything less is unacceptable to us. We would also regard any prohibition on certain methods of contraception which might result form the passing of this amendment as an infringement on the right to privacy and freedom of conscience.

We must express our anxiety at the effect which this amendment and the supporting campaign may have on ecumenical relations between the churches. The views of the minority churches have been stated in unmistakable terms, yet little has been done to meet their objections or to allay their fears. The Roman Catholic hierarchy has lent its support to the wording to which Protestants strongly object. For many people this will call in question the whole basis of ecumenism in Ireland, which is a matter to us of profound concern.

Further, we deeply regret the political consequences which will follow both in the Republic and in Northern Ireland. We have committed ourselves to the development of a pluralist society, in which the conscientiously held convictions of minorities will be respected and tolerated within the framework of an agreed public morality. The proposed amendment comes as a serious blow to our highest ideals and hopes. We believe that the constitution should be such that all citizens can subscribe to it wholeheartedly and without reservation - a bond of union rather that an instrument of division.

We therefore appeal to all, irrespective of creed, who have the best interests of Ireland at heart to vote decisively against the proposed amendment.

Speech by the Dean, the Very Rev. V. G. Griffin, at Liberty Hall, 2 September 1983

At the concluding rally in Liberty Hall when I was joined on the platform by Michael D. Higgins and Monica Barnes I said:

This unfortunate and unnecessary referendum has put a great strain on our tolerance and on our tempers. It has divided the whole community - lawyers, doctors, churches. Bitter words have been spoken, smear and scare tactics, emotive misrepresentation are the order of the day and Christian charity is the first casualty. St. Paul exhorts us always to speak the truth in love, and to recognise the right of everyone to their views and to show tolerance to one another.

I speak as a Protestant and member of the Church of Ireland. I spent most of my ministry, nearly twenty-five years in Northern Ireland. There I witnessed the sad results of religious segregation and sectarianism. Certain religious leaders in Northern Ireland believed that they had a 'hot line' to the Deity. They believed that they had a divine sanction to impose their will on the whole community, for according to them it was God's will and God's commandment. Even in sport and recreation where they appealed to the commandment 'to keep holy the Sabbath day' they insisted that, for example, the children's swings should be chained in the parks on Sundays and the swimming pools closed. This they held was God's law, they knew it, and no one had a right to offend against it. And so, having the Northern Ireland experience behind me, I am very much alive to the danger of doing anything which might seem to advance in any way the cause of sectarianism in the Republic. I do not want Protestant sectarianism in Ireland and I do not want Roman Catholic sectarianism in Ireland. I want Christianity in Ireland. Swift said: "We Irish have enough religion to make us hate one another but not enough Christianity to make us love one another". We need less religion in Ireland and more Christianity.

I am pro-life and like the vast majority of Protestants in Ireland, both North and South, I am utterly opposed to abortion on demand - indiscriminate abortion - as a means of birth control or simply to terminate an unwanted pregnancy. But no Protestant Church or Protestant organisation has campaigned for the inclusion of this amendment in the Constitution. Why? Because Protestants feel that the law governing abortion is really a matter for the Dail. Abortion is already illegal under present legislation, the 1861 Act. In this the existing law reflects public opinion. If the law proves defective in doing this it can quickly be changed by an Act of Parliament.

The Constitution is another matter. Protestants feel that the Constitution should keep clear of controversial moral issues. It should have wide acceptance, being the expression of a common unity and consensus, and it should avoid divisive issues. Such issues should be a matter of legislation, after debate and decision by the Dail, and not a matter for the Constitution. No Protestant Church or Protestant organisation campaigned for this referendum. On the contrary, all the Protestant Churches have made it abundantly clear, time and time again, that they are opposed to the holding of this referendum. The Roman Catholic Church on the other hand is strongly in favour and the Dail has concurred with the Roman Catholic Hierarchy's point of view. Therefore whether we like it or not, at the very outset sectarianism was introduced into the question.

When the referendum was inevitable Protestants unanimously supported the Fine Gael proposed wording, as being more acceptable from our point of view. This would, we feel, have met the stated intention of the Pro-life group in that it would have prevented any possibility of the Constitution being invoked to legalise abortion.

The Protestant Churches had compromised, when faced with the reality of the referendum which they from the outset had opposed, but even this compromise was insensitively rejected by the Dail and the Roman Catholic Church and we are left with the original Fianna Fail wording. The rejection of the Protestant Churches' willingness to compromise in an effort to solve this sorry problem can hardly be seen as an act calculated to reduce the sectarianism implicit in this whole business.

To turn to the present wording. Protestants see the present wording as ambiguous. Medical and legal experts disagree as to the possible consequences, if this form of words is inserted into the Constitution. We feel that on such an important question there should be no ambiguity, no uncertainty. The electorate should know exactly what it is being asked to vote for. And Protestants feel that there is a dangerous ambiguity. No Protestant would maintain that a mother has only an equal right to life to her unborn baby. For us the mother's right to life is superior and primary. Where there is a conflict, the rights of the mother's life and health, must take precedence over that of the unborn child. Her rights must be the primary concern, for she is in a real sense the heart and core of the family. Of course it is said that equality does not mean mathematical equality. We have biological equality, psychological equality, sociological equality, codology equality. That's about the height of it. The Irish people are being conned by codology! Also if the term 'unborn' is to be identified, not only with the foetus, but with a fertilised ovum, then there is a grave danger that certain forms of contraception acceptable to Protestants, will be declared unconstitutional on the grounds that they are 'abortifacients'.

The question is therefore how the Courts will interpret the amendment if passed.

The Pro-life people say that there will be no change in existing medical practice and that contraception will not be affected. They may be right. But they may be wrong. Legal and medical experts differ. Therefore, to say the least, there are very substantial grounds for Protestant fears.

As I understand it the Pro-life people want this amendment to guarantee the right to life of the unborn, but they would allow two exceptions, where the life of the mother is endangered either by (1) and ectopic pregnancy or (2) that of cancer of the uterus. These are the very exceptions and the only exceptions, recognised by the Roman Catholic Church and justified on the debatable theory of what is known as the principle of double effect. Indeed it is maintained that such cases are not really abortions at all. If these are the only exceptions to be permitted in an amendment prohibiting abortion then it is difficult to see such an amendment as non-sectarian, for such an amendment would enshrine in the Constitution only the Roman Catholic position. Such an amendment could hardly be regarded as non-sectarian when it would rule out other exceptions, which might be judged on medical grounds to threaten the life of the mother and which are acceptable to non-Roman Catholics. Thus the generally held Protestant ethical view which would allow abortion as a last resort in certain unfortunate exceptional cases. on the grounds of strict and undeniable medical necessity, would be narrowed and restricted by the Constitution. Protestantism is suspicious of rigid legalism and absolutism in dealing with complex moral issues. The individual case is all important and must be seen in the wider context of the sanctity of all human life and the mother must always be treated with compassion and Christian concern. I have been accused of deviating from the teaching of my church on this matter and an attempt has been made to depict me as out of step with the Church of Ireland's viewpoint. There is not one iota of difference between my views and the teaching of my church.

On this question of sectarianism, I am not saying that it was the intention of any political party or the Dail to make this a sectarian issue. What I am saying is that by the very nature of the problem it was impossible to avoid a sectarian dimension to this debate. First of all there was a sectarian division on the very nature of the Constitution and secondly, while there is a general agreement amongst Roman Catholics and Protestants that indiscriminate abortion is morally wrong, Protestants would not be so rigid as the Roman Catholic church as to the exceptions to be permitted. Protestants would judge the matter of exceptions on the ground of strict and undeniable medical necessity where the mother is at risk. Thus it was impossible to produce a form of words to accommodate the rigid Roman Catholic point of view. The best that could be done was to Constitutionalise the present position thus avoiding the need to produce a positive, definite form of words.

This was tried by Fine Gael, accepted by the Protestants but rejected by the Roman Catholic Church and the Dail. Sectarianism was unavoidable. I have said from the beginning over and over again that it was impossible to produce on this issue a non-sectarian wording.

We have to ask ourselves the question: What sort of State do we want? Do we want a Confessional State on Roman Catholic lines or a pluralist society in the true Republican tradition of Tone and Davis? We can't have it both ways. In truth, the proposed amendment has little to do with the question of abortion which is already prohibited by law. It has everything to do with the question of whether we are to enshrine in the Constitution a particular ethical view on certain moral issues. This I maintain is not properly a matter for the Constitution.

I do not want a Protestant Confessional State in Ireland. I do not want a Roman Catholic Confessional State in Ireland. Sectarianism and Confessionalism have been the curse of Ireland, North and South for far too long. I want a truly republican and pluralist Ireland. I will not desecrate the graves of Tone and Emmet, of Davis and Edward Fitzgerald, of Isaac Butt and Parnell and of all the other Protestant patriots who helped to form and fashion this Nation. These were men of wide and tolerant vision. There are those today who would turn that vision into a sectarian squint. I will not tarnish the memory of Shaw and Yeats, of O'Casey and Douglas Hyde and of all the other Protestants who have made a marked contribution to the cultural, artistic and intellectual life of this Nation. And because I will not do this, I will vote NO in this divisive, sectarian, unnecessary and futile referendum. And I hope all you who have the good of the Irish Nation at heart will do likewise.

Over the grave of Swift in St. Patrick's Cathedral there are these words: "Go traveller and imitate if you can one who played a man's part in the cause of liberty".

I appeal to you in the cause of liberty to vote NO and save the Republic.

Meanwhile, I had the full support of the St. Patrick's Cathedral Chapter, the only group or organisation in the Church of Ireland who endeavoured to inform and offer some guidance to members of the Church of Ireland and others who supported our views on abortion.

Are the churches serious when they talk of peace and combating sectarianism?

by Dean Victor Griffin

1. The air is full of voices, ecclesiastical and political urging us all to play our part to advance the peace process, promote reconciliation and combat the evils of sectarianism. All very praiseworthy. But, true to past form, such exhortations, especially the ecclesiastical ones are long on generalities but short on particulars. Lofty generalities evoke no opposition. All will approve. But should the speaker descend to particulars and point out that a particular policy pursued in a particular place by a particular organisation is an offence to the Gospel and should not be tolerated by those who profess and call themselves Christians, he enters stormy waters. In all our churches we have been scared to speak the Gospel truth about particulars and policies for fear of alienating our church members. (Protestantism in Northern Ireland is careful not to offend Unionists and likewise Roman Catholicism,, Nationalists). Many view their religion primarily as the making of a political statement. May I suggest some particular issues for urgent attention by the churches particularly in Northern Ireland, to advance the peace process and combat sectarianism.

(1) To give enthusiastic support to the cause of integrated education. Reconciliation is a long process and it must begin, as we say, at the beginning, that is with the children. The churches rightly tell us that we are all one family under one God. If this is so it is surely sinful to divide the family by separating the children on religious grounds from their earliest years thereby creating a 'them and us' attitude in their impressionable minds. To preach the Gospel of reconciliation while practising or condoning educational apartheid purely on religious grounds is far removed from the teaching and example of Jesus. In Northern Ireland religious and political divisions are accentuated and perpetuated by such segregation.

Do we hear too much from the churches on the need to preserve a "Protestant ethos" or a Roman Catholic ethos" and too little about having a common Christian ethos expressed in being together and practising together the Christian virtues of tolerance and mutual understanding without which, reconciliation is impossible?

2. To advocate and urgently work for the removal of confessional statements offensive to fellow Christians e.g. referring to the Pope and the Anti-Christ (Presbyterian Westminster Confession) or to sacrifices of masses as "blasphemous fables and dangerous deceits" (Anglican 39 Articles, No.3) or to Anglican Holy Orders as "null and void") Roman Catholic Papal decree 1896).

3. The Protestant Churches through their leaders to ask the Orange Order to lift the prohibition on its members attending services in Roman Catholic Churches. (Even a funeral or marriage attendance is prohibited - fortunately not always obeyed) and when parading or choosing a route to avoid any display of antagonism to the Roman Catholic community. To insist that if the Union Flag is flown from Church Towers on 12th July it must also be flown on all national occasions and public holidays. Limiting its display to the Orange marching season is tantamount to a public proclamation that the church regards the Union Flag as essentially a Protestant symbol, exclusive of all others. If a flag for church towers is desirable, the cross of St. Patrick is an obvious choice.

To take seriously the harm done to the public perception and integrity of Protestantism in general by the official connection between the Orange Order and the Unionist party whereby Protestantism is perceived as synonymous with Unionism and Unionism as essentially and exclusively Protestant.

4. Roman Catholic authorities to be more sensitive to the effect on the Protestant community of their divisive regulations on "mixed" or interchurch marriage continued right up to segregation at the marriage Eucharist and the religious upbringing of children all of which contributes in Northern Ireland to polarisation with religion aggravating political suspicions.

Irrespective of party politics to give due credit and support to the R.U.C. for its praiseworthy work in serving th e community in so many ways, which far outweighs any transgressions on the part of a small minority.

To support the call for the removal of the G.A.A. prohibition on R.U.C. participation.

To have done with the apparent reluctance to give any public credit or praise to the Government for the substantial educational benefits enjoyed in Northern Ireland compared with the Republic. Contrast this with the gratitude shown and rightly so by Protestant Church leaders in th e Republic and their laudable practice of inviting the Minister for Education to open a new Protestant school, a practice never reciprocated in the North by the Roman Catholic Church as far as I know.

5. Church leaders, following the Gospel teaching, to encourage politicians to participate in talks with political opponents at every level, at every opportunity, irrespective of venue and without any preconditions. Nothing is lost and much may be gained by talking and listening. While we were sinners God in Jesus talked with us without preconditions. He did not say - you must first promise to be good and then and only then I'll talk to you. A joint statement to this effect by all the churches urging restraint and calling for dialogue particularly on the Framework Document would have had greater impact.

"Did that play of mine send out those men the English shot?" asks Yeats. Did words of hatred in school or church or home, Protestant or Roman Catholic, send out men and women to murder? If so when we sit in judgement, remember we too share in their guilt. All churches must in humility ask forgiveness form one another and from the communities who have suffered so appallingly because of the religious or political sectarianism which they, the churches, to maintain their power and status, have inculcated, encouraged or condoned. Our communal guilt demands that the churches ask that judgment be seasoned with mercy in deciding on the release of convicted terrorists. Ancestral voices of sectarian religion and politics have played no small part in putting them behind bars.

6. To reject the political heresy promulgated by some Unionist politicians which narrows the concept of Irishness by implying that the term is somehow synonymous with being Roman Catholic, Gaelic and Nationalist, thereby concluding that Protestants of the British or Unionist tradition are not Irish at all. This causes bewilderment especially amongst Church of Ireland members in Northern Ireland. Protestants must emphasise that Irishness transcends religion and politics, is inclusive, not exclusive and is best defined as a sense of place, of belonging, of home. Recognition of common Irishness can be a healing and reconciling agent in a divided society.

7. To encourage the rotation of municipal offices such as Mayor or Chairperson between political parties in Corporations and Councils and to request all local authorities of whatever political colour never to allow constitutional or political niceties to take precedence over Christian hospitality by, for example, refusing to extend a civic welcome to distinguished visitors purely on political or religious grounds.

8. The churches in Ireland to get together, perhaps at Ballymascanlon and at least discuss and try to achieve some degree of consensus on such crucial moral problems as contraception, abortion, divorce, homosexuality. If consensus proves impossible, the churches in a spirit of honesty and tolerance should publicly recognise that on complex moral issues different views are sincerely held by committed Christians of all traditions and in public or private debate call for tolerance, mutual respect and charity, thus avoiding a 'holier than thou' attitude by any of the Irish churches.